A Childhood Memoir

Cover photo:
Melanie Lowy
October 1938

A Childhood Memoir

A Double Childhood

Melanie Lowy

authorHOUSE®

AuthorHouse™
1663 Liberty Drive
Bloomington, IN 47403
www.authorhouse.com
Phone: 1-800-839-8640

First published by AuthorHouse   10/20/2011

ISBN: 978-1-4567-8334-1 (sc)
ISBN: 978-1-4567-8335-8 (ebk)

Printed in the United States of America

DEDICATION

This memoir is dedicated to my precious niece Ruth, a courageous and gracious human being unique in overcoming adversity, unique in facing the bleakest reality with stunning perspicacity. Sympathetic to any sincere faith, she adhered to her very own, deeply felt Spirituality. She was my niece but so much more, my cherished friend and kindred spirit. My love and admiration for her will never fade.

Ruth Lawy. February 20th 1955–November 5th. 2010.

ON THE FRONTIERS OF HELL—A MEMOIR OF A FORTUNATE LITTLE GIRL

'Der Mensch denkt und Gott lenkt' wrote Johann Wolfgang von Goethe.

FOREWORD

I stood before the elegant five-storey apartment building in the Schweigerstrasse in Munich with my son, street and building unblemished. It has remained unscathed through all the bombing, a proud, once luxurious relic of another day. And I gazed speechless as my childhood flooded back and the edifice became a beast in chains. Within its breast cowed a world I longed to retrieve, to enfold and never, never let go again. We stood a long time in silence before we entered.

I had thought of writing a roman a clef but came to the conclusion that dodging reality and thereby the truth, was something no longer an option for someone of advanced years. I had been doing that far too long in most of my work in unison with most authors as we hide within our fictitious characters, peeking out from behind the curtain from time to time, tiptoeing warily into that reality from which by nature we shy away.

What and who has shaped my persona and beliefs is crystal clear. Of course parents and school certainly played a major role. But most of all it is that curse of twentieth century Jewry of which I became aware earlier than most and at a more tender age than most here in England. The holocaust has shaped my belief or lack thereof as well as my attitude towards mankind, animals, religion as it has shaped my general conduct towards everything. Deep down there is the Calvinistic throttle squeezing at my throat. I have not done enough—no, I have done nothing to make sense of my survival.

Never prone to put down to luck or any other such fanciful cause that might have protected me from disaster, I have on the other hand gone on plaguing myself with the unanswerable: why, why me? And worse still: since it was me, what could I give return? To whom was I supposed to show gratitude? How dared I be grateful for something that was denied millions? Who threw the dice? Back to square one.

Whatever term you may choose, fate is one that springs to mind unless you bring in God which from where I stand would be an aberration and a gross insult to the millions God deserted—then really there are no words for the bizarre destiny of the blessed few who scarred or not, reeled anaesthetised from Germany or the ghettos or camps to blink once more into the sunlight alive.

Of course the ultra civilised German people—the nation that produced Kant, Goethe and Beethoven but also Nietsche and Wagner—ceaselessly entertained for years by the march-pasts of black leather-clad automatons, jaunty caps with silver-plated emblem of a human skull atop, were entirely innocent of the ulterior motives of the regime they cheered till the rafters rang in the beer-halls of Munich—of course they were! Mesmerised to be sure but cognisant from day one none the less of the sinister undertones

I have chosen to tell at some length of the first ten years, added a few more vital incidents of the next two years; then several more years crept in almost unnoticed until I had finally shed all adolescence.

By any stretch of the imagination, they cannot be considered ordinary if far from unique. I have decided to speak now in advancing years because I am blessed, (sometimes I think it is a curse) with a retentive memory from a very early age. In earlier years although I was invited to speak in Munich, I obliged with only the briefest reminiscences. I preferred to tell of the Yiddish poet Josef Hillel Levi, my renowned father. But it is time to put down in writing for the coming generations who will hopefully find it difficult even to imagine what it was like not much more than half a century ago to be born a Jewish child in a Germany a mere four years before it would be devoured by National Socialism. And a most fortunate child at that!

From the outset it seems to me, I did worship a God and that God was and is my father. Occasionally I watch a film about Nazi Germany with the marching SA or SS hordes, the former in brown, the latter in black menacingly parading through city streets yelling 'VOLK AN'S GWEHR or DIE FAHNE

FLATTERT UNS VORAN'; the thousands cheering their allegiance to Hitler as he spits out his venom—and disbelief comes over me. Did I really spend my treasured childhood in the midst of all this and still manage to soak up such all-embracing contentment and love? Can I really still harbour the deep affection for these city streets that I do?

Ilya Ehrenburg has said that as long as there is one anti-Semite in the world he remains a Jew. Ilya Ehrenburg died a Jew and I fear that by the same token I too and many more after me will die Jews. For me the crux of Judaism too is certainly not religion but the shared burden of the pain and suffering of the millions. But equally it is the treasured tradition and culture this pain has produced as often as not transformed into wild joy and laughter, music and literature. Why then have I quoted Goethe? Goethe was a great poet and a great sage. I tend to think he used 'God' when he might just as well have used 'fate'. One thing is certain: man can steer his destiny almost all the way—almost. The rest is up to—?

BOOK ONE

HELL'S EDGE

Chapter One
(AN INTRODUCTION)

THE LOWYS AND THE TENNENBAUMS

MY FIRST, MOST TREASURED CHILDHOOD

At the time of my birth, my father JOSEF HILLEL LEVI was a poet of renown in Yiddish circles all over the globe. His rabbinical background stemmed from both sides. His father Yisroel Dov was a scribe (a SEUFER) whose beautiful calligraphy was admired throughout Galicia. He was also by all accounts a most righteous aesthete known in the Jewish community as a 'ZADIG. However, I was never fortunate enough to know him as he died the year I was born.

My father relates in a short biography in his post-war book GESAMMELTE SCHRIFTEN (Collected Works) how his grandfather, after a pogrom in Russia, settled in the Galician SHTETL of Tshebin. Not long after, he married the daughter of Rabbi Chajim Kluger, author of religious works. Upon the latter's death, he took over as rabbi. My grandfather Yisroel Dov Halevi passed over the rabbinate rightfully his after his grandfather's death, to his younger brother, out of sheer modesty and altruism. He himself chose instead to live in extremely limited circumstances, eking out a meagre existence as a scribe in Krakow.

Grandfather Ysroel Dov's utter devotion to Yiddish emanated from the religious conviction that Yiddish was one of the seventy holy languages given by God to Moses on Mount Sinai. It was only natural that such pious love would translate itself to his son in a worldlier yet equally tenacious dedication. All the more so as Josef Hillel adored his unassuming, gentle, self-effacing father.

On his mother's side, my grandmother Channa Henne was the great granddaughter of REB HERSCH LUBLINER, known as the IRON MIND and the granddaughter of REB YSROEL BIENENFELD who travelled with MOSES MONTEFIORE to meet with the Tsar of Russia in order to assist in persuading him to annul edicts against circumcision. However, on the way there he was arrested as a spy, stabbed with a dart and consequently bled to death.

Channa Henne was a remarkably well-educated woman with fluent Polish, German and some French. By the time I arrived, however, she was a forlorn, lonely widow residing in a cold water one—room apartment. Her grief at losing a beloved daughter, a renowned beauty and my father's only sibling, was etched as with granite on her small, white, pinched face which in early youth with those arresting large amber eyes, must have had its share of beauty. A tiny, slender figure she took up less space than anyone else in the entire family.

Grandfather Aaron Tennenbaum came from a wealthy Polish Jewish merchants' family and though I am less familiar with his background we were all very impressed by the fact that as a young man he proudly rode his very own white stallion through their estate. This easy-going, hugely optimistic attitude to life seems to have stayed with him and fortified him for the rest of his life. He was the most loveable, good-humoured, amiable, happy-go-lucky grandfather any child could ever hope to have. His love of music and song was to me as impressive as his sense of mischief. Simply to think of him to-day after all these years, still brings a flutter to my heart and a grin to my face.

My grandmother Chatshe (Helen) Tennenbaum nee TYDOR, born in a small STETL in Poland, with her lavender blue eyes and sculpted, regular features, beautiful complexion glowing with health, was as practical and down to earth as her husband was neither. Very much the way I would later on describe my own parents, they were complete, glorious opposites. They had been married when she was sixteen and he seventeen obviously with the help of a 'SHATCHEN' (a marriage broker) as was the custom and it was evident if not for her, their life would not have continued to be as comfortable as it appeared to be—for she was a travelling sales-lady. To think of it now fills me with wonder and pride. A Jewish woman wearing a 'SHEITEL' (a wig) travelling mostly on foot in leather lace-up boots and by tramway to the nearby, muddy villages scattered about Munich—selling haberdashery!

To me my grandparents looked as ancient from the day I was born to the day I last saw them in their eighties and nineties respectively. But the strange thing was that they never seemed to age either as the years drew on—not until grandma Chatshe reached the age of 94 that is. Only then was the change in her evident—and that solely in her complexion, not in her sweet disposition or mental acumen.

I know pitifully little of grandma Chatshe's background other than that as a young girl she was a beauty with her fair skin, ocean blue eyes, tiny, alluring features and gentle disposition. Married at sixteen to the proud, macho if diminutive merchant's son Aaron Tennenbaum, very slim and agile, with the charm of a vaudeville actor and the sense of humour of a burlesque comedian, it was an arranged marriage. Miraculously, even if far from perfect as would have been evident to any shrewd observer it nevertheless lasted to the end of their blessed, long days.

What I do know was, as told by my mother, that Aaron's family were wealthy landowners and little Aaron really did ride about his father's estate on a white stallion as he would go on telling throughout his life. Maybe that was where grandfather first came upon the notion that work and employment was only for others and song, entertainment and pleasure were what life was about. And the manner in which he celebrated and chanted his way through the religious rituals and sermons, the way he celebrated the great cantors of his day, endeared Jewish religious rituals that might otherwise have appeared puzzling to this grandchild. Of course in another era, another environment, Opa Aaron would have been a fulfilled, maybe celebrated entertainer of one sort or another. I realise now he was a very talented man in his own right, totally wasted in a country which unlike America that embraced foreign culture, his particular talent has never been applauded by more than a handful of fellow Jews stemming from similar backgrounds and remaining faithful to their culture. That, in particular, was not the case in a Munich already stuffed to overflowing, like a goose fed to bursting, for pate de foie gras, with anti-Semitism.

They came to Germany, the Lowys and the Tennenbaums, from Poland with their respective offspring in the wake of pogroms, to escape constant persecution. In my mother Miriam Marie's case as a little seven year-old alone from a small back-water shtetl called Titchin, with not a word of German. And they chose Germany as their anchor.

Miriam Marie was the second of four children, three girls and one boy. For some reason, most likely because even at a young age she was strong of will and fortitude, it was she who was chosen to travel on her own by train at the age of seven, to stay with an aunt in Munich. I was never to know who that aunt was or what she was like. Miriam Mary was not one to complain, even if complaint was indeed called for, by the time her own children came along. In fact Miriam Mary was not one to talk about her own woes. She was one to get on with things. But that first solitary journey from Poland to Germany, without a word of German at the age of seven, will surely have played a huge part in forming her stoic character.

My mother's three siblings were my beautiful, elegant auntie Rosel, the eldest, who married a wealthy furrier and lived in a sumptuous apartment in Leipzig. Their brother David, who like his father was a lover of song and all manner of music, especially jaunty Hungarian music, settled in Kemnitz with a pretty young wife and eventually three beautiful little girls, their ages matching ours. I hardly knew uncle David but recall a handsome, cheerful man much like his father, with a fine voice from all accounts and a charming disposition. I recall a pert moustache and a stocky figure and I clearly recall him trilling a lively tune I would recognise decades later as one of Lisct's Hungarian Rhapsodies. He seemed forever of good cheer with a warm smile.

The youngest was my flirtatious, vivacious and I was assured alluring auntie Ida, her head like mother's full of an abundant mop of chestnut curls in all those early photographs. Shortly married to a diamond merchant of great wealth but not of her choice, soon after the birth of a son, she divorced him and later married again in Israel, this time to a man of her own choosing, Paul Theilheimer, whom she loved until the end of his days and with whom she had their daughter Rochelle.

My father's first cousin Josef Bienenfeld had followed him to Munich as they had been like brothers in Krakow. He married a very attractive young woman with whom he had three girls, Golda, Traudel and Henni. But Mina was sadly disenchanted with the man I knew as Uncle Oiser and would curse him whenever she could find the slightest occasion, preferably in public. To be fair to her, Uncle Oiser was not the most dashing of men though his physique was good as he went mountain-climbing with my parents and both my father and he did a great deal of walking. But he seemed to be more often in our home than in his own, obviously avoiding Mina's company.

Uncle Oiser was part of the family so far as we were concerned and seemed inseparable from my father. So far as Mina was concerned, we hardly saw her at our house. Part of the reason may well have been that she refused to be bullied into all the religious rituals that were strictly adhered to. She may also have resented her husband's obsession with our family.

My own cousins from father's side left motherless at such an early age by my aunt Malka's death were close to my own siblings' ages. Their father was a wealthy, rather austere ultra-orthodox business man, who cared for his two sons and two daughters alone in a spacious but very unassuming apartment in an old, dilapidated building as he was a frugal, private man but a devoted father. The building was a stone's throw from my paternal grandmother and during aunt Malka's life-time Oma Lowy was able to see her beloved daughter and her children daily. Uncle Stiel did not remarry.

Trudel, the eldest girl, married a handsome, mundane dentist from Berlin, Kuno Roth, (at whose wedding I was apparently bridesmaid my first of several such honours but the only one I was too little to recall) with whom she emigrated soon after to Israel (then Palestine) Kuno was an affable man full of bonhomie. They joined a Kibbutz and helped build a new Jewish State. Louis and Jani STIEL were brilliant students and both became teachers also settling in Israel eventually; both miraculously surviving the war years in Nice, in the South of France. Hilde was the youngest and closest in age to my sister Henny. I would get to know her only later on. She and Henny were life-long friends. Their father, my uncle STIEL, left matters too late—but of that later—though detail is unsurprisingly scarce.

I was never to know the Tennenbaum children or Uncle David's wife as I was so tiny. My toddler's memory of the dashing moustachioed Uncle David was one of fun and singing, particularly Hungarian, Polish or Russian music

I would recognise and put a name to many years later. His voice as a young boy was apparently so fine that the great Cantor Jossele Rosenblatt, upon hearing him in the synagogue choir, wanted to take him with him to the United States to train as a Cantor. My grandparents, however, were at that time reluctant to part with their only son. Of what is known of David and his family's fate—later. (Yet again details agonizingly wanting.)

I would not meet my Aunt Ida's son Bernie until many years later when he had become a dashing RAF officer of precisely the same age as my own brother Abi. Auntie Rosel's two children, Abi and Hanni both of a similar age as my brother Abi and my sister Henniy, were regular visitors to Munich but it would take several more years until I grew to love and get to know them more intimately.

What Miriam Mary Lowy nee Tennenbaum was about, was to get on with things—to get on with life. The fact that she too was supplanted at such a tender age struck me only much later as a sad coincidence. But in no way could I profess to have the admirable tenacity I spotted so early in my mother, even if it took almost a lifetime for me to appreciate it.

Josef and Mary, yes, those were their German names though father called mother Miriam, or better 'Maryem' in its Yiddish form, her second name, were both profoundly artistic from an early age and it was inevitable that they would meet at one of the many small Jewish arts clubs then abounding in Munich.

Josef Hillel Levi, as was his Yiddish name by which he would be known throughout literary circles from the age of seventeen, had already published his first book of poetry in Krakow at the age of seventeen. The reviews were extremely positive and from then on he would have no problem publishing poetry and articles all over the Yiddish speaking world. And it was that world alone that mattered to him and would go on mattering to him until the day he died.

I have a programme from the Jewish Arts Club in Munich in which Marie Tennenbaum is named as a leading lady and Josef Hillel Lowy as artistic Director. But I know that my father had a good singing voice and was an exceptionally good orator. His bohemian good looks, slim physique, dark longer than average bohemian hair-style and arresting blue eyes made him very popular with the ladies. Mary Lowy's velvety almond complexion, head of chestnut curls, flashing sorrel eyes and a perfect set of white teeth teamed with a buxom figure if shorter than what to-day would be considered average but at the time probably average; her irrepressible energy and spirit would make her a key figure in any public establishment. What was more as she was educated in Germany her German was perfect, her hand-writing exceptionally fine. She was the born leader and instigator as he was the born romantic dreamer.

Josef and Marie fell deeply in love; he was penniless but what did that matter? They would and did build a prosperous life together and raise a cherished family inspired by his passion for music and culture and her indefatigable energy and optimism.

Chapter Two

1929-1935

MUNICH MY CITY OF MOTION
'HAUPTSTADT DER BEWEGUNG'

Melanie aged Two with Kitten

Born on the 27th of January 1929, the year of the Wall Street Crash and the day of Mozart's birthday, I am the fourth child of Miriam and Josef Lowy, named MELLA LOWY (the o with umlaut)singly and unadorned (there is no christening in Judaism obviously). I know for a fact I was born on the first floor of a four-bedroom apartment in the TIRSCHPLATZ, an old, imposing section of Munich as I was frequently shown the stucco-decorated building that stood opposite the Gymnasium a few years later. The wide street was bright, tree-lined and elegant with similar proud buildings each side. I would walk along it later with my father as he spun his glorious tales and sometimes after school with a friend or on my own as it was not that far from the HERZOGRUDOLFSTRASSE. Just one of many shapely, symmetrical old streets with which Munich abounded in those days. The large, four-storied buildings were whitish grey, resembling in fading daylight over-laundered and wrung out giant sheets, all the more so as lighting was muted. I could swear I recall the interior of that apartment although we moved to the modern, far grander one in the SCHWEIGERSTRASSE when I was still in my pram.

I cannot be held strictly to account for the accuracy of my depiction of that bright, if over-furnished front-bedroom with huge beds and feather duvets, surely two generous single beds pushed together or even separated by bedside tables. And those enormous goose or duck-down pillows you could smell a mile off. All bedding covered in pristine white linen. And that heavy mahogany wardrobe that took up one entire side of the room matching the head-boards of the beds as they did at the flat in the Schweigerstrasse, most likely the selfsame. I never thought to ask.

I know I was born in one of those huge beds. Maybe that particular recollection owes more to the many stories I have since heard as well as later on, before returning home from school secretly entering and examining its downstairs lobby with the curiosity of a fox seeking out its lair. One could also see through open balcony doors in the summer, as they lead from front bedrooms.

The building was tall, grey and imposing, maybe somewhat forbidding to a child's eye but along with so many similar ones, a lovely relic of a past century. It was generously spacious, with high, decorative ceilings; the bathroom and toilet accordingly very dated by to-day's standards, but in perfect working order as German plumbing invariably was.

These buildings, each with two copious three to four bedroom flats on every floor, one to each side, housed friendly, hopeful, burgeoning young families. The war was over and now the path was clear for uninterrupted progress. Occasionally a genteel, white-haired couple whose children had grown up there and had left to form families of their own could also be spotted, standing rather forlorn by windows or on balconies of their rambling, apartments.

My sister Trudel told me later that all three children were called in to see the new arrival hours after I was born. She spoke of a miniscule head almost hidden by the mass of black cluster of curls, the tiny intruder wrapped in swaddling at mother's side. She must have felt the first tinge of jealousy as until then aged five, she had been the family's baby. But it was not something Trudel would ever admit to.

To both mother and father my late arrival appears to have been an absolute blessing and right from the start my father let me feel and understand that to him I was very special indeed; it was the same year he lost his revered father. Nor could I doubt that never for a moment was I not in absolute possession of mother's love.

My first genuine memory is one from the end of my second year or was it the first month of my third year which would have been 1932. That particular year was one in which I experienced what to many tiny tots might have been a terrifying accident but left me with little more than the memory of a frantic 'Papi' and a great deal of fuss all around me. The word 'pain' could be heard frequently and I was curious to know what it meant.

MY FIRST ACCIDENT

We had set out on one of our regular days' outings 'AUSFLUG' (a word evoking fun and outdoor freedom as soon as pronounced.) into the countryside outside Munich. A country-side awash with sunburnt meadows, isolated, pine-scented woods, fields and far-flung villages with cows, geese and chickens emitting their various faeces and tragic rhapsodies of terror and complaints all over the area. The stench seemed to seep right into the pores as one approached but after a while became an olfactory kaleidoscope attacking the senses with so many mashed aromas. Pigs were generally not seen roaming about freely in picnic areas but it was easy to sniff out where their sties were. My time to meet these hard-done by animals was still long distant.

The farm-houses were primitive stone buildings or made of wood with doors open to reveal families eating at tables as large as the room and the aroma of unmistakable SAUERBRATEN reaching far and wide. I disliked the cloying smell. The farmers spoke 'MUNCHNERDEUTSCH' a special Bavarian dialect, difficult to comprehend. But my parents and in particular my maternal grandmother Chatshe, the travelling sales-lady with the glowing complexion of a country woman, seemed to converse with them easily and familiarly. She was invariably treated with the respect of a native—one of them, her entire appearance in particular her complexion being far more rustic than my mother's Mediterranean hues.

I was left to play in the meadow, pick daisies and those flirty, fluffy flowers whose head you blew off. It was a hot day and the picnic table on which grandmother and mother had spread out the food so meticulously over a white linen cloth prepared and packed up early that morning, stood not far off. My father whom I called PAPI from the day I could prpononce the word, sat nearby on some collapsible green stool and as usual, with a pad and pencil on his lap making notes for his poems. He could never sit idle. Grandpa Aaron had seated himself a little further off emitting great swirling clouds of smoke whose yellow matched his finger-tips and the daisies in the fields. I am not sure if Papi and Opa had all that much to say to each other but there was rarely unpleasantness between them perhaps more due to father's quiet, uncritical manner than grandpa's boisterous, devil-may-care character, forever finding something to joke or laugh about. Failing that, he would sit smoking and gently chanting cantorial ditties or bits from his latest Jolson record to himself in a most pleasing trill of a tenor. My siblings were rarely present at these outings.

I was very proud of the daisy chains I had presented to my mother and grandmother and was stooping down to pick more daisies for Papi and Opa in the adjacent meadow, when I felt a needle-sharp sting in my right arm-pit. I must have cried out at quite a pitch more in surprise, as my father was at my side within seconds and lifted me up in his arms to inspect the cause of my obvious discomfort. By now, egged on by Papi's consternation, my tears flowed freely. So this was what they called pain.

In fathers arms all the way to his doctor friend's house that evening and from there to his surgery next door, I felt another sharp sting of the needle this time from the anaesthetic. Father's kisses and later that evening, mother's, helped to get me to sleep. I had been stung by a wasp which had embedded itself in my arm-pit and had to be excised. Apparently this was quite a dangerous accident hence my parents' panic. The lovely doctor, father's friend whom I had known since birth, had had to cut out the unfortunate creature. As for me, I still have the scar under my arm-pit. But the recollection of it all was not one of pain and fear but of being wrapped in a blanket of protective love.

LOST

The attractions of the ENGLISCHE GARTEN, one of Munich's prime open-air attractions and its only real park—the others were the OKTOBERWIESE and the ANLAGE—were evident. There was the AU the other side of Munich, the less salubrious area near the DEUTSCHE MUSEUM, standing alongside the river ISAR over the REICHENBACH BRIDGE. But for me the ENGLISCHE GARTEN was a magnet. There were the green open spaces; the milling crowds all of great cheer and reeking of MUNCHNER BIER and WURSTL. The little green chairs around small tables with people munching SAUERKRAUT and SCHWEINSBRATEN, a stench that dominated an entire area and had become as familiar as their rowdy Bavarian chatter. There were other green spaces near the MUNCHNER OPERNHAUS but none could boast the wonderful Carousel blasting out the same tunes over and over from a scratchy barrel-organ: tra la la la la la, tra la la la la la—as soon as those bewitching notes began taunting my ear-drums from afar, I was in Utopia. My hand unclenched itself from Papi's and I would skip ahead in the direction of the music. The Pied Piper of Hamelin had nothing on that primitive old barrel organ. I knew my way back to front and Papi would no longer restrain me by the end of 1932, allowing me the much-appreciated freedom of giving vent to my bursting excitement.

That early October was clement and would most likely be our last visit before the snow took over from the magic of the Carousel and we would go sleigh-riding on our huge sledge, rolling down the snow-covered slopes of the river Isar so close to our part of town. Those coarse notes screeching forth from the bowels of the Carousel sped me magically ever onwards in a trance. I needed no ZICKEZANGE—I needed no-one when those chants of the Carousel took a hold of me. There were a great many people about that sunny autumn afternoon, maybe more than usual and I fought my way ahead without remembering to look about me, enchanted by the magic strains but still not getting closer to the Carousel.

When I did stop for a moment I could not see Papi. But I continued, a little less sure now of my destination. No sign of Papi or of the gaudy, galloping horses and little side-cars and coaches of the Carousel. Even the familiar drone of the tunes had become fainter. I began to feel chilly in my favourite gold—embroidered coat that just covered my behind and which Mutti had said would have to be laid to rest next year as I was 'growing out of it.'

I shook my head of carefully dressed ringlets several times as if to confirm my suspicions: I did not know which way to go. I began to whimper in spite of myself. I could hear my tiny sobs as though they belonged to someone next to me: all those people and no Papi. But I carried on walking.

"Papi" I sobbed to myself

"What's the matter little one?" came a deep, comforting bass.

"Are you lost?" I looked up at the tall, friendly young police-man and nodded.

"I can't find my Papi—I've lost him. I'm very hungry too!"

"O dear me, lost your Papi have you—and hungry too? Then we'll have to get you an ice-cream before we take you to the station where I'm sure your Daddy is already waiting" I nodded looking up at him hugely relieved. He took my hand in his just like Papi, stopped at the next ice-cream vendor and purchased a chocolate wafer ice, before we walked hand in hand, with me licking my ice-cream held tightly in the other hand.

"Papi" I cried rushing up to my pale father standing outside the station. "Papi, look what the nice policeman has bought me!" All was forgotten save the delight at the police-man's generosity as I ran into my father's arms, clinging expertly to the remainder of the cornet.

Papi thanked the policeman and made a lame effort at chastising me. I knew even then that it was something he simply would never master.

"She's a little corker" I distinctly heard the bobby whisper aside. "She really is. She's going to break some hearts with those huge green eyes and long lashes!"

Why would I do such a terrible thing? The policeman's remark, which I took to be a dreadful prediction, secretly troubled me. Did that nice man think I was really so bad? I think Papi paid for the ice-cream before he marched me off with unaccustomed brusqueness.

"The—the Carousel—" I asked a trifle weepy aware we were nowhere close to my beloved jingles.

"We are going straight home" Papi said in an unfamiliar tone. I felt momentarily like grumbling to my 'special friend' ZICKEZANGE' but this was Papi, and I hardly ever resorted to other company in his presence; ZICKEZANGE was reserved for longer walks with Mutti. ZICKEZANGE had turned up one day only a few months earlier. I'm not exactly certain of her birthday, nor what she looked like; she was not a physical presence. But she was always there when I needed someone to talk to and in those early years she was the only contemporary friend who seemed to understand everything that went on inside my head and to whom I could confide ideas grown-ups might ridicule—excepting Papi that is.

I promised with all my heart, that I would never, never walk more than a few paces away again but there would be no ENGLISCHE GARTEN with its spellbinding Carousel until early spring in the New Year.

"Weren't you scared?" Trudel wanted to know that night.

I shook my head adamantly.

"No, not a bit" I insisted.

"But you cried—Daddy said so." Again I shook my head.

"Maybe—I only pretended. That nice policeman—he bought me an ice-cream" I bragged, "a big one!"

Trudel had a way of wriggling things out of me that I would not admit to others. Like the time she listened blank-faced to some little story that I assured her was a joke. When I had done and she still did not utter even a chuckle, I wanted to know why—"because that's not a joke." She explained not unkindly.

"Well" I replied outraged: "It's not a joke to be laughed at!!" To make matters worse, Trudel repeated my words to the whole family over and over and it took me a very long time to understand what they all seemed to find so risible. But she was always so kind afterwards and would kiss me on the nape of the neck until I complained and made her stop, pretending still to be offended when actually I liked it.

The year slipped by. I had made friends by then with the little girl in the apartment below us and far more importantly, with Alize Goldfarb, known as Lizzy from the top apartment. Lizzy was a year younger than me and also Jewish. At first I looked upon her as a baby when I was invited to play with her in her flat. But as the months drew on, Lizzy seemed to mature with miraculous speed and we enjoyed each other's company enormously. For me the Goldfarb's apartment was a never-ending paradise with its spacious rooms, its few inhabitants as Lizzy was an only child; its stylish, bright showroom-perfect interiors, its affable maid when parents were out and o' those expensive toys! I would frequently arrive around break-fast time and be asked to take breakfast with Herr and Frau Goldfarb and Lizzy. I could not wait to get my teeth into the new, warm rolls so generously buttered and spread eye-poppingly thickly with home-made raspberry jam, simply gliding into my mouth, washed down by the most chocolaty cocoa, where only one floor down in my own apartment, I would frequently refuse breakfast altogether. The Goldfarbs showed me great affection as my parents did Lizzy. It was a most desirable friendship for both our parents as we knew how to behave, not to ruin expensive carpets let alone the parquet floors and to respect the salons that had to be kept child-free, better known as 'DAS GUTE ZIMMER': the special room.

In my own home it was the music room with the piano and the best dining-room furniture and shimmering emerald green velour—covered chaise longue. Furniture always gleamed in both our homes, especially in the sunlight and our tables seemed to me big enough to hold a hundred diners.

Several ornately gilt-framed oil-paintings graced the walls of our 'GUTEN ZIMMER'. One was a very large oil painting of an imposing rabbi with dense, flowing white beard clad in a black, floor-length caftan blessing a handsome young scholar wrapped in a 'Tallith' (prayer shawl) kneeling at his feet. But the picture that invariably trapped my gaze as soon as I would enter was a large, gilt-framed sepia photo of my paternal grandfather Ysroel Dov who had died the year I was born. The pallid face seemed other-worldly, saintly and at that time I was secretly in great awe of it, tip-toeing beneath it, standing there staring for only a moment or two and then hastily retreating as if I were intruding. It was particularly unearthly to me because I knew he had died so recently and the thought of death, whatever it meant, terrified me. That saintly face of the man Papi so revered would continue to hold me in its spell as the years rolled by.

There were three bedrooms, one bathroom and a toilet next to the small bedroom intended for the maid. But as Abi was the only boy and Maria the maid did not sleep in, that room was his until he went to the Jewish teachers' training college in Wurzburg. My parents' bedroom was the largest and furnished with an elaborate, gleaming mahogany suite. Two huge single beds with matching head-boards stood next to each other not separated by the bedside tables that were placed on either side of each bed. Two separate his and hers wardrobes partially glass-fronted and a kidney-shaped dressing table with complementing stool elaborately satin-covered stood in between the wardrobes. Discreetly folded, that stool was generally taken up with one of my mother's flesh-coloured corsets, something I was determined from very early on, I would never wear.

The dining-salon was grand and spacious and the living room next to it, with a balcony, was 'gemutlich' (comfortable) to a fault. The living room lived up to its name: a true living room where one did not have to mind the furniture or the carpet or even the couch along the wall that smelled of every member of the family though it was frequently aired and beaten as well as recovered. I shared the bedroom with my two sisters, where we each had similar beds with red and gold iron bedsteads and smelly duvets filled with duck-down. The room was large enough to allow comfortably for one bed along each wall leaving one wall for the cupboard. My clothes were generally kept in Mutti's drawers. I loved having the large empty room to myself and did a great deal of fanciful dreaming on such rare occasions.

Two floors down lived Herr and Frau Loewenberger. I had recently made great friends with them too, especially their little golden Dachshund with the strange red appendages drooping from behind. The Loewenbergers had no children of their own and seemed to have taken me to their heart. Herr Loewenberger was Jewish and his wife Catholic. I am not quite sure how I knew that but fact is I knew it quite early on as it was never considered anything to be secret.

I loved the sharp little face of FRITZL, the dog, but was not at all sure about his smell although he was washed and groomed meticulously by his owners. I became so friendly with the Lowenbergers that I was eventually allowed to take Fritzl round the block on my own with my parents' permission too, of course.

But I could not love Fritzl as much as that velvety black and white kitten I had been allowed to cuddle on our last outing to the country and which I could kiss and stroke to my heart's delight. It was so smooth and soft, so indescribably lovable as though it needed me. The photo Papi took of me holding the kitten became a family favourite and cats have ruled my heart from then on. The photo was duly dated: I was all of two and a half years old. There were few cats about in my direct neighbourhood, however. I had plenty of love left for any other member of the animal kingdom I might come in touch with including lady birds we collected in little match boxes and believed we fed adequately with bits of leaves and grass.

RINGLETS

I was convinced my mother enjoyed dressing my thick, long black curls every morning before she went to the mattress and bedding shop in the LINDWURMSTRASSE which she ran with my father. She would go earlier because Daddy had to type out his Yiddish articles and poetry on his Hebrew—lettering typewriter and mail what had to be posted or taken to the publisher's office in person if it was here in town. Sometimes of late he would even take me with him on the tram which I loved. And I began to realise quite early on that he was a highly respected and admired Yiddish writer and poet frequently invited to speak, sing or read poetry at social functions. And quite early on too I was proud of my slim, handsome, distinguished—looking father with those china-blue eyes and fine, even features. He was also Invariably immaculate, his shoes polished to a high sheen.

The daily kerfuffle with my abundant, stubborn locks was not one of my favourite routines as I am now sure it was even less so my dear patient mother's. Often enough it would end up with me in tears by the time she had rolled my ringlets one by one in some fragrant lotion. When done she would take out a mirror from her bedside cabinet—the entire procedure was carried out in bed before she rose and I had to sit still on her goose-feather duvet. I loathed the smell of those goose-feather pillows and duvets. They were considered the crème de la crème of bedding and naturally as became the owners of a bedding—store, all our beds were blessed with equal luxury. I was then asked for approval, shaking my freshly dressed, bouncing and still somewhat damp ringlets this way and that as Mutti awaited my delighted thank you. There were times, however, when I thought she might have taken just that little bit more pain and I would ask her to improve on her chore which she unfailingly did. My busy Mutti's patience must have been brought to breaking point.

It appears that the little girl in a downstairs apartment with whom I sometimes went on the swings in the spacious back yard had begged Mutti to dress her hair like mine and as I only discovered years later, my dear mother duly obliged although that child's hair was spaghetti-straight in absolute contrast to my own. Somehow Mutti worked her patient magic to the girl's satisfaction and it was something that girl never forgot.

Of normal height for my age, quite skinny but with sturdy, well-shaped long legs, I was getting used to people saying nice things about my looks, especially about my huge green eyes, long lashes and of course, Mutti's pride but hardly her joy: my curls. In fact I grew quite blasé about the whole matter and it was left to Trudel to put me in my place. Henny humoured me as I saw far less of her and Abi played with me whenever he had a spare moment. I liked him very much. Our ten-years age-difference gave him plenty of opportunity to treat me like his own toy but Henny, nearly eight years older than me, appeared often to feel hard done by, overtaken by the all-important boy of the Jewish house-hold and now by this spoilt little newcomer. But I looked up to her: she was my clever, well-behaved and always polite elder sister, who could be called upon by Mutti to help out whenever necessary.

18

I thought Trudel was beautiful with her straight, smooth shiny chestnut hair and fringe and wished my hair would behave better. I liked the freckles in Henni's pale face and the way her thick chestnut hair was worked into a kind of sausage every morning. Mutti too, whose hair was much like Henni's, wore her hair in that sausage style although to begin with I simply thought that their hair grew that way. Trudel's fringe which grew right down to her eye-brows seemed to me the height of what a modern young girl should look like although I had to admit that she did look a little wild at times, with her large blue-green eyes peeping out provocatively from that fringe.

Our maid's name was Maria but ever since I had begun talking I had pronounced it Magiga and that was what for me she would remain. She was gentle and kind and part of the family. Everything was an adventure and I could not wait for the day to begin and fought bitterly to make it last as long as possible. Maria arrived softly, very early every morning and left after supper just as unobtrusively. Bed-time was my least favourite time unless Papi had time to tell me more than one story. His own stories were far better than the fairy tales others would read to me but which I still swallowed up greedily. In the day-time I would pour over the brightly—coloured picture books, especially those of Hansel and Gretel and Cinderella. Many of them frightened me, especially 'STRUWELPETER' with his horrid long uncut nails and hair and RAPUNZEL.

Sometimes Mutti would come home early and take me with her on a shopping trip to town. On fine days we would walk as no one thought anything of walking through our lovely city for an hour or more. Or we would take the tramway which to me never failed to be an adventure. I loved the tinny clatter of its wheels, the exciting jolts as it turned hither and thither and I particularly loved looking out of the window into shop-windows and buildings and theatres like the REICHENBACHTHEATER the sight of which thrilled me ever since I had been taken to see Cinderella there.

I was eager for Mutti to complete her shopping at the stylish, up-market store like OBERPOLLINGER where the haute couture fashion department had its own separate floor and the enormous carpet and furniture showrooms took over another two floors. The parquet floors gleamed and the steps up to the floors were thickly carpeted. The owner was Jewish and Mutti seemed to know everyone. We were invariably made very welcome. These stores had a most pleasing olfactory effect on me as smell and sound seemed to be a part of me from the very beginning perhaps thanks to my parents' exceptional cleanliness and father's perpetual singing what later I would recognise to be not merely snippets but whole sections of operas, lieder and operettas. I found faces far less interesting and could often not tell one from the other whereas tunes, melodies of any calibre and fragrances, once come across, found a permanent home with me.

But the return journey was the best part of such shopping expeditions. Trailing behind Mutti for what seemed like hours might have brought ZICKEZANGE into my life. I do not know. Maybe I needed someone to marvel with me at the sun-kissed FRIEDENSENGEL (Angel of Peace) gleaming across at us from the REICHENBACH Bridge. That gigantic golden angel looming over all Munich was its instantly recognised landmark and from where we lived, with the choice of two bridges across which we could reach our street, we were treated to its magnificent spectacle no matter which bridge we crossed. In the summer with the sun highlighting its gleam as though newly polished, you could not ignore its overpowering predominance. In the winter it was still conspicuous enough unless it snowed thick flakes and the air as well as the angel was white. Yes, I needed to tell someone other than Mutti. Someone other than Mutti who might not have been interested as she was always so preoccupied with countless other tasks, how much I liked that angel and how I hoped its broad beautiful golden wings spread over us all in perpetual protection.

But once we reached my favourite café in KARTNERPLATZ and sat down at a little table outside on the pavement, with sun beaming down, I had no need of ZICKEZANGE. My mind was on the scrumptious hot chocolate with dollops of snow-white whipped cream and at its side a plate of my chosen chocolate éclair with yet more fresh cream. Skinny as I was I could handle sweet delicacies from the cradle as my mother and grandmother were such wizard bakers of every manner of patisserie. Yes, the return journey was eagerly anticipated each time and it was very rare that Mutti would disappoint me by depriving me of this treat.

OUR APARTMENT

We lived in the SCHWEIGERSTRASSE by the AU, a bright green stretch of meadow where a DULT (fair) was held regularly. An ancient church stood on the other side. But of course I could not visit the church although I know Trudel had secretly done so. The REICHENBACHBRUCKE flanked the banks of the sea-green river ISAR in the opposite direction. Beyond lay the shady, tree-lined ANLAGE, a boulevard that ran all along that side of the Isar right up to the ENGLISCHE GARTEN. WE were embraced by outstretched emerald arms wherever I chose to look. And of course the golden FRIEDENSENGEL brooded over everything.

The SCHWEIGERSTRASSE prided itself in several brand-new apartment houses, all of them flats with the most up-to-date services: with porters living in the basements, marble walls and floors in the entrance halls and fine wide wooden stairways. AS soon as one entered, the sweet smell of polished wood and its lapidary surrounds would caress one's olfactory senses

Right on the corner opposite stood the old, sprawling Convent very grey and grimy. To me it looked forbidding and ghostly. Tall, powerful chestnut trees ran along the rest of the street. In winter they were dark and a little too mysterious not to be frightening but in summer their bright verdant crowns seemed to glow in the golden sun. On our own side following the three apartment buildings a tiny bakery had squeezed itself into a gap announcing its existence with its irresistible yeasty redolence. Even the pub on the end of the road could not vie with its BRATWURST stench against the sweetness of the bakery smell. How I loved the aroma of the fresh rolls known to me as 'SEMMEL'; the enticing sugary odour of the fat doughnuts and the unmistakable smell of the fresh rye-bread with aniseed my parents liked so much.

The fair that came to our 'AU' every festive occasion was like a special gift only given to the few fortunate ones. The Punch and Judy show; the little ghost train I was too young to brave. The pitiful circus with the sickly, tortured animals! It was all so exciting all the more so as my grandparents lived just up the hill on the GEBSATTELPLATZ and we would have to go via the fair whether my parents wanted to or not, unless they crossed over and made the whole walk longer and denied us the pleasure of the DULT. And my parents were not made of such tough fibre. Even the Gothic gargoyles grinning ominously over the stone water fountain on the GEBSATTEL Bridge, did not faze my enthusiasm; in fact as time drew on I came to regard them as little devilish pals. Munich was not short of such weird embellishments.

My little world and its surroundings, the colourful, exciting people that formed our social circle—snugly ensconced in the warm cushion of my family, little Mella Lowy was as happy a little girl as one could hope to find in all of the German Reich.

Chapter Three

MY TRAVELS, SCHOOL AND FIRST FILMS; GOETHE AND TOBOGGANING WITH ABI.

Since I turned four there was an awful lot of discussion on what the adults called 'politics'. I hated the word from the very start as it took Papi away for hours on end with fellow poets or artists, generally to the 'GUTEN ZIMMER' as the salon was known. Naturally I could not follow. I heard too of a THIRD REICH headed by a man named Hitler who did not like Jews. I even began to recognise his voice and accent as it was so exceptionally mean and menacing as soon as it came on the wireless. It reminded me of the screeching witch in Hansel and Gretel as she was generally portrayed. The other man who spoke on the wireless was a Dr. Goebbels. His voice was thinner but equally menacing. I was surprised how a doctor could sound so unpleasant. Our family doctor was such a cuddly, kind man with a voice as reassuring as Opa's or Papi's.

Of course I knew I was Jewish and a great deal of our daily, weekly, or special celebrations—to me they all seemed like celebrations as I would be dressed festively for synagogue and mouth-watering cakes would be baked with friends and family sitting around festive tables—were all centred around being Jewish. It was good: there were so many festivities and they invariably went hand in hand with delicious pastries and cakes immersing the entire flat in a chocolaty yeasty fragrance. Of course I knew that a great many other people in Munich were Christians and went to church to pray as we went to Synagogue. It did not ever occur to me that they might dislike me for being Jewish as everyone was invariably so nice to me and my family. I was very proud of my family. But I never entered a church. In fact those huge, dark Gothic structures housing charnel chambers in the back (as Trudel had one day informed me) frightened me, whereas Synagogues seemed friendly and unassuming although I was never to enter the oldest and most ornate Synagogue in Munich. The Synagogues I was familiar with were humble rooms in old, tumble-down houses or quite new, plain almost naked buildings as though purposely designed not to draw attention, like the one in the Reichenbachstrasse I was taken to most frequently.

There was one time of the year when I would secretly have been happy to metamorphose into a Christian child whose home sported one of those magical pine trees adorned with twinkling stars, gilded fairies and sparkling tinsel wrapped around mysterious, fabulous gifts. They were to be seen in most shops and department—stores and I truly wished I could come home at Christmas to find just such a gigantic woody pine tree in our own living room. It was hard for anyone to tear me away from the window of OBERPOLLINGERS, the elegant Jewish department store at this time of year. Or there was ULFELDER and EPA, more large stores, the former Jewish, with equally beguiling frippery on their lavish trees in their windows. I could not quite understand why I could not be visited by 'NIKOLAUS' (Father Christmas.) And it was at this time of year and then only for the briefest time, I began to regret that we were a little 'different'.

Christmas—time in Munich in 1933 with the snow gently falling and church—bells ringing; multi-coloured lights twinkling invitingly from even the smallest shop-window decorated with a myriad of desirable baubles as soon as daylight faded—yes, that was when I would have exchanged my own Jewish status for one whole day—mother's cheese cake and all. The chanting of 'STILLE NACHT, HEILIGE NACHT' (Silent Night, Holy Night) too, resounding from every street corner it seemed even if it came from the numerous mysterious churches, added to an eerily enchanted spectacle I could only glimpse from the wings. All this mystery, like the Gothic churches certainly frightened me, but even more did it somehow leave me with the yearning to be a part of it.

As it happened I was to be more fortunate than most Jewish children troubled with similar sentiments of deprivation. The Loewenbergers, whose unofficial doggie—walker I had become, invited me to celebrate Christmas morning around their tree. As they had no children I was a little surprised by the invitation. A tree—I had thought those wondrous fragrant green giants belonged solely to Christian children who would then be visited by

Saint Nicolas in the night so that their presents might be found under the tree the following morning. But it seems my fertile imagination had quite misinterpreted the Christmas puzzle. My excitement was intense. There was, however, the problem of permission from my parents. Could a Jewish child be permitted to accept such an invitation?

My pleading expression must have been too much even for Mutti with whom the final decision rested—as she gave her permission but not without all too obvious misgiving. Thus the Christmas before my fifth birthday with Hitler already Chancellor and the streets beginning to sport men in jack-boots and brown and black uniforms that I found no more than baffling and rather rowdy, as their clanking marches disturbed the erstwhile serenity of my Munich, I was to experience my first Christmas at the Loewenbergers. What I was also soaking up as was my nature, were the poisonous chants they marched to—the rabble-rousing words seemed glued to the tunes—and how they both stuck! But fortunately I was immune to the poison.

I was not to be disappointed. If anything the reality exceeded my expectations. I was to arrive shortly before lunch-time Christmas day, so that Saint Nicholas had had time to bring me his gifts as he was so busy. Actually it was also so that the Loewenbergers had time to attend church as it appeared they always did together even though he had not converted to Christianity. It was also a time much preferred by my mother who did not like me going anywhere alone in the evening even if it was only a couple of floors below our own apartment.

My parents' faith was firmly rooted though even small as I was, it was obvious that my mother oversaw religion whilst my father lived for nothing as much as family and his 'MAMMELOSHEN' Yiddish, in which he practised his art and for which he would forsake all worldly riches. But equally I comprehended from the moment I could understand anything, that my father's loyalty and devotion to the saintly Ysroel Dov, his father, was unshakable.

Christmas morning finally dawned though it had seemed to take forever coming. I rang the door-bell at noon as instructed, praying I was not too early. The Loewenbergers had been to midnight mass, a very special service they had informed me with beautiful choir-song and hymns. As I had loved anything musical from the cradle thanks to Papi's perpetual singing and humming, I secretly wished they had taken me along too though the local church in the Au was in my eyes surely thousands of years old and anything and everything connected with 'church' made me feel alien and uncomfortable.

As the door was opened to this Jewish four-year old by Herr Loewenberger, heart threatening to burst out of her skinny body, raven curls especially carefully fixed into resplendent ringlets and clad in very best red velvet dress that reached just past my bottom I was led into the 'GUTE ZIMMER' without further ado. Their apartment being smaller but far smarter and immaculate as only a childless home can be, I stopped short at the threshold. In the middle of their resplendent salon stood the largest, most beautifully decorated Christmas tree even I could have dreamed of. Frau Loewenberger bade me enter as she stepped towards me with open arms to hug me to her generous bosom. From out of nowhere it seemed, fairy-lights formed a halo over the tree, twinkling in every colour of the rainbow, but crowned in golden glory by the beauteous fairy on the tip of the tree.

Frau Lowenberger's embrace eased me out of my tongue-tied stupor"St. Nicholas has brought you a present too." She said softly, pointing to the many exquisitely wrapped little parcels on what seemed a bed of snow under the real pine tree whose overpowering scent permeated the entire flat.

"For me—" I repeated in disbelief. "But"

"Of course—"she interrupted again. "He loves all children." She seemed instantly to have comprehended the source of my 'but': I was not a Christian child, could Saint Nicholas love me?

With what delight I took her word for it. St Nicholas loved Jewish children too. She pointed to a little package in gleaming silver wrapping paper and I knelt down to take it.

"You can unwrap it later." She said in that comforting voice while little Fritzel yapped his hellos and made efforts to jump up. I giggled with delight as I thanked her, but secretly anxious Fritzel might tear my new red stockings or scratch the brand new black patent shoes I would be wearing to Synagogue that Sabbath, for it was Chanukah too.

That morning I was to become acquainted with the wonders of German Christmas fare and the ensuing tummy—ache so richly deserved. But I loved every morsel of the MARZIPANSTOLLEN, the coloured sugar-coated LEBKUCHEN cookies and all those marzipan animals I loved above all else!

And the tinsel-wrapped gift from St. Nicholas? A newly-baked outsized ginger-bread St Nicholas which I had not the heart to eat and only nibbled at long after it had grown stale. After all, St Nicholas loved all children.-

The snow was thick, white and wonderful that Christmas. Abi was home and we would go tobogganing on our huge family sleigh. Usually Papi took me on a Sunday as all my siblings were busy seeing their friends or in Trudel's case going to ballet classes. Abi was a member of his LYZEUM'S football team and he was a prominent member of the Synagogue's choir. He had a lovely voice, was generally considered talented and highly intelligent and made sure I was included in any plays he directed for the PURIM and Chanukah festivities. Later he would write the plays too. Yes, I was certainly fond of my big brother. He did not treat me like a baby, nor did he tease me as Trudel often did. I also thought him very handsome.

He was always immaculate like Papi and looked particularly fetching and stylish in his brown tweed knickerbockers. He was of athletic build with broad shoulders and very good at football as well as a first rate student. But I had to admit he often gave Henny a hard time, teasing her and bullying her far more than Trudel ever did me. I think Trudel and Henny got on well enough though I could sometimes hear them squabble late at night.

Going tobogganing on a fine, frosty sunny day, with the golden FRIEDENSENGEL reigning benignly over Munich, the river Isar frozen and countless children queuing on the banks to toboggan down the steep slopes, was my idea of winter heaven! Everyone was impatient for their turn, yet rarely were we pushed before we were ready, maybe because Abi was broad-shouldered and athletic for his age and not one to be fooled with.

To cling on to Abi's back as we sped down what seemed to me an enormous height but in reality was little more than an average slope; my fingers and toes were frozen in their respective boots and mittens yet arms remained wound tightly around Abi, as the snow softly yielded to our vehicle—I experienced a sensation of euphoric freedom tinged not a little with fear. By the time we reached home fingers and toes would be entirely dead but by then Papi was home to rub my frozen extremities back to life and make me the anticipated cup of hot cocoa its vapour deliciously chocolaty.

Dr Ziegler was a friend of my father's and shortly before I was to start school, he gave me my first piano lesson as he had been teaching Trudel for some time. But Trudel, musical as she was, fell in love with the accordion and neglected her piano practice. She was promised an accordion if she did her school-work satisfactorily, or so I was told. Dr Ziegler, a fine, distinguished-looking man with thick whitish hair and wonderful long fingers, would lift me up on the piano stool and I would begin excitedly with flushed cheeks, anticipating the forthcoming praises the avuncular man never failed to heap upon me.

I had just mastered 'GUTER MOND' with every finger in the correct sequence and played it every chance I got when Papi told me with that sad expression he had of late, that Dr Ziegler would come no more as he was emigrating to America. If there were two words that secretly puzzled and frightened me they were 'emigrate' and 'America', though I would not admit as much. Somehow I sensed that it was to do with the increase almost daily of those marching and chanting automatons in their rowdy, empowering jackboots. I found them mesmerising like giant metallic toy-soldiers and gradually could repeat every word and tune of what was becoming a kind of repertoire. They had become part of everyday life; part of everyone's life in Munich.

ITALY (ABBAZIA, NOW W. CROATIA)

Before I was to start school at the Jewish VOLKSSCHUHLE (the Jewish State School in Munich) in the Herzogrudolfstrasse, Mutti and I were booked go on holiday to Italy. Mutti had some female complaints it was rumoured by my sisters and needed the warmth and rest. A child my age sharing a room with parents would not be charged so Mutti had decided to take me along. Of course I had to promise to be exceptionally good and quiet. I was very excited. A long train journey stopping first in Merano where my parents' close friends the Konigsbergs had now been living for some time Uncle Moshe much preferring Mussolini's Italy to Hitler's Germany. We would be staying with them one night as Mutti did not want to put them out longer. Of course I had to promise to be very good. As it was they were a large family. Passing briefly through Trieste and Fiume, we would finally arrive at the modest pension in Abbazia.

Had I had a choice I would have preferred to go with Papi but then again he would have nothing to do with dressing my hair although he was meticulous where washing and general cleanliness was concerned and it was generally he who washed my hair. When he read my unspoken disappointment he said:

"Someone has to stay behind to mind the shop in LINDWURMSTRASSE."

Even though it was an open family-secret that Mutti ran the business and Papi spent most of the time in the shop writing poetry on printed business paper. I just looked sadly at his dear face and waited for him to take me in his arms.

"There won't be anyone to tell me stories and make up fumy rhymes" I grumbled as I clung to him.

I loved coming to the shop which was opposite the OKTOBERWIESE to which I would soon be allowed to go with Trudel. But I had also made friends with a few children from neighbouring shops and we would get together in the communal back-yard, where we would play mothers and fathers or doctors. I always ended up marrying the handsomest boy and the other girls would have to be maids or perform other menial chores. I never discovered whether any of my friends there were Jewish but I do not think so. I knew that once I began school there would be little time for such indulgences.

Mutti took me to see a Shirley Temple film where the lovely little girl with the perfect golden ringlets sang 'The Good Ship Lollypop' and all I could not take my eyes off her hair. The rest of the film eluded me as I could not make heads or tails of the plot and at any rate I was hypnotised by the lush American settings and Shirley's lovely dresses—but most of all her perfect ringlets that never seemed to fall apart like mine.

Mutti took me to another film soon after called 'The Good Earth' with Paul Muni and Louise Rainer. And for some reason I followed the contents sufficiently to burst into bitter tears more than once. Something about seeing people being executed, the earth being scorched and the main characters in constant peril and misery upset me deeply. Mutti had to calm me and put her arm about me.

"It's only a film—"she whispered. "A very clever lady called Pearl Buck wrote the book and then it was made into a film." Maybe it was the brilliant acting of the stars and the terrifying spectacles on the screen but this film would continue to move me for many a year.

When Trudel took me with her to see 'Ramona' sneaking through a back entrance without paying, I fell in love for the first time. Don Ameche seemed to me the most handsome man I had ever seen (almost surpassing my father) and Loretta Young simply the most beautiful woman in the world. I would return home and chant the tunes enraptured until Trudel hushed and threatened never to take me with her again. At the time I did not comprehend why I could not sing the lovely tunes I had picked up from the film. Obviously I had not yet learnt that everything had to be paid for any more than had my big sister.

This was to be my most exciting year: first, my trip abroad and then that long-awaited first school-day. The journey to Italy was hot and sticky but when we reached a stop and I was given a genuine Italian ice-cream, I was a very happy girl. There was much bustle and commotion in Fiume the frontier and I clung to Mutti's hand without having to be reminded. But I could not fail to be struck by Mutti's relaxed attitude when she spoke to the Italian frontier guards, their charming smiles and the fuss they made of me. They looked a bit like Don Ameche, I thought.

"Bella, bella—"they beamed as they stroked me. I took it they referred to my perfectly dressed ringlets as that was the only thing I ever paid attention to when I looked in the mirror; that and the lovely little dresses and coats my mother made sure I was dressed in. I was actually quite baffled by the fact that so many people referred to my huge green eyes and thick long lashes as I never noticed them in the mirror Only my hair which could at times become quite unruly as it was so thick and curly.

"We are in Italy" my mother said with a deep sigh of relief as she settled herself and me back on the train. "It's lovely here." She gave me a hug.

"O" I exclaimed in horror as Mutti said we would soon be arriving in Trieste. I had been looking out of the window of the umpteenth train, enjoying every moment of this warm, welcoming scenery gilded by constant sunshine.

"What's the matter?"

"We forgot something very important!"

"What is that?"

"We forgot to bring the NINIVEA CRÈME!" I spilled out the word with some difficulty. Several heads in the carriage turned towards us and to my consternation, they were all smiling broadly

Mutti put her arm about me and assured me that she had packed a small jar of NIVEA crème in her own travel bag. I blushed wondering why everyone seemed to be so amused at what I had just said.

"O, that's good." I said in a very small voice as I hurriedly turned my head back to stare out the window.

The Koenigsbergs had sold their business in Munich and had for the moment rented a very modest villa in Merano. The place seemed to burst at the seams with Eva, who was my age, Hannah Trudel's age, Rachel Henni's and Eli Abi's age. They were such a happy and hospitable family and so thrilled to be reunited with their friend Marie and hear all her latest news. But Auntie Hedda as I called her missed Munich, as she was a genuine MUNCHNER KINDL born and bred in Munich like all of us children. What was more Hedda looked more like a local Bavarian woman than any of my parents' other friends. She was a large, buxom woman, with a broad, open face and a huge welcoming smile and laugh. Uncle Moshe on the other hand, had a far more exotic, refined artistic appearance with a handsome moustache and a thick heads of dark hair. The couple were as different in appearance as in their accents but when they looked at each other they seemed to melt together with love.

I thought their villa was exquisite with so much flora back and front and the dining table on the veranda. Such al fresco living in such lovely surroundings struck me as magical. Uncle Moshe appeared to prefer it here in Italy and he insisted that Italians were not ant-Semitic nor would Mussolini ever cause the Jews the kind of misery Hitler was causing. Auntie Hedda seemed not quite that convinced.

We were to visit a kosher restaurant near-by for supper and as it was such a lovely day, it was suggested we took a walk. I would have been quite happy to stay with Eva and Hanna who were not coming but Mutti would not leave me.

I trundled behind the adults marvelling to Zickezange at the blissful fragrance of orange blossom and jasmine. I was told those magnificent pregnant rose-red blooms hovering tall over our heads as we passed the grand villas were camellias. "Yes," I whispered, "Italy is very beautiful!" And I almost wished we could all move here away from the noisy din of the goose-stepping marching marauders, which is what Papi called them—even though Munich was my real love.

Our 'Pensione' in Abbazia was only a steep walk down a hill from the ocean. I had a little bunk-bed and the room was modest in the extreme. But Mutti explained that we needed to be frugal as there were so many expenses and this was the only reasonable place so near the ocean.

"These are difficult times." She had added with one of her frequent little sighs.

I was very excited when we walked down the hill rather more slowly than usual as it seemed my poor mother's female complaints caused her great discomfort but there right below us, shimmered the lavender blue Adriatic. I found myself jumping up and down and begging my mother to let me go in.

Mutti purchased a red rubber swimming belt on the way down from one of the many shops and placed it round my waist over my brand-new bathing costume, when we reached the beach. She herself wore a bathing suit I had seen many times as we often went en famille to the swimming pool in MARIAEINSIEDEL. My parents were good swimmers and until this year had also regularly gone mountain-climbing with their friends from the Jewish Arts Club. Now here, to my delight, in the soothing cool of the Adriatic, in obvious pain as she was, my mother patiently explaining and guiding, taught me to swim. She stood in the warm waters of the gentle ocean, held my chin up high if it threatened to drop and directed my movements. The salty ocean did the rest as it supported me so that within a few more days I could dispense with the swimming belt and swam confidently under my Mutti's tender watch. That holiday, in spite of a face swollen with mosquito bites and away from Papi, was idyllic.

A BIKE-RIDE TO STARNBERGERSEE

Abi had promised to take me for a long ride on the back of his bike before he returned to the Jewish teacher's training college in Wurzburg and I would begin school. But I had not reckoned with the beautiful lake in STARNBERG and the woods surrounding it.

It was a very long ride on a lovely warm, sunny summer's morning and I was allowed to wear my favourite blue dirndl. Sandwiches packed mysteriously in the saddle in the back and Abi clad in stylish grey-green knickerbockers and short-sleeved white shirt, I clung tightly seated in my own special saddle to the back of him, much as I did on a sledge.

With the glimmering lake on one side and pine trees opposite, we finally came to a halt at a small inroad into the thicket and Abi lifted me out of my saddle to which by then my hot bottom had seemed to be stuck, clad as I was in my dirndl dress which like all other dresses, went no further than the start of my thighs.

Once Abi had taken great trouble to search for a dry, grassy as well as shady spot for us to settle and had parked his bike with utmost care by a tree, he spread a small blanket he unfolded from the saddle-bag and out came the large grease-proof bag of sandwiches. My eyes flew to it with great longing.

"Not yet," he said with a broad grin. I liked his smile. He had such fine white teeth.

"O"—the disappointment in my voice was unmistakable.

"Are you hungry?" Well, maybe we could just have one sandwich now and save the rest and the fruit and Mutti's cake for later. My happy grin was sufficient reply.

My sixteen year old brother that day was as tender, caring and solicitous as any devoted parent. After that first snack washed down with lukewarm home-made lemonade, we settled down on the grass and Abi took out a thick book and began reciting from Goethe's poetry:

'UBER ALLEN GIPFELN IST RUH-

UBER ALLEN WIPFEL HOHREST DU KAUM EINEN HAUCH.

DIE VOGLEIN RUHEN IM WALDE.

WARTE NUR BALDE RUHEST DU AUCH."

I understood none of the poetry. But I loved to hear him recite. It was work he had to prepare for school but I was so flattered that he should honour me with so much attention. However, I gleaned from the sombre tone of his voice that this was a very sad poem.

We finished the last remnants of our picnic after the sun had begun to disappear behind the tall, masterful trees and I tried to stop myself from shivering.

"You are getting cold"—said Abi, as he began to pack up, scrupulously crunching the grease-proof paper back in his rucksack to discard in a suitable receptacle later. Litter was not something tolerated lightly in Germany.

"No, no—" but I was quite happy now when he lifted me into my very own little saddle and I clung once more to his back as we set off back home. He had wrapped me in his sweater and I felt very happy as we began to sing "Das wandern ist des Muller's Lust" (Wandering is the joy of the miller.) The gleaming STARNBERGERSEE lay behind us, darker and more mysterious now in the waning light and I hoped we would come back here very soon.

A few weeks later Abi arrived home for a week-end and gave me a cuddle.

"You see," he said beaming" you helped me with my Goethe and I came top!"
I didn't quite see how I had helped him but if he said so then it must be true.
I was very proud of my big brother.

FIRST SCHOOL DAYS

It seemed as if I had been waiting for this day all of my five and a half years—my
life-time. The weeks, the months could not go fast enough. I would be six in
January of next year and it was decided to admit me a few months early.

The Jewish school (JUDISCHE VOLKSSCHUHLE) the only one available
in Munich was in the HERZOGRUDOLFSTRASSE right in the centre of
town. HERZOGRUDOLFSTRASSE was just off the main road in which
stood the grandiose HOTEL VIERJAHRESZEIT, adopted by the Fuhrer as
his preferred sojourn when he was in Munich.

It was customary to bring along as large and fancy a cone filled with goodies
as one's parents could possibly afford on that first, momentous occasion.
Thus one could see tiny tots dragging along silver or gold cones often taller
than themselves, stuffed with enough chocolate and marzipan animals and
boxes of assorted chocolates to feed an entire class which must have been the
initial idea though rarely carried out.

This was the fourth time my parents had gone through the ritual but I
was fortunate as there was a reasonable gap since Trudel had had her
turn. Mutti had insisted on accompanying me as far as the top of the long
HERZOGRUDOLFSTRASSE but I wanted to do the last lap on my own
so I pretended I had not noticed Mutti a good few paces behind me whilst
I dragged the over-loaded silver cone reaching almost up to my shoulders,
to the school entrance. My heart pounded furiously when I stopped and
graciously waited for Mutti to give me that final kiss before I braved the
jostling mass of over-excited little strangers.

I loved my school from that first moment I set foot in my allotted class-room.
There were about thirty children, seated in two double rows with a passage

in the centre for the teacher to walk down. One side was taken up by boys and the other by girls. That first day we were told to sit anywhere in the girl's section.

The teacher introduced himself as LEHRER BERLINGER. His voice was soft and gentle, the face if not exactly handsome, was immediately sympathetic. Nor was he very elegant but there was something so kind and fatherly about him that I adored him from the start. In fact he was the first man I truly loved other than my father. Neat in his somewhat frayed greenish serge suit, with a clean white shirt and polished brown shoes, it would have been difficult for any child to take a dislike to this man. His eyes that first year still had a twinkle and he was never averse to a joke even if at times it was at the expense of one of the less bright students, it was never overtly mean.

Eventually we fell into our seating arrangement naturally. The best students sat furthest back and to my delight I was one of them. It was all there: the excitement, the real world of lots of new friends I had so longed for. I had my cocooned home-life with older siblings and a couple of friends in the building and now I was presented with a new, a never-ending, ever-changing daily excitement and drama.

I loved singing and reciting and picked up tunes quickly as our home had resounded with music from the day I was born. And reciting poetry was second nature Papi having always encouraged me to learn poems by heart and Abi who wrote little CHANUKAH and PURIM plays, had given me small walk-on parts almost before I could understand a single word of what I was saying. But one thing I knew even then: I loved attention and I loved reciting.

Lehrer Berlinger obviously detected this flair early on and it helped that I had a good musical ear. I made friends with Evi Ballin, a doctor's daughter, from the first day. And there was Bertel Sandbank, to whose beautiful villa near the ENGLISCHE GARTEN I would eventually be invited for birthday and Chanukah parties. All three of us sat at the back, Eva next to me and Bertel in the last bench with Annemarie. Bertel Sandbank was a star pupil and she was also the sweetest natured girl anyone could wish to meet. There was Steffi Weil too at the back, with the fairest complexion and golden ringlets that certainly put mine to shame I thought. But she too was such a friendly, sweet-natured child that instead of jealousy I was filled with admiration. She was certainly fairer than any other pupil there. At any rate I thought her very lovely and she was always so beautifully dressed. She too would become a good friend.

I excelled at gym and could do a head-stand at a moment's notice. Being thin I could also perform one of the highest jumps in the high-jump tests for juniors. To top that I was a fast runner and it was planned to put me in the junior Jewish Olympics for which we would be training regularly at the wonderful sports grounds the school used in the outskirts of Munich.

Birthday invitations abounded from the day I started school. And of course when my own birthday finally came round Mutti promised me a party too.

Each day was an adventure. I loved walking home with several school chums who lived close by although I was given money for the tram. But walking home on those halcyon summer days with a gentle, fragrant breeze cooling our heated cheeks, we would dawdle along the ANLAGE gathering lady birds whose age we were assured could be defined by the spots on their backs, was all part of the new school experience I so treasured. We made sure those creatures were comfortable in their little cardboard boxes which we stuffed with leaves and grass. When they died days later I was genuinely upset. It never occurred to me that I might have overstuffed the tiny boxes and that above all, they required fresh air and their freedom.

Sometimes when the river under the REICHENBACH Bridge had dried up with only the FRIEDENSENGEL as witness, we would sneak under the bridge our sandals in our satchels and it was then that Erich Kupfer grabbed a hold of me and kissed me on the lips. That was when I decided that Erich Kupfer would never become my husband because I did not like that kiss at all. It worried me that we might have committed some unspeakable sin.

So much happened in 1937 that I thought no year could ever be more eventful. Mutti had taken me to visit Auntie Rosel in Leipzig and I had stood below the rather formidable statue of Felix Mendelssohn who looked very old to me although it said he had died at the age of thirty-eight.

My lovely auntie's home was the most palatial flat I had ever seen. Some of the villas of my school-friends were certainly sumptuous but as we lived in an apartment ourselves and a very fine and modern one at that, I took it that as apartments go, our apartment and certainly the Goldfarb's could not be bettered.

But my auntie's home was the closest I had come to a small palace, the kind I had begun reading of in fairy tales. I had been able to read basic Children's Tales like SRUWELPETER & RAPUNZEL a good year before I had started school. By now I could read well but learning to write thanks to LEHRER BERLINGER was becoming my latest accomplishment and not merely in German script but in Hebrew lettering too.

Auntie Rosel's flat had sliding-doors that lead into the glittering salon with the most beautiful red velvet chaise—longues and antique Louis Quinze mirrors and chandeliers took my breath away. In the music room stood a full-sized Grand piano which auntie explained proudly was a BECHSTEIN. And I had never imagined a kitchen could be so sculptured, all in white and no huge black stove towering over half the kitchen. There was no table as meals were taken in the dining room, just gleaming white or glass work-tops. The floors of the apartment were parquet as were ours but I had never seen such a shine on any floor. And all those wonderful, colourful Persian rugs all over the flat—was this how Shirley Temple lived?

I thought my auntie very beautiful too and cousins Abi in pristine white casual flannels and navy shirt and Hanni in a gorgeous pleated white skirt and blue pullover looked like the models in the window of the finest shops in Munich. They were so beautiful I thought including my elegant uncle Bernhard. They made us feel so very welcome and I was showered with gifts of pretty dresses as well as more chocolate than I could possibly eat.

Auntie Rosel was obviously thrilled with our visit and she and Mutti went shopping. Then I overheard that they too were planning to emigrate and uncle Bernhard hoped to move his fur business to London where they would settle.

We returned to Munich a few days before start of the Easter term. What I liked best about all of the Jewish holidays was the never-ending stream of exquisite fancy cakes and pastries baked by Oma and Mutti. The cheesecake was everyone's favourite. It was a mouth-watering confection that melted sweetly in the mouth!

No, I thought nothing could beat the sheer excitement of this year when I had also excelled in my poetry and song recital and was frequently asked to stand in front of the class and sing 'SCHNEEFLOCKCHEN' (little snow-flake) or 'MAIREGEN' (the rain in May) a particular favourite of my own mother as it told the tale of a little girl explaining to her mother that she was standing in the rain so that she could grow taller as she was told that the rain in May made children grow taller:

"MAIREGEN MACHT DASS MAN GROSSER WIRD

GROSSER DOCH MOCHT ICH SCHON SEIN,

WAR' ICH O MUTTERCHEN GROSS GENUG

GING ICH GEWISS NICHT HINEIN."

(The rain in May makes you grow taller

And taller I wish to be.

Were I mother dear tall enough

I would surely not stand in it.)

I anticipated the new term with enormous impatience and simply could not wait to tell my friends all about Leipzig

Chapter Four

"Let her through—let the little one see the Fuhrer!"

AN ENCOUNTER WITH THE FUHRER & HIS CLIQUE; GRAF ZEPPELIN! MY PATERNAL OMA'S FLAT; A BRUSH WITH CRIME.

The words anti-Semitism, emigration, Zionism, England and America were becoming more and more frequent in our household. Yet no-one explained what any of them actually signified. I knew that England and America were far-off countries where good people lived who loved my father's Yiddish poetry and where people were now flocking in ever more increasing numbers. I was sure I understood enough not to ask silly questions. In truth I understood little if anything.

Yet nothing in my happy, insouciant life had changed much. I was growing out of some of my favourite clothes and was taken to OBERPOLLINGERS the stylish, up-market Jewish store where my parents were always treated with great respect. Or BATA, the shoe-shop in ROSETHAL (a shopping centre) where the owner treated my father like royalty and made a huge fuss of me. They had been friends for years and were members of the same Jewish Arts Clubs where Josef Hillel Levi was one of their most prominent artists.

Papi seemed to be out more but when one night he had not returned, Mutti was beside herself with anxiety although she did not tell me why. When Papi returned the following night he looked wan, unshaven and sad as he took me in his arms and clutched me very tightly to him. After that he seemed to be less jolly, his songs less cheerful and my siblings too were a little more restrained. The atmosphere in our home generally buzzing with noises of one kind or another too was more muted. But there was still plenty of singing and Papi went on playing his few records as before. Only he did not compose quite so many funny rhymes unless I pestered him. Opa alone was his cheerful old self and loved being called Opus but Oma was a little more irritable with him than formerly, chiding him when I thought he was just being funny. If he dared criticise any of her culinary masterpieces, she would really lose her temper. As it was her cakes were delicious as was everything she cooked that we all thought Opa was being very naughty. But Oma losing her temper was out of character because unlike other family members she seldom raised her voice. Papi's absence that night—he had been held in Stadelheim jail over an article he had written in German. He gave us little detail of the interrogation but somehow he had managed to appease his interrogators. Or maybe he had simply been extraordinarily lucky when finally, with a serious caution he was told he could go.

As I did not care for meat except chicken, the discussions over the difficulty of obtaining kosher meat hardly touched me. My siblings were forever arguing who would have what part of the chicken, but Papi made sure I would have a little of his if things grew seriously out of hand between Henny and Abi. Naturally poor Henny lost out as Abi was not as gentle with her as he was with me. Mutti seemed always to think that Abi was entitled to the largest and best portion. Trudel like me, was not as interested in the whole matter.

One day I stood on the swings in the back garden of our apartment building, bragging about my skills on the swing to the girl who lived below us, and swinging, swaying ever higher, higher standing upright, gazing up at the sky in a daze—until I lost my balance and fell onto the concrete. I blacked out but as there was no-one else about other than the girl, I don't know how long it took for me to come round. My parents never found out and the little girl obviously did not think the fall anything to talk about either. I was very pleased that my fall remained our secret as I would certainly not have been allowed to go on those swings again unsupervised. But it did teach me not to show off quite so much on the swings in future.

Another time I rode Lizzy Goldfarb's spanking new, gleaming red scooter straight into a lamp-post, my right eye colliding fiercely with the rusty post. I pretended I was unhurt when I rang the door-bell of our flat, shielding my eye with the palm of my hand as I felt it swelling and throbbing. When my poor mother forced my hand away she screamed—which had been precisely what I had attempted to prevent. I knew Mutti was inclined to get somewhat overwrought when one of us hurt ourselves. My siblings called it Mutti's hysterics. The doctor said it was touch and go and I was incredibly lucky not to have damaged my eye permanently or even lost it. So no more rides on Lizzi's scooter.

Papi and Abi when he was home, continued to take me tobogganing and these outings never ceased to be the crowning glory of winter for me. The thrill of the crunching, pristine snow as we glided down the slopes of the banks of the Isar now a golden pane of glass in the winter sun; the thrill of the momentary panic as my heart beat furiously! Before I was to start school we continued visiting the public open-air swimming pool in Maria EINSIEDEL just outside Munich in the summer, until it suddenly Papi and Mutti told us that sadly we could no longer go there as Jews were not allowed. I secretly wondered how they could tell who was a Jew. But there were just too many things I did not understand and some even my to me omniscient parents, failed to explain just shaking their heads sadly.

Our strolls in the ANLAGE, the lovely tree-lined boulevard that could take you from one end of Munich to the other side near the ENGLISCHE GARTEN, were a constant solution to the adults' frayed nerves and presented children the relative freedom to run about freely as long as they made as little noise as possible and drew as little attention to themselves as possible. It was where on fine Saturday afternoons Jewish families would take leisurely walks after they had been to Synagogue in the morning and then enjoyed their specially prepared Sabbath luncheon followed by a nap. Thus the Anlage on sunny Saturday afternoons could be indulged unhindered by Jewish families as few Jews appeared to work on the Sabbath and few Christians did not.

My parents' many friends who would come to suppers and parties at our flat seemed to grow fewer as that word 'emigration' cropped up more and more. So there was less baking and less festivity. The marches, however, through the neighbouring streets of our building seemed to multiply by the day. Opera and theatre visits too, had become a rarity for the parents. Mutti in particular adored the films with Greta Garbo and she would persuade Papi to go even if he was now reluctant to go to these public entertainment places. And when we passed the cinema where a gigantic picture of Garbo was displayed, Mutti would grow quite animated when extolling the star's beauty and talent. When I told her she was just as pretty and not nearly as skinny she laughed and kissed me.

Papi's Yiddish songs, which I soaked up like sweet syrup, had always been plaintive and sad. But there were also the comical ones about little boys who didn't learn their Hebrew alphabet and were scolded by the rabbi. Or the little boy who was so sweet and clever but still wet his pants. One of Papi's early childhood friends from Krakow was a brilliant Yiddish poet called Mordecai GEBIRTIG. We heard his name often as Papi sang his moving songs, in particular one called KINDERYOHREN (Childhood years.)

"Childhood years, sweet childhood years—"it began and its plaintive tune was hummed and the words known to every member of the family. Henny in particular loved that song and she would sing it soulfully to herself in her gentle voice over and over. Many of these songs were workers' songs, vowing to improve their lot and if necessary fight for their rights. There was one about a father sending greetings to his little boy from Siberia and telling him to be strong so that he too could fight for freedom. It was a chilling song and Papi sang it softly, wistfully in his lovely baritone:

"Vun Sibirien schickt dein Tate Dir ein Brief mein Kind" (from Siberia your father sends you a letter, my child.) Yet at some precious moment Papi might still burst out with:"SANTUZA REIZE MICH NICT, BIN ICH DEIN SKLAVE, HOR' AUF MICH ZU QUALEN!" rolling his eyes in Mutti's direction, awaiting the inevitable goodnatured admonition. ("Santuza stop teasing me, I am not your slave, stop torturing me!" from Pagliacci by LeonCavallo.) How we loved and laughed at this ever rarer little chunk of mirth!

I was fortunate too, not merely in living a mere stone's throw from the German 'VOLKS' Museum, but that Papi decided to take me there when it became daily less advisable for Jews to visit such public places and exhibitions. It was a brief visit, however, as Papi solely aimed to introduce me to the difficult life of the coal miners. This was something he seemed to take particular interest in as he told of Emile Zola's wonderful novel GERMINAL that dealt with the hard life of the French miner.

As we entered the museum from the back entrance, the mine shaft which to me looked like slide going down a dark vast void was practically the first thing we came upon. I was very keen to go on that 'slide' but Papi warned

43

me it was steep and very dark below. No, no, I assured him, I was not afraid though I would have to go on that slide alone as adults were not permitted on it. But as we slid further down what seemed a bottomless pit, tears of fear welled up in spite of my insistence to ZICKEZANGE that I was definitely NOT afraid.

It was very short visit as apparently I was very pale upon return and Papi took me straight home. But I assured him that I enjoyed that visit to the museum enormously and would never forget it. To have to go down those black pits—those poor miners!

One Saturday morning I had gone with Trudel or rather, I had tagged along much to her irritation as she had a friend from school with whom she liked to roam about the town—centre to explore the large stores like UHLFELDER or EPA in ROSENTHAL, quite a distance from our home. The last person she wanted to be lumbered with as she made abundantly clear time and again, was her precious little sister everyone made such a fuss of. There were times, however, when she was told she must take me along as there was no-one to take care of me at home. Thus with the absolute reluctance Trudel was an expert at displaying, she would agree as she certainly did not want to stay home alone with me. Much as I adored her, I sometimes wondered if the feeling was mutual. But it did not worry me for long as we always ended up having such fun. I was never bored with Trudel and she was never really mean to me.

We had just reached the road near our home opposite the DEUTSCHE MUSEUM, when we heard the approaching din of the clanking jackboots and the accompanying roar of their customary repertoire:

"VOLK ANS' GEWEHER" (People to arms) or the HORSTWESSELLIED, or any of the numerous chants I had learnt to hum as though they were harmless music. The words meant little to me excepting when it came to "REACTION ERSCHOSSEN" which was part of the HOSTWESSELLIED. Why had someone been shot dead for having revolted? What did it all mean?

Normally we would take little notice of these marches as they stopped traffic but not pedestrians in our section of Munich's suburb. Yet this time we realised the pavements were black with bystanders and the Swastika—flagged windows n our road were wide open with people craning their necks to get a better view. Practically every window sported the enormous blood—red Swastikas I loathed because from afar Munich had begun to look like a blood-spattered butcher shop. Fortunately our flat was to the back of the building so none of our windows faced front. Otherwise the nude windows might have raised eye-brows or worse.

It was obvious that big brass was marching with the usual troopers. Trudel drew me aside, firmly holding on to me with unaccustomed grip, as we stood stock-still trapped in the thick of the crowd. We were at least four rows from the front and of course I could not see a thing but the singing, stomping and frantic, carnival atmosphere was enough to excite us too. And there was no way out. The excitement of the crowd was palpable—any effort to leave was unthinkable as Trudel fully comprehended even if I did not.

"DER FUHRER, DER FUHRER!" came the muffled chants from the crowd, as though afraid to utter the sacred words too loudly. Trudel nudged me. Suddenly a gigantic roar went up from the neighbouring street, the drums beat frantically and the big woman next to us pushed me forward almost roughly, clearing the path for me. People yielded to allow me to the front.

"Let the little one see the Fuehrer!" she demanded in strident Bavarian fashion as with my heart threatening to jump out of my skinny Jewish frame, I was shoved right to the edge of the pavement within enviable view of the approaching Hitler, Himmler, Hess, Goring and Goebbels heading the procession!

Did they look at me? Did they see the Jewish girl standing so close, mesmerised, fighting back tears of fear? Rooted to the spot I did not budge. My eyes were glued on Hitler as he was the only one I recognised. Besides I knew he was a very evil man, the leader of the terrifying Nazi Party and he looked so absolutely macabre. That stiff dark front lock of hair looked stuck on. His waxed moustache was that of a menacing brigand. But his cheeks were so red—just like our maid Maria's after she had plastered them with rouge! The others were equally repellent, apart from the fat man in a uniform which was too tight and made him look comical as he beamed at the crowds like a star performer. He was the only one who seemed pleased with life. It was surely a hallucination; it simply could not be happening to Trudel and me! We were so close to these men I knew were dreaded by every Jew in Munich. If I had put out my hand just a little further I could have touched the one closest to the pavement flanked only by one huge SS guard with a rifle in his holster.

And there I stood where the woman had pushed me, with Trudel only paces behind, with my perfect raven ringlets in my favourite blue dirndl dress. I felt very unhappy, terribly nervous in my prime position and longed to tell the over-affable, bossy woman standing close behind me that really I had no right to be here as these people didn't like Jews. In fact they might hurt me. They might look like evil puppets my brother would activate in his Purim plays but these people were no puppets—they were real. But something told me to almost literally bite my tongue and smile sweetly at my 'MUNCHNER' benefactress. She grinned back after the crowds began to disperse.

"So," she said stroking my burning cheek, "Now you'll have something to tell your children about eh." I nodded edging my way back to where Trudel stood.

A man, the leader of the nation with rouged cheeks! They had marched past looking more like a group of circus clowns. And they were all so hideous, particularly that awful Adolf Hitler! Trudel was unusually silent on our way home as I clung to her.

"Did you see," I whispered afraid someone might hear. "Hitler wore make-up." But Trudel remained uncharacteristically silent.

Opa continued to chain-smoke rolling his own cigarettes and blowing yellow sky-high smoke-rings to please me. His fingers were equally yellow and his coat in particular smelt of nicotine. I loved the way he smelled and the way even his goatee was yellow at the edges. It was all part of my Opus. As I only had one grandfather Opa was all the grandfathers rolled into one and I thought he was very special the way he could grunt like a bear pretending to be the big bear from the archaic stone statue on the GEBSATTELPLATZ close to his apartment and only a little way from our own. Beneath it was the terrifying grey stone gargoyle with an integrated water-fountain with drinking water. I could not understand how anyone would dare go close to it let alone lean over to sip its waters.

Opa played rummy a lot while Oma was away on her travels. I believe he had several favourite cafes where he met up with his friends and there they would play cards, drink coffee and smoke. Sometimes Oma did not return until late or even days later. She was friendly with several of the farmers' wives and had little difficulty finding hostelry there. Money was never mentioned but sometimes Opa would come to our home in very celebratory mood and hand out bars of lovely milk chocolate wrapped in silver paper. From that silver paper redolent of the chocolate I had just guzzled, I would fashion little doll's dresses to wrap around my two favourite dolls. One was a white doll with straight blond hair and the other, my favourite, was what we called a NEGERPUPPE (a Negro doll) with pitch-black frizzy hair and a lovely, smiling dark brown face with beautiful full red lips. I had never seen a human being like her but like ZICKEZANGE she fitted well into my dream world.

Opa and Oma resided in an elegant flat only a short walk up the Gebsattlebrucke (bridge) away from us, which Oma kept immaculate and where she baked her inimitable cookies and pastries that could compete with any of the top patisseries in town. Opa loved music and when he bought his velvet-brown mahogany gramophone, he played me his first Al Jolson record 'Sonny Boy'. I loved the instrument, the singer and equally the wonderful scent of new wood and as I was so appreciative of his beloved gramophone he would reward me with playing his new records as soon as he had bought them. Sometimes they were arias by famous cantors like Jossele Rosenblatt. I had to pretend to enjoy this music but the mere honour paid me was quite sufficient.

Oma Lowy's home was very different to that of the Tennenbaum grandparents. I was rarely taken there as she spent Sabbaths and High Holidays with us and would walk to her home and back, no matter what the weather, no matter what the hour naturally accompanied by Papi. She wore sturdy black boots and her skirts were long and black or dark grey. Like Oma Tennenbaum she wore a Sheitel (wig) which sat darkly atop her little head and made her face appear even more pinched and pallid. Her eyes were large, dark and fiery overshadowing every feature in her face. But her thin, pale lips which always had a plaintive smile for me disturbed me, though I had no idea why. She was so petite and tiny of stature and yet she had a commanding presence as her fine amber eyes alighted on you.

Papi might have taken me to visit her on a couple of previous occasions, but this particular visit one early Sunday morning in September was the first time her tiny flat in the drab, dilapidated, ancient grey building actually registered on my memory. The flat was so like the black and white movies with not a hint of bright colour anywhere. No pictures on walls excepting photographs of my Auntie Malka, Papi's sister who had died tragically a few years after my cousin Hilde's birth, on a side table. Oma herself was dressed as she invariably was, in black cotton long-sleeved blouse and long black cotton or woollen skirt. Her voice was softer than anyone else's in our family. She offered me one of the sweets she always carried in the generous pockets of her wide skirts. As they were barley sugars I was not exactly eager but never failed to accept and thank her.

"May I keep it for later?" I would ask and she would smile sadly as I in turn stuffed it in the tiny pocket of my coat where it remained until Mutti dislodged the by then sticky mess.

Her standard reply was "leb' lange, Meidele" (live long, little girl) as soon as I addressed her. Whereas Oma Tennenbaum would hum to herself the live-long day, this Oma had about her an aura of late autumn stillness.

And of course at the time I could not reach out to her with the same kind of affection I felt for Oma Tennenbaum.

The flat was a medium-sized bed-sitting room with table and wooden chairs, a small bed with metal headboard to one side, a single brown wooden wardrobe that looked a hundred years old on the other. A tiny undecorated recess led to a stove and white sink to one side and a door leading to a tiny lavatory. There was no heating in the recess and after swift exploration I retreated hastily shivering with cold. I believe there was a communal bathroom outside the front-door shared by the tenants. There was no running hot water and no central heating, a black stove in the corner of the bed-sitting room providing the sole heating. As Papi talked to his mother I was free to explore and that was how I became familiar with my grandmother's strikingly modest life-style. Was it necessity or was it her devout faith that prompted her to frown on the slightest form of hedonism? Instead of humming, trading, cooking and baking, obviously cherishing every moment of her life, grandma Channa prayed to God. She prayed incessantly, her face deep in her SIDDUR

(Prayer Book) when she was in our home and she prayed as soon as she had done talking to Papi and me in her own home. She wished a long life to any of her grandchildren who chanced to address her and she made every effort to smile. But it was the least felicitous smile I was ever to encounter.

I found the austerity of the flat quite startling but I never remarked on it. I accepted as my father must have done that that was how she chose to live. It was what she was, who she was. Her modesty and outstanding lack of interest in her own comforts was self-evident. Yet I knew that she was the better educated of the grandparents having attended high school and learnt French. Her background was illustrious yet her entire personality was one of outstanding modesty and asceticism. Like her flat, she was scrupulously clean on her person and her worn clothes were spotless. My own father's fastidiousness was obviously inherited from her. There were moments when I felt in awe of her because I simply could not warm to her apparent austerity as I did to Opa and Oma Tennenbaum and of course I had never known the revered Scribe everyone spoke of as a 'ZADIG' (saint) She was so devoid of joy but her kindness was evident in so many ways. I sensed too that my father failed to understand her mode of life and that there was a gulf between mother and son though never acknowledged.

Nothing much had changed in my life until 1935 when finally I started school. By then I could sing quite a few stanzas of the bitter-sweet HEINRICH HEINE poems Franz Schubert had set to music and which Papi had ingrained in me for all time. "FREMD BIN ICH EINGEZOGEN

FREMD ZIE ICH WIEDER AUS." a stranger I came, a stranger I leave. He sang in a particularly doleful manner, as though telling of his own fate.

He loved HEINE and Byron and I knew earlier than I had a right to that HEINE had translated Child Herald, was a brilliant satirical poet and had written sad and beautiful love poems. I also knew that Heinrich HEINE had converted to Christianity from his Jewish roots and later lived to regret it as he lamented in one of his poems: 'KEINEN KADDISCH WIRD MAN SAGEN—'(there will be no (Jewish) prayer for the dead for me) There was Schumann too, who had composed the haunting tune to Heine's heart-breaking poem about the Kaiser (the emperor Napoleon) having been captured:

"MEIN KAISER, MEIN KEISER GEFANGEN-"(My emperor, my emperor captured!" And through my father I could mourn or love with these great men, picturing beautiful maidens whose tears fell on the poet's hand so that he sank to his knees with contrition.

There was however, one opera I did not like and I was not slow to make my disapproval known to Papi. Above all I did not like the music but I also disapproved of the name of the hero. Brecht and Weil's DREI GROSCHEN OPER (Threepenny Opera) which Papi seemed to like so much, was so different to all the gentler, more melodic music I was accustomed to, that I would voice my dislike in no uncertain manner. I must have detected its raw vulgarity subconsciously.

"How can you like that music, Papi? And that silly name Meckie Messer—it's—"I would chide.

Now I have to admit that the German pronunciation of Meckie Messer (Mac the Knife) was dangerously similar to a rude Yiddish word for male genitalia and I simply could not help being shocked every time Papi sang it.

No, the music did not die in our home no matter how much more terrifying the voices over the wireless spattered and raved. Sometimes they did send a shudder down my spine more because of Papi and Mutti's ashen faces than to knife-edged words I simply could not fathom. But I hated Hitler's guttural squawking that seemed to grow more manic each time he spoke. I could recognise it the moment he opened his mouth on the wireless. Germany's Fuhrer had begun to give me nightmares. I could not understand why most people seemed to like him and why he hated the Jews so much. Were Jews bad? When I could make out the word 'JUDEN' from his twisted pronunciation, there was no need to comprehend his language—he was predicting something terrible. Mutti and Papi looked at each other without a single word but their white faces spoke for them. They stood around that little wireless set on Papi's desk in the living room as though it was a beast about to pounce on them.

No-one ever bothered us so far as I knew. No-one I had ever met looked remotely like the STURMER Jews depicted in that horrible rag that could be seen at the paper-stands and on bill-boards in town. Why, why was this happening? Why was our lovely life suddenly changing to one of fear and apprehension?

Papi continued to put a brave face on everything though he now rarely sang my favourite silly ditty to me. He had composed it when I could barely walk:

"DIE STRUMPFE UND DIE SCHUH

UND ALLE DIE DAZU

WOZU HAB' ICH SIE AN

WOZU HAB ICH SIE AN

WOZU (Socks and shoes and all the rest;
What for do I wear them; what for—what for?) It was so beautifully silly that none of us could help laughing each time he sang it to his own little tune. I can sing it still.

However, much as he tried, Papi rarely felt like fooling around now. Mutti talked quite often of that wonderful little Jewish prodigy violinist called Yehudi Menhuin, She and Papi had heard him play the violin not that long ago like an angel from heaven. He was clad in a lovely blue velvet suit. His face was beautiful, framed by blond curls. She spoke of him in an unaccustomed tone of awe. But now he was in America she had added with a sigh.

But she lost her temper more often especially with Trudel and even with Henny who could be brought to tears at the slightest provocation. It made me sad because Henny was generally gentle and maybe too meek, though she could grumble and complain quite effectively and then Abi would provoke her and make fun of her. But in my eyes Abi was very nearly perfect. He was smart and he wrote lovely little plays in which I always had a part and he was never impatient if I forgot my lines or walked through the wrong door. I was inclined to mumble too audibly: "now here I enter" or "here I exit" to the intense amusement of my audience. Most likely both my brother and elder sister were more troubled by what was going on all about us than they let on to me so life in general remained unchanged so far as I was Concerned.

Trudel and I had wandered off to town. She was to meet her friend in UHLFELDER. We would just look around at all the countless trinkets, bric a brac, make-up and just about anything and everything one could think of—which although as cheap as it was possible to find, was still beyond our wildest dreams. Just looking around the vast store was in itself a real adventure. Trudel had a meagre stack of cash Oma Tennenbaum had given her and I too had ten pfennig in my piggy-bank. So off we had set to ROSENTHA where we enjoyed doing the rounds of both EPA and UHLFELDER, the two cheapest stores. UHLFELDER was larger, owned by a Jewish family and just that bit more alluring with its fairy-tale array of goods. Trudel's friend was waiting there for us.

I was always enchanted by the little china figurines, the colourful beaded necklaces and matching bracelets set out on tables to be handed to the saleswomen for the necessary sales transaction. But it seemed there was no sales-staff on hand as it was lunch time. We strolled leisurely along the vast ground—floor. To my surprise I was sure I saw Trudel and her friend inspecting and then deftly pocketing items. I nudged my sister but she brushed me off. In that case it seemed to me I could do the same and did so with enormous pleasure and dexterity.

Trudel, noticing what I was doing, took my hand decisively and together with her friend we all three marched out of UHLFELDER. I did remind Trudel outside as an afterthought, if we should not have handed over some money but she shushed me and when I felt the fabulous booty snuggling in my coat pockets that was now all mine, I was so elated I could not wait to reach home to set it all out and enjoy my new-found wealth. I loved playing shops and now I would have goods galore to pretend sell.

Perhaps it was my fault that utopia collapsed so soon; perhaps Trudel too had been less than careful. But suddenly Papi stormed into the bedroom where I was setting out some figurines carefully and lovingly on my bed, talking to pretend shoppers interested in my wares. My generally pale father's face was flushed and he looked angrier than I had ever seen him. His handsome face was quite contorted with anger.

I had heard some ominous slapping noises coming from the bathroom but engrossed as I was in my game I soon dismissed them. Now confronted by this alien Papi, for the first time I experienced fear of my gentle father.

"How did you get these—these—"his voice scissor-sharp, cut into me. He picked up a bracelet, my favourite haul as it was probably the most expensive.

"Uh—Uhlfelder—"I stuttered as I began to cry.

"And how did you pay for them?"

"I—I—"

"You did NOT pay for any of this—you stole—"His face was white as he struggled with the enormity of the problem.

"Trudel—"

"I have dealt with Trudel," he interrupted not looking at me as my sobs increased.

"Stealing—my daughters thieves and at a time like this, dear God!" And he raised his hand as he turned me round and smacked me on the bottom three times.

"Promise you will NEVER again take anything that does not belong to you and for which you cannot pay—promise!"

"Yes, yes!" I cried bitterly. "Papi—"I wanted him to pick me up and cuddle me to make me feel better. He looked back at me once as though in pain then with parting words of:

"Trudel knows what to do first thing to-morrow morning. It is too late to do anything else now." He was gone. I cried a great deal that night because he had not returned to comfort me. But I knew too that never again would I take anything that was not mine or that had not been paid for, no matter what

Trudel or her friend did. The enormity of the insult of my beloved father having smacked me was almost too terrible to bear.

Very early next morning Trudel told me to get dressed and we went downstairs and across to the ANLAGE closest to the river bank. It was a chilly morning and the river raged and frothed eager to devour my precious loot. Trudel began throwing item after item into the foaming water.

"C'mon!" She commanded. Reluctantly I took a tiny glass horse and threw it in.

"Get on with it, Mella!" She said impatiently. I've emptied both my pockets. We have to. Papi—"

I don't know if there was ever a more reluctant thief ridding himself of his loot. I found it excruciatingly hard to part with even the smallest glass thimble. Trudel had to examine both my pockets until finally the job was done. I could not understand why I could not at least have kept one of these ill-gotten spoils. But Trudel, so deft at misleading me, was now equally skilled at setting me straight.

There was not a school day I did not anticipate with excitement and pleasure. Most of all I loved LEHRER BERLINGER'S religious studies. He made the Old Testament come alive as vividly as any film. As Abraham stood poised to sacrifice his beloved son I had great difficulty restraining tears. And when finally God relented I was so thrilled I clapped. Lehrer Berlinger did not teach belief in religion, he simply taught the Old Testament as a ripping yarn and he taught it with such realism that few of that class had difficulty remembering any of it. Genesis was a spell-binding tale of adventure, of right and wrong, good and bad and then there was the judge—God. In fact, everything he taught, every poem, song or historic tale was a spell-binding adventure to me.

Gymnastics was another of my favourite activities. I could stand on my head from a very early age and I could do it for longer than any other girl in my class. We did not take gym with the boys. It was mooted that I was to be in the Jewish Junior Olympics. Every day at school was a new adventure and I therefore anticipated each new day eagerly.

As I sat next to my best friend Evi Ballin in the last row but one in the back, we were fairly near the large window with a view of the school-yard below and a vast expanse of sky above. I would not infrequently gaze up into the blue sky and do a little secret dreaming or hold a mute chat with a much neglected ZICKEZANGE, as my new school friends were fast replacing her.

It was the early summer of 1937. I loved the special scent of early summer as I made my way to school through the empty Munich streets in the morning. And only a few weeks ago Erich Kupfer, one of my class-mates who frequently walked home with me, had stolen a kiss, my first kiss, under the bridge in the ANLAGE. I had felt dishonoured and thoroughly ashamed to be treated thus—especially as he was not the boy I had a crush on. Thoughts of our maid Maria who was judged a loose woman for some unknown reasons came rushing to the fore. I had run home as though possessed, telling no-one of my shame and vowing not to go home alone again with this ginger-haired eight year old villain.

Now, as I sat day-dreaming a little more than I had a right to at my desk, a gigantic, silvery grey monster appeared suddenly hovering directly towards the building. Others had also spotted it and began shouting: "GRAF ZEPPELIN—it's GRAF ZEPPELIN!" and we all rushed close to the window.

"It's going to crash into the school!" Someone cried in horror and even though I said little I was terrified the closer this giant beast soared towards us. Through the vast windows of the air-ship I could see people moving about. The excitement in the class was electric. I stood stunned into petrified silence. Now I really knew what fear was.

"It's going to crash!" One of the boys exclaimed. We all huddled a little closer to each other. Lehrer Berlinger stood at the back. He was a short man but he was still taller than any of his little charges.

"No, no" he said with what I think purported to be a chuckle but did not sound quite like one.

"The GRAF ZEPPELIN—that will never crash!" We all screamed in unison now as the monster soared literally feet by our window—any closer and it would devour us—before slowly, o' so agonisingly slowly, it finally shuffled into the distance.

"Well, children—"said Lehrer Berlinger in his old voice with a sigh of relied, "We're really lucky to have had such a close up view of the GRAF ZEPPELIN. Lehrer Kissinger will be jealous!" But his words were accompanied by another deep sigh.

As for me, I don't think I had ever been so frightened or felt so threatened by what seemed to me a supernatural grey bird of prey about to swallow us all up. And we had just stood there petrified—its' willing fodder for the asking.

Chapter Five

THE GOLDFARB'S VOLKSWAGEN, PASSOVER.

CZECHOCHOSLOVAKIA, MY NEW WINTER COAT.

Miriam and Josef Lowy with Abi aged two

Lizzy came knocking on our door at seven, well before school-time at eight and asked me to come downstairs with her as she had something to show me. She was flushed with excitement, her apple cheeks even more ruddy than usual. Mutti had barely finished dressing my hair and I ran down with Lizzy midst unfinished ringlet. It had to be something very special to judge from Lizzi's wide grin. I loved my friend with the pretty face that glowed with health and none-stop joi de vivre. She seemed never to be sad or ill-tempered. And I secretly coveted her short, silky smooth trouble-free head of hair with the fashionable fringe adorning her forehead. I was beginning to think that

57

ringlets were babyish and too much bother and I knew I fussed too much but could not help myself.

Together we pulled open the heavy front portals of the building. And there it stood right outside the house—the beautiful, brand-spanking new gleaming black Peoples' Car, the Fuhrer's much heralded gift to his beloved German people—if they had the money to pay for it. Mr Goldfarb sat at the wheel beckoning us to jump in. I sat in the front with Lizzi, both of us squeezed against each other as much in delight as sheer affection and excitement. The fragrance of the new leather and paint delighted my ever alert olfactory senses.

"It's—it's just so wonderful, Herr Goldfarb!" I stuttered. "Can we—?"

No need to finish my sentence as Mr Goldfarb started up the engine and away we went. We only drove round the block but I was sure that that was how royalty felt. To ride in a brand new car—to ride in any car; it was not something I was accustomed to doing apart from the day I was bridesmaid at my cousin Trudel's wedding. But then dressed in some uncomfortable fussy dress, I was squashed between another bridesmaid and some adult I did not know and the car was a hired impersonal limousine with an austere driver in the front. That had been quite a while ago. Trudel Roth and her new dentist husband Kuno had left soon after for Palestine. This was different This was a car owned by the handsome Herr Goldfarb, immaculately attired and groomed and always adding the fragrance of his French After-shave to the surroundings.

Lizzi and I hugged and cooed continuously like excited little chicks, during that short ride, until all too soon we were back in front of our house.

"Oh" I could not help exclaiming disappointedly, "already?"

"I'm afraid so. It doesn't take very long in a car, does it?"—"said Herr Goldfarb opening the door for us. "I have a lot to do as I have to arrange for the car to be shipped to the States."

"To the States—" I repeated in disgust. "Yes darling, we are leaving next week!"

As elated as I had started the day, my dejection at this news was I think one of the biggest blows I had yet experienced. I ran upstairs with a heart that had been so light earlier and was now unaccustomedly heavy.

"Next week!" I repeated before I fell completely silent as Lizzi and I climbed up the stairs to our respective homes. The Goldfarbs were really emigrating. They had talked of it for a long while but so had so many people. Mutti too kept urging Papi about the visas. I did not understand the word visa and no matter whom I asked, no one gave me an explanation that made sense to me. They were some kind of documents Jews needed to leave Germany. Why, why on earth should they need documents to get out of Germany? I knew people needed Passports and that I was on Mutti's.

But that was not what troubled me, rather the opposite. The Goldfarbs had obviously acquired all the documents required to leave—and they were leaving in a few days' time. We would meet again soon, I was assured. But where—hey were going to America, a land so far away, so glamorous and unattainable in my imagination that the only way there was if you were a film star like Shirley Temple. The Goldfarbs were probably connected with the film world even if they had never said as much. Herr Goldfarb to me was very glamorous. They spoke of New York and as that was the only city ever mentioned I took it that that was just another word for America. We had not yet begun Geography lessons.

It all happened with nightmarish haste. The Goldfarbs had gone and new people moved into their lovely flat. They were not Jewish. At a party of my school friend Bertl Sandbank who sat behind Evi Ballin and me, the talk was once again of Bertl's imminent emigration to America. Bertl's home was a villa near the Englischer Garten and the most beautiful house of any of my friends. Bertl herself was an exemplary scholar, far more efficient in simply everything than I was. By then I was the one always called upon to recite a new poem or sing a new song not because my voice was particularly fine but because I had a good musical ear and it was obvious that I loved performing before an audience. Students like Bertl, exemplary in every subject, were far less eager to stand up in front of the whole class whereas I was more than ready. Steffi Weil, the girl next to Bertl in the last row, was the most beautiful girl in the school with her golden curls and her pale peach complexion. Her voice was soft and she was very shy but like Bertl, a fine student. So many of us were at the party in the Sandbanks' rambling villa that Sunday early 1938 not long after my own far more modest birthday party.

Frau Sandbank asked if we too were leaving soon. When I said I did not think so she looked sadly at me but made no comment. I enjoyed the cakes and the ice cream and playing in their lovely garden but somehow the atmosphere that day was less boisterous and jubilant than was usual at such parties. When Papi called for me I felt inexplicably sad. I did not know that it was the last time I would see Bertl as they left the following week. Everyone seemed so secretive about their actual dates of departure. I found that very unfair.

Now it was Eva Ballin's turn and all at once I had a dreadful premonition that things would never be the same again. The doctor's daughter with the pitch black, short, gleaming satiny hair, in direct contrast to my own mop and those huge dark eyes and olive complexion, was my very dearest friend. I admired her. She was exactly my age almost to the month, but I thought of her as someone very special because she had an innate air of class and distinction about her and behaved far better and with more modesty. A doctor's daughter and an only child, she was so polite and impeccably well-mannered without being prissy. Lizzy had been two years younger but Eva was my peer; a precious school chum and we spent as much time as possible together, each occasion more enjoyable than the last.

Now Evi too gave a small party—a farewell party as she explained. The Ballins resided in the centre of Munich in an old, elegant building, one floor of which served as her father's surgery. The flat was sprawling and beautifully furnished with antique furniture. Eva's bedroom was a child's utopia with all of the toys one could dream of. I was not in the least envious because I had always felt a part of all this, as though we were sharing all these wonderful toys as indeed we frequently did. And was not my father a famous poet?

Delicious chocolate gateau was served with hot chocolate. Each child was handed a small, daintily wrapped package of goodies upon leaving as was the custom, consisting mostly of coloured paper whistles, balloons and sweets. We promised to write to each other and hugged and kissed. And before I knew it Eva too was gone. But for some reason it was unthinkable that we would not meet again. We had sworn to write often and tell each other all our new adventures. It was simply not possible that I would lose her for ever.

Why o' why did everyone have to leave their homes? Surely no one would hurt us? Not even those increasingly menacing SA and SS men who were everywhere.

The class-room was several pupils short by October and Lehrer Berlinger seemed permanently depressed. But I still loved going to school even with Eva and Bertl and so many others gone. There was still Steffi Weil who sat behind me and who now seemed to want my friendship more. And there was Erich Kupfer, Eugen Goldberg who frequently walked home with me too and Uncle Oiser's eldest daughter Goldi, with whom oddly enough, I was practically a stranger as our families did not socialise and only Uncle Oiser, as I knew him, came frequently to our home. He was Papi's cousin but of course I was entirely ignorant of his unhappy marriage. And Goldi sat in the front rows which seemed at the time like a different country with which one did not fraternise. Was there some snobbery on the teachers' part? As it seemed that the children in front, both boys and girls, were less well-dressed and altogether less well turned out than those further back. I for my part had always thought that it was more to do with their learning achievements. But if truth were known I was not above quite a sizeable slice of snobbery.

Abi was in Wurzburg in the Jewish Teachers Training College. Henny was no longer in the secretarial office job she had been so proud of and where she had made many friends. And Trudel had broken her leg in several places at the Ballet School she attended. She had been a very talented dancer and her teachers thought she had real potential as a professional dancer. It looked as though the fractures might be more serious than first diagnosed and she would require an operation and lengthy treatment. The parents were terribly upset. This was not a good time for a Jew to have to go into hospital.

Munich, formerly so bright and cheerful, seemed to have grown darker by the day. Henny was home a lot looking bewildered and forlorn and generally keeping to herself with a book or doing chores for Mutti. Mutti herself was very busy in the shop trying to wind things up though I did not understand what that meant. I believe she was attempting to sell as much left-over stock as possible. I knew that Jews were now being discriminated against in every walk of life, no matter what their station. I knew and yet I understood none of it.

Kosher meat was not merely a rarity but impossible to obtain as kosher butchers were forbidden to ply their trade. Even my ever-cheerful grandma Chatsche could no longer bring home fresh chickens or even eggs although her loyal customers went out of their way to help when the High Holidays arrived. But to my constant dismay, Oma still brought home live carp from the market that splashed miserably about in our bath-tub until they were swiftly dispatched. I refused to eat the fish and never failed to show my disapproval of the entire practice as did my sisters. I knew as soon as I entered the flat and heard the flapping and desperate splashing of the distraught fish, what I would find in the bathroom. I don't think Papi approved either but it was Oma's perpetual present to the family for the holidays, so no one could object. And Opa above all loved his carp. The adults seemed to enjoy the sweetly prepared fish. Opa ate every part of the animal, including head and eyes much to my never-ending protestations. I simply could not comprehend how one day the fish was so alive and the next in bits and pieces on plates. But Opa was so funny, purposely exaggerating the whole process to provoke me, that everyone ended up laughing and I had trouble keeping a straight face. He assured us that the eyes and head were particularly beneficial to our health and I really should learn to eat them. I would look over at Papi but he remained impartial as he often did when Opa was involved.

Passover, never my favourite holiday as Mutti adhered so adamantly to every nuance of the rules as she had been taught and Papi frequently objected to the pettiness of it all even though it was he whose back-ground was far more ultra—religious. What was more, as the youngest in the family, it fell to me to ask the ten questions of the 'MA NISCHTANA. I was invariably nervous as the slightest slip-up would elicit sniggers from Trudel and Henny well-meant, I'm sure, but enough to set me in a panic and in earlier years even bring on tears.

"Where's the sense of it all—"my dear father would moan not quite under his breath that April in 1938, much as he had grumbled as far back as I could remember, as yet again we were expelled from the flat so that the spring—cleaning could be put in motion, the 'CHOMEZ' (none Passover) china and cutlery replaced by Passover dishes that had been safely stashed away since last year. Early on the morning of the first Seder-night, when Passover would officially begin, we were cast out after a meagre breakfast in order for the last crumbs of bread and other 'CHOMEZ' to be finally swept away. Our gentile maid Maria had been forced to quit and Mutti, with the far from enthusiastic assistance of poor Henny, worked even harder without Maria's help.

Trudel had to stay home of course, until a place was found for her in hospital. But she was better off resting rather than hobbling about and making things more difficult. Abi would be home for the holidays later that day. So Mutti and Henny had the kitchen to themselves to prepare things exactly as Mutti seemed convinced God had decreed and Oma Tennenbaum would come in later to bring some lovely 'PESSACHDIG' (suitable for Passover) pastries she had prepared, mostly from almonds and she and Opa as well as Oma Lowy (I never saw Oma Lowy cook or bake for herself) would all be gracing our table over the two 'Seders' even more reason for me to be nervous when it came to reciting the 'MA NISCHTANA.'

But this year nothing seemed to help make the ambience festive, even though we sat around the table in the living room as previously, relaxed and unafraid of the inevitable spillage of a few drops of the blood-red wine from four glasses the adults would drink and Trudel and I would be allowed to sip, whilst Henny was permitted considerably more and soon became giggly and grumpy in turn. Abi was by now treated like an adult but he too admitted that the wine went to his head in a most pleasant way.

Papi helped me into my old winter coat. He was humming something from Pagliacci by Leoncavallo. I recognised the piece as I did most of the numerous songs and arias Papi would chant softly, more to himself, no matter what he was doing. He was extraordinarily musical and he adored every kind of opera as did Mutti. But Mutti rarely sang to herself though when she did, she revealed a pleasant voice as did her sister auntie Rosel. Uncle David's voice was considered beautiful. Unfortunately I never heard him sing as he lived in Chemnitz and had not been to visit us for a very long time. I had really only met him once.

Sadly Mutti and Papi could no longer indulge in visits to the theatre. The miracle was that Papi knew so much of the libretto too and as time went on I had actually picked up his huge stock of favourites quite unawares. All those Schubert songs; especially those written to Heine's poetry! I am not even certain I liked the music at the time, certainly some more than others, but all of it clung to me as though it were a part of Papi that I could never let go—and never have.

Soon I might have a really nice new coat, as Mutti and I were due to travel to FRANZENSBAD in Czechoslovakia after Pesach, before my school holidays were over. It would be only a weeks' stay at a Jewish Hotel where yet again I was to share Mutti's room and food. I loved going to new places and was very excited at the prospect of this trip. Especially as Mutti had hinted there was some really nice and reasonable children's wear to be found in Czechoslovakia. I would finally be rid of the old, scratchy one I had had to bear with such reluctance.

So now I slipped into the old coat grumbling.

"It's warm outside—"I protested but Papi shook his head and I demurred.

We strolled leisurely to the ANLAGE, close to our home, just over the REICHENBACHBRUCKE on the other side of the river Isar. We had time to kill. Settling down on a bench protected by the tall tree's dense foliage so that even rain could not trouble us, Papi took my hand in his.

"You are very pale." he studied my face frowning. "Are you hungry, darling?"

I shook my head but he must have noticed me greedily imbibing the unmistakable aroma of newly baked rolls and ham and sausage with which no Munich resident could be unfamiliar. It reached us from the small grocers' way back on the other side of the wide road, defiantly bouncing over mighty trees and traffic. The little shop was always awash with fresh fruit, fresh rolls and cooked cuts of meat and sausage. The tantalising smell was familiar as there were countless such shops in Munich and it was impossible not to recognise such wafts of sausage and pigs' meat when going to Munich's market for fresh cheeses and fruit and vegetables. Never having tasted these forbidden foods they became nevertheless more mouth-watering the hungrier one was.

My father, frowning, studied my face for a further few moments in silence. Then he rose.

"Wait here—I'll only be a few minutes!" He said. I nodded smiling. I suspected that he was going to get us some of those fresh rolls and even though there would be nothing to put on them, the prospect was very welcome.

As we were outdoors and it would not officially be PESACH until nightfall, there was no reason why we should not indulge in bread-rolls even if Mutti had already made our home a CHOMETZ-free (breadless) zone. And if truth were told I was very hungry by now.

I looked about me listening to the chirping of the birds and wondering when the first lady-birds would begin crawling on the new leaves. And I thought yet again how much I loved my father who never ceased to think of our welfare. I wondered why Mutti was always pressing him to write to his friends in England again and urge the authorities to send those precious visas. Why England and what was the hurry? I loved Munich and anyway, those friends who had gone or were going had all gone to America and one even to China. I knew no-one who had gone to England. But Papi had many writer friends there and two or three were childhood buddies. I hoped so much that we would not leave at all. That the horrid soldiers would disappear from our streets and that the ugly man Hitler and his evil followers would be chased out of my good country.

Papi made his way back carrying a small paper bag. I watched him as he came closer and thought again how handsome my father was. He was always immaculately dressed and shaven, even if we just went a few blocks. And he generally wore a fedora which made him look like a film star. He was slim and elegant and his features even. His eyes were sky-blue unlike mine which were green or Mutti's that were flashing grey-green. Only Henny had blue eyes like Papi and apparently my grandfather Dov. Abi's I thought were exactly the colour of Mutti's. As for Trudel, I could never be certain whether her eyes were green like my own or grey-green like Mutti's. She never seemed to stay still long enough for me to make up my mind. But they were nice, large, bright impish eyes, though as Trudel herself always pointed out, my lashes were the thickest, longest of anyone in the family and apparently that was something to be proud of, especially for a girl.

With an unaccustomed secretive grin, Papi sat down beside me carefully holding on to his purchase. To my surprise I noticed grease—stains forming on the bag.

"Here," said Papi, handing me a roll out of the bag. I looked at it in surprise as I could smell sausage. It was just the bag, I concluded as I accepted the fresh roll eagerly. But as I opened the roll a little there was no mistaking its content.

"Pap" I exclaimed keeping my lips away from the roll with difficulty, "Do they sell kosher sausage?"

"Eat Kindele—(little one)" I bit in so eagerly that some of the grease of the sausage nearly dripped on my coat.

"Careful" Papi hastily tore some of the paper-bag and placed it on my lap as a napkin.

I ate without further ado. I don't know when I had enjoyed a simple repast more. The sausage tasted better than any I had ever tasted. Papi watched me closely in absolute silence before handing me the second roll into which he placed more sausage he took out of the bag.

"But what about you?"

My father shook his head solemnly.

"No darling. You are a little girl and you need nourishing food. I can wait until to-night just as Mutti is doing. But you have to make me a promise: this has to remain a secret between us for ever. You must NEVER tell anyone ever! Can you promise me that?"

I huddled close to him, kissed him and nodded emphatically. I knew then what my common sense had told me all along. That sausage had not been kosher but it had tasted delicious just the same. Even more so perhaps because it proved if more proof were needed, how much my father loved and trusted me.

I understood that day that love and loyalty were paramount to this man. He visited his father's SCHTIEBEL (small, modest ultra orthodox rooms) on High Holidays, whereas the rest of the family and the Tennenbaum grandparents worshipped in the REICHENBACH Synagogue. Only Oma Lowy would be at the SCHTIEBEL with him and I was allowed to come there on SIMCHAT THORAH (The festival of the Torah.) It was the high-light of my Jewish festivities as I loved the old men with their TALLITHS over their frail frames and half covering heads as well; their gnarled hands stroking my cheeks and plying me with all manner of sweets. I alone of the three sisters was still young enough to be allowed into the men's section to visit my father after which I would fleetingly go across to the screened-off women's section to kiss Oma Channa. My father prayed at the SCHTIEBEL out of loyalty and devotion to his dead father and his pious mother, though his wife and family worshipped in the less ultra-orthodox Synagogue across the street. The men who prayed here were men wed to their belief as grand-father Isroel Dov had been and as my father never would be. Oma Channa of course maintained her place there because that was where she and her late husband belonged. For my father, human decency and loyalty to those you love were paramount as I had often heard him say but maybe understood a little better that eve of Passover in 1938. He would skip from one prayer house to the other to be with the rest of the family. I was inadvertently learning from him that what mattered was the absolute loyalty to those you loved and the satisfaction and comfort derived from the togetherness and affiliation of all these occasions.

Passover was not such a jolly affair between us siblings as in former years. Somehow no-one felt much like joking and laughing even after a few sips of the sweet wine I too had been allowed to sample for the past two years. Mutti used to be the jolliest of all and her laughter would elicit a fond caution from Papi:

"Now, now Marileben—the children" and that would really send my siblings into hysterics. I would by then have been in command of Papi's knee again, snatched sneakily by Trudel previously. This, however, was a very different Seder.

Back home that late afternoon, Papi and in turn the rest of us bathed and dressed in our Sabbath best. Mutti was last when she had finalised all the endless preparations. Kissing the equally festive grandparents upon their arrival, we neglected none of the usual ritual. Mutti had already prepared the Passover dishes and placed some on the table. There was that awful bone that was to represent the Passover lamb for slaughter. I did not like that at all.

Of course I would take centre stage reciting the MA NISCHTANA by heart proudly but not without the usual trepidation. I knew I would have to go on doing this for many years to come as the youngest of the family. And the air of excitement that evening was more poignant than ever as Papi, his face taut and troubled but immaculately shaven and in his best suit, was handed the traditional 'KITTEL' by Mutti. He donned the white, voluminous robe before seating himself ceremoniously in an armchair as was tradition, to begin the reading of the HAGADA (the special book for Passover) that related the tale of the Exodus of the Jews from Egypt and the many miracles God had led Moses to perform. The white robe wholly enveloping my father's sparse frame gave the proceedings an aura of momentary other-worldliness, though I could not understand at the time why it affected me so strongly. For a man who generally frowned on petty observance as superstition, the wearing of the white robe during the two Seder nights was as indispensable as Matzo and 'Morau' (Bitter Herbs).

I asked the ten questions as was expected of me. And even Trudel refrained from taunting me. All three grandparents sat silent, just managing only the smallest encouraging smiles for me. No-one stopped me this time from being the only one to hide the special piece of Matzo from the master of the Seder and thus demanding a ransom at the end of the evening for its return. Papi still played along until I found it for him and was promised my ten pfennig. But something had gone out of the Seder celebrations: the fun and laughter had died.

That night I went to bed with one comforting thought: FRANZENSBAD. My mother and I were booked to go to the Spa in Czechoslovakia two days after Passover so that she could take the waters which were considered so beneficial and rejuvenating for women. I never could make out what exactly ailed her as she seemed the most energetic, radiant and fit member of the family. In fact both my parents were great mountain climbers, swimmers and walkers. It was only of late that they could no longer roam freely as in earlier days. Outside I could hear marching SA chanting DIE FAHNE HOCH (Hoist high the flag). They were some way off as they rarely marched directly down the SCHWEIGERSTRASSE leading to the AU (a suburban part of Munich virtually out of town.) I wondered what Czechoslovakia was like. I had heard there were no Nazis there.

FRANZENSBAD CZECHOSLOVAKIA

Mutti patted my knee:

"This time you are not worried about the NIVEA Crème?? She smiled. Her smile was so carefree that my heart jumped.

"No," I said, "I saw you pack it."

We were sitting on the train, I as usual having been allotted the window seat by my kind mother. I hooked my arm in hers and cuddled close.

"I'm so excited. Will I really get a new coat and maybe shoes too?" I remembered to whisper as this was our great secret. Mutti nodded but said nothing pursing her lips.

FRANZENSBAD was a small, sleepy Spa promising little excitement for me from what I could judge when we settled into the small hotel, a little more up-market than the one in Abbazia; tables in the cramped dining room carefully set up with starched white table-cloths and silverware, to which I had already been told I would not be going. All I could do was steal the occasional glance at the adults enjoying the rich food from which I was most grateful to be exempted. I was to share some of my mother's meals which she would save from her own portions and then bring up to our room. As the deserts were delicious, especially the chocolate gateaux and Mutti always saved these for me, I was more than content. Mutti was supposed to get plenty of rest after she had taken the waters and during that time I would play quietly and very happily with the contents of her handbag, pretending they were for sale and talking to my customers. As Mutti was eager for her new hotel acquaintances to meet me she would ask me to come down to the foyer and on occasion I might be invited to share a snack at table. There were no other children to be seen so I took it that this was a special favour.

The Spa Centre consisted of several handsome stone water-fountains spurting this special medicinal water. They were spread out in well-tended gardens with colourful flower beds. Fronting these gardens stood a resplendent white mansion where the ladies could receive various treatments. Mutti had bought a special spouted cup upon which was inscribed in bold letters: FRANZENSBAD 1938. Sometimes she would let me take a sip of the water and I did my best not to pull a face as I found the water quite horrible though strangely enough it left no after-taste.

We would often sit on a bench in the garden with the sun beaming down and that is where we made friends with an elegant woman and her daughter from RIGA in Lithuania. She too had come for the waters and like us she was Jewish. I was happy to have a new friend and we would saunter behind the two ladies chatting.

Both my new friend and I were waiting for the day when our mothers would take us shopping—the piece de resistance of our holiday. The streets were narrow and the shops small but displaying some beautiful children's wear.

"O' look" I exclaimed practically every window we passed. "Mutti, there's the perfect coat for me, really just what I need!"

"Darling," said Mutti. "It is so expensive. You know we have to . . ."

I nodded sadly. "But couldn't we do without"

"Let's see. Maybe they will reduce it a little. They are all so nice but too expensive. You are developing expensive tastes my little daughter. You mustn't forget we are a big family—and these days-" But by Mutti's tone I could tell that she too liked the look of this last coat.

"Let's go in." She said suddenly, excusing herself and arranging to meet our new friends back at the gardens later for the waters which the ladies took four times a day. My mother was convinced as was her nice friend from Riga, that these waters and some of the treatments which included mud baths were doing them the world of good. So far as I was concerned the mud baths struck me as absolutely disgusting and I would have to sit outside my mother's cubicle in the luxurious marble hall and inhale the terrible stench of the tar-like mud. Even after Mutti had been cleansed, massaged and showered I was convinced I could still smell the black goo on her for days. But as the lady from Riga underwent the self-same torture with equal equanimity and claimed remarkable improvement, I was happy for Mutti who was after all, the best mother in the world whether she smelled of mud or not. And indisputably my mother had the smoothest, softest complexion though the taller, slimmer lady from Riga might have won a few points on elegance.

The moment I put on the coat I knew I had to have it. It fitted so perfectly and when I was asked to twirl around in front of the mirror, the owner of the shop said it could have been made for me. I looked at Mutti entreatingly:

"It feels so comfortable, so soft and so warm. It's REAL camel hair, isn't it?" I could think of nothing more luxurious in the world. And then the shop owner came and placed a little sailor hat in the self-same navy colour carefully on my head, making sure my ringlets were left undisturbed.

"O" exclaimed my dear mother "doesn't she look beautiful!"

I have to admit I thought the hat looked pretty good on me.

"Can we—?" I looked from one to the other of the two women in whose hands the fate of my beautiful coat lay. My mother and the shop owner walked into a small office deep in conversation whilst I waited dressed in the coat and hat.

Soon Mutti was back and I was told to take off the coat.

"We are coming back to-morrow. The lady has to discuss with her partner whether she can let us have the coat for the price I offered." She said. My eyes filled with tears.

"Does that mean . . ." I tried hard not to cry.

"We are coming back to-morrow afternoon." Mutti helped me into my old coat and said we would go and have some hot chocolate and cake further up the street where there was a fashionable café. But I had lost my appetite. I could speak of nothing but that coat all the way back to the hotel.

"We'll see to-morrow." was all my patient mother would promise.

There was nothing I wouldn't do for my mother the next day. I was silent as a church mouse when she took her siesta not even whispering to my pretend customers. All I could think of was that wonderful coat. The material was smooth against my skin, the navy colour velvety like a night sky. The present coat, apart from being too short, was of rough, scratchy wool that itched. I had never realised there were such lovely, caressing, none itching garments made for children.

We returned to the shop punctually at four o'clock next day after their late luncheon break—I with beating heart now and my dear mother with all the notes she had to spare stuffed into her purse. We were welcomed cordially and I was given a sweet and told to sit down and wait while Mutti and the shop-owner once again stood aside for serious conferring.

I looked anxiously about me, studying the rails of delectable clothing but unable to find MY coat. THEY'VE SOLD IT! But then Mutti came holding the precious coat.

"Try it on again" she smiled. "O' and the sailor hat—she looks so adorable in it." She turned to the shop owner. The latter nodded returning my mother's smile and conjuring up the matching navy sailor hat with two wide navy silk ribbons ensuing from its rim, she placed it expertly on my head and turned me towards the long mirror. "There, see how nice you look!"

"I—I love it!" Was all I could say as I turned to examine myself back and front "maybe—isn't it a bit too long, Mutti?" I was almost afraid the small criticism would undermine the purchase. But to my relief both women nodded and the charming shop owner began pinning the hem. She promised the coat would be ready by the next day.

"That will leave you plenty of room to grow." She assured my mother rather than me, surely aware that that was the last thing that concerned me. "We will leave a good hem."

And so it was all settled. The coat and hat would be mine. I thought I was walking on air. I had never before cared so much for an item of clothing.

"You know you are my MASELDIGE MEIDELE (lucky little girl)" Said my mother not for the first time. "She gave us a very good price." I loved her very much that afternoon and readily agreed to go without the hot chocolate and cake at the café.

"Of course," I agreed only too readily. "We have to save every penny now mustn't we?"

When we were back in our hotel room, mother sat me down.

"Darling," she said her face strained as it was most days lately, even on holiday. "You can wear the coat as soon as we get it to-morrow morning and every day till we leave in two days' time." I nodded eagerly not bothered even if it turned out to be sweltering.

"Now at the Customs—"she sighed obviously trying to find the right words. "If they ask you if you have had the coat before you came—you have to say yes."

I looked up at her but said nothing.

"If they know it is brand new they will either take it away or charge as much again as it cost and I do not have enough money. So that would be—"

"O' don't you worry Mutti I'll say I have had it for ages." Mutti smiled and heaved another of her more and more frequent sighs. "I know I can count on you."

We parted from our Lithuanian friends having gone out for coffee and cake together the night before our departure. They were staying a little longer before returning to Riga. Mutti pointed out that they were fortunate not to be living in Germany at this time. We kissed and hugged promising to keep in touch and meet again here in better times. Mutti seemed sad as did our friends as we kissed and hugged.

I think we bought some small items for my siblings and Papi but I was hardly interested. I know as usual, Mutti bought nothing for herself. And so, with our one suitcase and a couple of bags, dressed in my treasured coat and jaunty hat, we reached the Customs. Asked to alight from the train, we opened our suitcase in a special cubicle. We were back on German terrain.

The blond young German uniformed Customs officer smiled at me.

"So young lady," he said most affably, "I bet you got some nice new clothes?" I looked him straight in the eye. "No" I said regretfully. "Mutti said we couldn't afford it.—everything is so expensive."

"And the coat you are wearing—have you had it for some time?" I nodded emphatically. He had made it easy for me. He smiled and said:

"It looks as good as new. I like your sailor hat—next!" And he turned to the next waiting party.

We returned to the train and Mutti kissed me without a word.

"My MASELDIGES MEIDELE" She whispered. (My fortunate little girl)

"I hope we'll go again next year Mutti and meet up with our friends from Riga." I said as I settled back in my window seat on the train contentedly.

Mutti heaved one of her sighs as she gave me a hug.

Chapter Six

POLEMABSCHIEBUNG (EXPULSION OF POLISH JEWS)

(OCTOBER 27th 1938)

My birthday had come and the subdued party was tinged with sadness at the absence of several dear friends, especially Lizzy Goldfarb. The party's highlight as ever was Mutti's unique chocolate marble cake with thick chocolate glazing that gleamed like soft fairy lights and a bouquet so tantalising, that it was always torture to keep from cheating until that final moment when everyone including myself, was already replete with all mother's other delicious pastries. I knew of course by the delectable fragrance days earlier, that baking was going on, but somehow, tired as she must have been after a day at the shop, Mutti would wait until after I had gone to bed not to spoil the excitement of my special day and I never caught her preparing my birthday cake let alone discovered where all her other multi-coloured, star-shaped delicacies were hidden. Even Trudel would not reveal the secret though I was sure that of anyone knew, it was she. And we always somehow found room for a huge piece of birthday cake because once tasted, it was impossible not to eat up.

Now I was nine. The star gift was an exquisite little linen autograph book I had long wanted given me by my parents. It was covered in blond linen and embroidered with bluebells, poppies and corn the colours of which were so realistic that you felt they had just been picked. I would get my best friends to write little messages and poems so that I would never forget them. Sadly it was too late for Lizzy—maybe one day.

I had very few dolls and never asked for more. There was my NEGERPUPPE (black doll) and a fair-haired one. They had no specific names, nor very fancy clothing. Yet I would spend hours dressing them in the silver and gold wrappings of the abundant bars and boxes of chocolates always at hand. I loved designing their clothes. But I seemed to have no need for more dolls. Opa always kept silver and gold paper for me and I would go and invent new clothing and thus a different persona of the same doll.

I was loyal to my two dolls and gave them all the affection a mother had to give. It seemed to me that I had no more to give to more dolls yet I would stare in the shop-windows with longing at some of the huge, life-like expensive china or porcelain dolls but never asked for one. I had had my share when I was smaller and they had broken too easily and had to be taken to 'hospital' which had always upset me. I was quite content now with my two babies.

Ever since I started school ZICKEZANGE my special friend, had taken a back-seat and now she was gone. I had so many friends who could come and play with me and who did not need to be hidden away and whispered to. So ZICKEZANGE had left and did not return.

Back at school after the Easter break, the class had shrunk some more. With my best friends Evi and Bertel already gone and several boys too leaving or about to, Erich Kupfer alone was always there to walk home with me even though I even preferred Eugen Goldman, so meek and word-shy, who would at least not attempt to kiss me under the bridge.

I still enjoyed school, especially when Lehrer Berlinger was around. I was sadly wanting in needle-work and it was the only subject in which occasionally I would suffer the ignominy of being kept behind to finish a piece of darning or embroidery. Knitting was less dull but still demanding patience and manual dexterity it appeared, I was not blessed with sufficiently. I no longer chatted to the extent that warranted the cane on my hand as was the practice. But most of us regarded it as a stamp of honour rather than the opposite, as so reluctantly meted out by Lehrer Berlinger. I knew, however, that being caned by either Kissinger brother in the upper grades was a very different matter as my poor sister Trudel was all too ready to testify. But then the Kissingers—we knew them as the 'fat Kissingers', especially the younger one, were awe-inspiring in their obesity to small children. As the diminutive Lehrer Berlinger was roughly half their size even had he wanted to, he could not have achieved the dread and trembling the unfortunate Kissinger students experienced. As inevitably I would one day be confronted with one or the other of the two brothers, I secretly resolved never to put a foot wrong by the time I reached the upper grades which necessitated leaving the dear junior building and moving over to the large, unfamiliar one next door.

The summer passed and I for one anticipated the first snows with the usual excitement. Although it looked as though Papi was no longer quite so keen to take me about and altogether the atmosphere at home became so much sadder as that awful Hitler or Goebbels screeched on the wireless almost daily and even I could make out the word 'JUDEN' almost every time they ranted on the wireless. The voices were threatening, ugly and I simply could not comprehend what they wanted from us as all we did that was different so far as I knew, was attend Synagogue instead of church.

Papi continued singing his plaintive, beautiful songs: DIE GEDANKEN SIND FREI. Or Heinrich HEINE'S poem made even sadder by Schubert's magical tune: FREMD BIN ICH ENGEZOGEN; FREMD ZIE ICH WIEDER AUS.

(A stranger I arrived; a stranger I leave.) Papi loved that particular song. But I complained because it made me feel sad. Maybe saddest of all, however, was 'DER ERLKONIG'—Goethe's 'EARLKING', brought to life by the magic of Schubert's musical genius. Papi would sing it with eerie realism until I could visualise the little child dead in his father's arms. Invariably I would grumble that I did not like that song but he would always explain that it was a masterpiece of both poetry and music.

Unfortunately he no longer indulged in his little games with Mutti, when he would sing Schubert's 'DEIN IST MEIN HERZ' (yours is my heart) his head close to Mutti's and she would respond as was expected of her with:"hor' doch auf!"(stop it!), never quite able to hide her amusement.

I overheard heated discussions and Papi assuring Mutti that there was plenty of time and that the visas were definitely being prepared for every member of the family including Oma Lowy. The Tennenbaum grandparents' visas were being arranged by Uncle Bernhard, Auntie Rosel's husband.

Auntie Ida was in Palestine with her new husband Paul. My cousin Berni, Auntie's son by her first marriage was in Belgium with his father. Uncle David, my mother's brother in Kemnitz, (Chemnitz) was apparently staying put with his young family. Papi too felt that the Nazi rhetoric should not be taken quite so seriously. After all, this was the civilised nation of Goethe, Kant and Brahms. There really wasn't much further for them to go with their heinous anti-Semitism. Somewhere, somehow something had to give. The average German was decent and humane, wasn't he? How much longer would a decent man stand by and watch his neighbour being plundered, humiliated and beaten?

Papi continued to send his Yiddish articles and poetry all over the world. There was not a Yiddish journal that did not have either a poem or an article by Josef Hillel Levi in their weekly or monthly pages.

Our family summer picnics and trips to the outdoor swimming baths were no more. 'JUDEN VERBOTEN!' became an evermore prevalent sign on public entertainments and even hotels and restaurants. But how could they tell who was Jewish I had asked until I finally gave up. The STURMER printed some dreadful rhymes about Jews not eating pork and being despicable.

There were few parties that summer and at last, school recommenced. Lehrer Berlinger seemed to have grown thinner but he was as ever riveting when he taught us about Andreas Hofer, the shackled hero awaiting the firing squad.

"ADIEU MEIN LAND TYROL" chanted Hofer with his last breath and I cried bitterly. Lehrer Berlinger seemed to be drawn to tragedy.

The first snows came quite early and I walked alone up the ANLAGE towards the banks of the Isar where soon there would be tobogganing though I was not sure who would come with me. Maybe I would be allowed to go on my own. After all I would soon be ten. I was sure I could drag the enormous sledge up the hills on my own even if I was all skin and bone as Oma Tennenbaum maintained. I was sinewy and I had muscles so I was surely strong enough.

Trudel's leg was broken in two places. Our Jewish doctor, about to leave for America, had to put her in the care of one of his Arian colleagues. Her leg was in plaster but it was more than likely that she would require an operation if the leg did not heal or she would be left with a limp. That would mean a lengthy stay in hospital. My parents were devastated.

I spent much time with my sister. We sang together and laughed and played games and I argued because I hated losing at a game called 'MENSCH ARGERE DICH NICHT' (Don't get annoyed) which is precisely what happened each time. Trudel was promised an accordion if she rested and did as the doctor had advised. As her dearest wish was to play the accordion and she was sure she could teach herself, she gave her word with utmost sincerity. I too could hardly wait for her to get her accordion. We could have sing-songs as they did at the OKTOBERFEST. Trudel was so musical that no-one doubted that this was something she would achieve without difficulty even if she had frequently fallen behind in her school—work, unlike Henny who was an exemplary student. But there was no getting away from it: Trudel would have to have an operation if she was ever to walk normally again.

The bell rang forcefully several times downstairs just as day was dawning. The concierge will have opened the entrance door to the flats immediately perhaps identifying the commanding urgency of the caller. I had run out of bed following Henny who went into the bathroom. Trudel could not move out of bed without her crutches and stayed put. I could hear the heavy foot-steps gradually growing louder with each floor left behind. Mutti's anxious voice came from the bedroom.

"Yossele" (My father's Yiddish name)

"I'll get my dressing-gown" came my father's steady voice. Though his oratory could carry far and wide his voice at home was scarcely ever raised. The foot-steps outside our front door were accompanied by hefty ringing followed by impatient banging. Papi opened the door to two plain-clothes men with Gestapo badges.

I did not hear the first part of the conversation as the two men stopped short at the door. But without hesitation I ran into the hall in my nightdress to look. They stood there like statues without a single word, ignoring me. But I stared straight at them. I was so accustomed to being smiled at that their immovable expression took me aback.

Mutti came out while Papi hastily threw some clothes on. My parents had been conversing heatedly in whispers and I could not make out just what was happening.

"My daughter Trudel has a broken leg and cannot walk." Mutti addressed the men sanguinely. "And she cannot be left on her own."

The men looked at each other and nodded.

"You'd better stay with her." One said.

"And my little girl—she is only nine."

Again they looked at each other, at my mother and finally at me.

"She can stay with you. But your son Abraham," they pronounced the name with obvious distaste.

"He is in Wurzburg in a Teachers Training College."

They studied papers they were holding and nodded.

"And the woman Henny Lowy"

"Henny is here but she is still . . ."

"Tell her to get dressed. She must come."

Meanwhile I ran into the bedroom where Papi was already dressed and sorting out a few papers and his Polish Passport.

"Papi, Papi why do you have to go?"

"It's because we are Polish and not German citizens. It won't take long-" He sighed.

"But I'm German. I was born here. Yes, you can stay here."

"No, I want to go with you!" I suddenly insisted, as he went into the hall and I followed.

Henny was there in her quiet, unobtrusive way, standing silently next to my mother. I had scarcely noticed her as I ran after my father. But by now I was clinging to father's hand and I had no idea why I was so adamant to go along."

"I want to go with Papi!" I sobbed.

"Please yourselves." said the older of the two stony-faced statues shrugging. "But get a move on—we'll be waiting downstairs.

"Ten minutes!"

Mutti, ashen-faced looked at me. I ran into the bedroom followed by my poor mother.

"Mellale, they said you can stay" but the rest of my mother's sentence hung heavily in the air as she heaved one of her sighs and helped me get dressed. It was obvious that for once she simply did not know what was best.

"I want to go with Papi!" I insisted stubbornly as the tears ran down my face. I had no idea why I was crying. I only knew I wanted to be with my father.

"Anyway, we'll be back soon, the men told Papi, didn't they?" Mutti nodded as she helped tidy up my hair and then kissed me.

"My MASELDIGES MEIDELE" She whispered in m y ear as she had done at the Czech border. "They said it wouldn't take long. They are checking up on all Polish citizens." Her sighs mocked her steady tone. "If you are with Papi maybe—"but the remainder of her sentence failed to materialise. I understood what she meant. I would bring 'Masel'. I almost believed it myself as she had reiterated it so often. I was lucky.

Once dressed in my blue school dirndl dress which with winter approaching, would soon be put aside and my old scratchy coat and school shoes, I ran back and grabbed Papi's hand.

"I'm coming with you" I reaffirmed. Papi picked me up rubbing his unshaven face against mine. No-one thought of taking anything other than the documents they had asked for. Food was the last thing on anyone's mind.

"What can one do with you?" Papi said with so much love in his voice.

"We'll be back in a couple hours. If she wants to come . . ." Papi turned to my mother as he embraced her. "You mustn't worry. Once they've cleared everything up at headquarters." He paused. "I don't understand Marileben. What exactly do they want to clear up? My papers are in order." But there was no time for my mother to reply. The ten minutes were up and one did not keep the Gestapo waiting. The three of us rushed out of the flat. I looked back at Mutti and waved. I felt very grown up.

With the door open, we were ushered without a word of explanation into the back of a sombre black official car and driven to Headquarters in town.

"Look Papi, back there is the LIndwurmstrasse—our shop!"

From there, however, to Papi's consternation, instead of the expected interrogation at Headquarters, we were instructed to board the waiting coach already filled with other tired-looking unshaven men and dishevelled women. I looked about me to see if there were other children but could not see any. There were rows of more waiting coaches. We watched them slowly filling up. We were in a part of Munich I was unfamiliar with: tall office buildings and wide elegant modern streets. I took it all in with interest intending to tell everyone at school all about my adventure. I was sure there would be few other children with such an interesting experience.

People began to recognise my father and they greeted him and patted me. I could hear the word 'STADELHEIM', the name of the local jail outside Munich. The thought of seeing the jail excited me. This really was turning out to be a unique adventure. Fear was the last thing on my mind. I was with my Papi. Henny had found a seat somewhere in the back. She must have met some acquaintances. I could just make out her pale freckled face. My modest, shy sister, with her tidy hair-style of a sausage roll in the back of her neck reaching half-way to either side of her cheeks keeping her ample frizzy chestnut hair always in fashionable good order, would never make a fuss in public even if at home she was not so reluctant to complain. At that time our close to eight-year age gap was virtually unbridgeable. She was my 'good' sister and I loved her.

The drive seemed to take quite a while, accompanied by muted discussions with the occasional raised voices soon lowered again. Papi was quiet, speaking only spasmodically in polite response. But his dear face looked drawn and increasingly anxious. Obviously he did not regard this trip the adventure it seemed to me. I had managed to squeeze into the window seat beside him, with two or more people next to Papi. I took no notice as I was fascinated by the bucolic scenery suddenly taking the place of everyday Munich as I knew it. It was not long before we came to a halt, however, behind several other coaches in a muddy, drab courtyard leading to endless buildings whose rows and rows of windows all had black thick metal bars across. A real prison—STADELHEIM!

We were impatiently ordered into this vast pile of repellent brick which looked to me as though it was covered in grey soot. People filed in stunned silence into open cells. Papi clutched my hand firmly. Henny had disappeared with other girls and women to somewhere further back. Someone suggested I join the young women. I clung stubbornly to my father without a word.

All the cells were open, fetid and filthy with the barred windows and window-sills covered in grime. The few taps in the gang—way disgorged only a trickle at a time of brown water stinking of rust. I looked about me: only one prevalent colour throughout and that was a dank, filthy grisly grey and only one odour and that was the smell of urine mixed with sweat. So that was what a prison was like.

Papi looked suddenly very anxious, the knuckles of his hands white, but as ever, he was one of the least vociferous. He seemed to be taking stock. An orator of renown when it came to social gatherings he was invariably reserved in private. People were circling around him asking for his opinion of what was going on, what he thought would happen next. We were free to walk about and Papi and some of his acquaintances and I believe his cousin Uncle Oiser was there too, strolled outside into the yard forming a kind of small private cell. I did not let go of Papi's hand. The talk between the men and a few women was so muted that to me it seemed like a grey hum matching the bleak colour which surrounded us. My father spoke very little.

It was growing dark and still nothing; no interrogation, no one to say it was time to return. No food although we had been here since mid-morning. But it seemed everyone expected the coaches still parked at the gates would soon be employed to return us all to our homes. A mistake must have been made by the authorities as no-one could think of a feasible reason for entire families with never a single complaint against them being held in jail. Of course they were all Jews and it seemed all of Polish origin even if their offspring were born in Germany.

Then women from the German Jewish Council arrived with some food, mostly chocolate, bread rolls, bananas and milk. I refused the banana but greedily devoured a good deal of chocolate. I may have had some milk but soon abandoned the lukewarm liquid handed me in a metal mug tasting of rusty metal.

I realised that no-one had any notion what exactly would happen next. It was growing very late and very dark. We returned to the open prison. The dank odour of perspiration in the gangways now filled to bursting with people roaming about aimlessly rubbing their hands, searching for more familiar faces, seemed like a fetid black cloud spread over the entire area.

There was nowhere to wash and I had no idea if there were toilets as I did not at any time need to go. The one tap near us disgorged only the faintest trickle of cold, lead-coloured water. Papi told me to lie down and try to rest on the bunk in the wall but I could not. It was filthy and stinking. Someone said I should go down and join my sister but I shook my head vigorously. I had no idea where Henny was. I did not even feel tired. I did not know what I felt if truth were told. The excitement of seeing a real life prison, of actually being in it, had gradually turned to overpowering bewilderment. I was covered in dirt and I missed Mutti. At some time of the night I must have fallen asleep.

Up until that day, the entire nine years of my life here in my birthplace had been blissful. I hardly knew the meaning of pain and I certainly could not fathom unhappiness no matter how many tears I shed over Cinderella's misfortunes or worst of all, Hansel and Gretel's. My home-life was filled with love, music and the banter of my older siblings. If my mother would sometimes lose her temper with the older ones, especially Trudel and Henny and even slap their faces on occasion it, never seemed to happen to me and my siblings accepted it with the usual lack of grace and screaming that went to make up our delightful KINDERSTUBE. My school was for me a place where learning and friends mingled with ever new adventures. My skill at gymnastics was an added bonus and there was nothing that stood in the way of my happiness. As for that saddest of films THE GOOD EARTH, which I had seen with my mother and had cried my heart out at every scene that depicted cruelty—it was simply beyond my comprehension. Just something that happened to people in another far-off place—another world. At any rate it was based on a book written by a clever author called Pearl Buck. It was impossible for me to relate to such tragedy even if it made me cry in sympathy.

Had I been asked if there was anything I would change I might have said only the constant jack-booted marching and droning of those uniformed metallic soldiers that had little by little usurped our precious, peaceful city—and the terrible word 'emigration' that was taking away my dearest friends to places that seemed alien and I did not think I would ever be able to visit. But I did not comprehend the terrifying significance of any of it. My parents had sheltered me to the extent that left no room for fear or mistrust of my surroundings. Even now in Stadelheim jail with Papi at my side and Henny somewhere nearby; Mutti and Trudel at home, Abi in Wurzburg—I may have been momentarily bewildered but not afraid. I simply did not understand. My parents had been told I was a top student: I grasped quickly, I adapted without difficulty and I was not impertinent. Above all I was a happy child—but I grasped none of what was staring me in the face.

Some members of the Jewish Council, all German Citizens, came and went apparently freely, with little information of any use to the bewildered crowd of Polish Jews standing, sitting on the floor, clustered in groups, heads close together discussing, discussing in whispers until the bleak, shrouded night changed to dawn and beyond.

At a moment's notice we were ordered by the guards to assemble outside: we were leaving. I believe the news was greeted with relief as we soon found ourselves inside the self-same coaches that had brought us. We were going home! Exhausted, dishevelled, hungry and unwashed—but all would soon be back to normal.

My hands were covered in grime and sticky from all that chocolate. Papi had tried to squeeze water from the rusty tap but even he was no magician. He used a handkerchief to wipe the chocolate off my face. His own face already unshaven when he had been dragged out of bed the day before, now had a second supply of stubble and because he had not even been able to wash as he would on High Holidays when he also could not shave, it did not have his pleasant Papi odour. It did not matter as soon we would be able to enjoy a nice warm bath and resume our normal lives. I wondered fleetingly what I had missed at school yesterday and if I could still make school this morning. I was sure Bertel would be wandering what had happened to me and Lehrer Berlinger would be most surprised when I told him that I had spent the night in Stadelheim jail. I could describe it to the entire class. For some reason it had not occurred to me that there might be others in the same situation. I had seen few children and none I recognised. No, I saw myself as the sole recipient of such an adventure.

I squeezed into the window-seat next to Papi as before. It seemed to me that as we left the jail the route somehow differed from the one we had taken coming. I could not see the LINDWURMSTRASSE where our shop was, or the OKTOBERWIESE opposite and we appeared to be approaching the town centre. A little while later we came to a halt—outside the MUNCHNER BAHNHOF—the station!

As if with one voice came the sudden puzzled exclamation: "DER HAUPTBAHNHOF!" Some people rose but most remained seated. Papi gripped my hand more tightly but also remained seated. I did not see Henny.

"RAUS, SCHNELL—AUSSTEIGEN!" The order came from the armed, black uniformed SA men who had opened the coach doors. Up until now I had not noticed any SA, only prison guards and before that plain-clothes GEATAPO. The order was given in a fairly low, almost normal tone as though they were bored with the whole thing. The bedraggled, soporiferous passengers filed out glad to breathe in Munich's familiar fresh early morning air before being marched inside the station just as they had hoped they could make their own way back home. I heard no complaints but there may well have been. Most people were too dazed, hungry and exhausted to take in the situation. As yesterday morning I experienced a throbbing sense of excitement, Papi scarcely spoke, as though waiting to see what would develop. No-one thought of approaching the armed masters of our fate for explanation. Yet I could feel only excitement—the adventure was not yet over.

Obediently we assembled inside the station—how many of us? I had no idea but there were several hundred. I loathed that station. I had been inside only for our exciting trips to Italy and Czechoslovakia and could never wait for the trains to pull out of the fetid, smoke and soot infested bleak hole the station seemed to me. It was always dark. The grisly clouds of smoke and the constant spitting, rumbling trains had a nasty life of their own and the entire station was always terrifyingly bleak and spooky. In short it never failed to make me feel uneasy even if in anticipation of a pleasant journey. I had decided a while back I did not like these great big smoke—belching iron beasts. Some people liked trains; I did not. Invariably some of the grit would land in my eyes. Nor did I like the monotone of their soporific, soulless clickety-clack forever accompanying our journeys. No, I did not like trains.

We were made to stand around for how long, I do not know. Time to me then was either something one awaited eagerly with impatient anticipation, or something having just enjoyed and now having regretfully to look back on. This senseless standing around with so many other sad-faced, anxious people had no name, no time-scale.

The sooty station made me feel even more soiled. Papi, dignified as ever, was shockingly unable to put an end to this inexplicable episode that had begun as an adventure and was now turning into—what? I wanted to go to school. It was nearly morning and there might not be time for me to have a bath and have my tangled hair washed and for Mutti to dress it as expertly as she always did. The lotion she used on my hair was so fragrant. I could smell it now in my imagination. I began to miss her and to feel weepy. But I would not let Papi see me cry. And anyway, I would not want to leave his side until we returned home. I never wanted to leave his side. But I would at least have liked Mutti to be here too.

Now we had boarded a train—it had happened so quickly and I was so tired that as soon as I had been lifted onto the train and squeezed in beside my father, I fell asleep.

I awoke spasmodically and was given more chocolate and a roll which I accepted and managed to eat. I looked about me. The same miserable frazzled passengers I had seen in jail. I could hardly tell one from the other; they all seemed to look alike. Every time I awoke I heard the word POLAND. Were we going to Poland? Were we not going home at all?

"When are we going back, Papi?" I asked drowsily between dropping off again. But my father merely stroked my cheeks and told me to rest more.

The train had come to a halt with the usual noisy quiver and all its accompanying belches and scraping noises. I woke instinctively clinging to Papi whose hand I had let go during sleep. I looked at him hoping he could explain where we were. But as we looked out the window and saw only stretches of untended earth and overgrown grass even I understood that we had not actually arrived at any recognisable destination.

"Where are we, Papi?" I asked nonetheless hoping that Papi would have an answer.

There were no houses to be discerned from the windows as people craned their necks to see if they could identify the area. Then someone exclaimed: "We're in Poland!"

"Can't be—Came from someone else." Where is the frontier? Where are the Customs? There's nothing—it's a no man's land!"

Doors were opened and the same SA men had alighted and now bellowed: "RAUS, AUSSTEIGEN!" as before. People hesitated as there was no sign of a platform only dirt and gravel. It was a steep climb down from the train but Papi, having heard the word Poland, lifted me off the train having been one of the first to alight. He had detected a few Polish guards in a hut or cubicle obviously serving as some kind of make-shift custom building. Everyone was made to leave the train and people spilled out from a part of the train in the back that must have joined us after we left Munich. Amongst them was my brother Abi who at a moments' notice had been made to board the train from Wurzburg where he was studying at the Jewish Teachers Seminary.

"This is not the frontier—this No Man's Land!" could be heard with ugly regularity. "We're in No Man's Land!" But the men in the little booth just over the fence were unmistakably Polish guards in uniform.

"We are going to Krakow!" Said my father to me with what was the closest to a smile I had seen on his face in twenty-four hours.

"Mellale—it will be alright. We will all live in Krakow where I was born." I knew how much he loved the city of his birth and had a hankering to return there. His most renowned poems were about his home town and his revered ancestry.

"Krakow—"I repeated. "And we will all live there?" Papi nodded and stroked my sticky face.

People began to take out their Passports, resigned to walk through the dirt-roads and fields of this No-Man's Land into what appeared to be Poland proper. There was only one draw-back. The Polish customs men refused to let us through and awaited instructions.

Now almost for the first time, my father became animated. He was angry that these men had to await instructions to allow a Polish citizen entry into Poland. He wanted to go there. He told some of his acquaintances who had gathered around us how he would be delighted to get his family out of Germany.

I do not know how long we were made to stand there, unkempt, unwashed, hungry, humiliated in an unpaved waste-land that looked as bleak as a grave-yard. I know, however, that my father was genuinely furious at being denied entry into his birth-place.

Finally the bawled order: "ZURUCK IM ZUG!" (Get back on the train).

An uncharacteristically disgruntled father lifted me on the train. It appeared the Poles had taken more than their full quota of Jews and simply refused to accept this last train out of Munich. I do not know how long the train journey took. Maybe I fell asleep again. But by night-fall I was back in my lovely clean bed with its immaculate white linen sheets, having been bathed and fed and kissed and fussed over by a Mutti who somehow seemed far more pleased with the way things had turned out than my father. What was more, Henny and Abi were home too.

October 27th 1938 17,000 Polish Jews including 2,000 children were expelled under HEYDRICH'S orders, the second in command of the SS. presaging KRISTALLNACT. (Night of Broken Glass) None of them returned; most of them perished in the holocaust.

Chapter Seven

MY SCHOOL IS BURNING! (10.11.1938)

There was great disappointment in the class over the cancellation of the Junior Jewish Olympics. The Jewish Council had probably known for some time or anticipated as much. But we junior pupils were informed only a few days after my 'adventure'. It was strange really how rarely if at all the subject came up and how none of my fellow class mates had apparently been on a similar trip. So far as I knew no one else at all had been to STADELHEIM or to the Polish border. But instead of being invited to elaborate, Lehrer Berlinger avoided the topic in class as though it were something shameful. There were, however, several more pupils missing. Whether they had boarded earlier trains that were allowed to enter Poland, or whether ours was the only Munich train that day having stopped en route also to pick up people from WURZBURG including Abi, I don't think anyone knew. What I do know is that from that day my mother had put my name down for the KINDERTRANSPORT to England which though suggested earlier, had been rejected by my parents chiefly on my frantic pleading and Papi's assurance that the visas for his entire family and that included his mother, would not now be long in arriving. The PEN Club and his colleagues in London were doing everything possible to speed up the procedure. But for my practical, prescient mother, the time for waiting patiently was at an end. No matter how much I pleaded with both parents, this time Mutti's decision prevailed. Papi too appeared to have changed his mind.

"No matter what" he had taken me on his knee only a few nights ago, "you must never agree to be adopted." He impressed on me with unusual severity.

"But what does that mean?"

"It means that strangers can become your parents."

"O' no" I cried horrified. "I will never let them do that—Never, never!" I hugged him with tears running down my cheeks. "No-one will ever ad—adopt me! I love you both so much!" Papi had clasped me very tight.

Lehrer Berlinger seemed to grow more haggard with each passing day, though we went on singing those plaintive, generally heart-breaking songs together and he would continue to ask me up to the front of the class to recite a favourite poem. I worshipped the man: he was the essence of kindness and effortlessly inspiring teaching. I felt it then even if I would not have been able to put it in words. I knew him to be a rare, very special man.

'SCNEEFLOCKCHEN, WEISSROCKCHEN JETZT KOMMST DU GESCHNEIT

DU WOHNST IN DEN WOLKEN DEIN WEG IST SO WEIT'

(Snow-flake, white—skirted one, now you've come a'snowing.

You live in the clouds—what a long journey you have.)

I could see the thick, clean snow-flakes of our beautiful winters falling once again as soon they would be and it felt so good when we all sang together. And yet I felt like crying when I looked at Lehhrer Berlinger.

The boy was taller than me and obviously a couple of years older. I had noticed him waiting at the corner a few times previously and had grown a little anxious. Even I had now come to the realisation that it was dangerous to be alone on the street but until this boy had so obviously waited there just staring at me, I thought little more of it. I did not think he was Jewish but he was not in Hitler Youth uniform and with his nicely brushed thick, chestnut hair and perfect features, he was decidedly handsome. What was more, he did not look like someone who meant me harm. Yet our meetings seemed to become more regular as though he was purposely waiting for me on the corner of my street as by now he must have seen me enter my apartment building and knew where we lived. My heart began to thump when I saw him from afar. What did he want? Was he going to attack me? The intrepid side of my character to the fore, the thought of another adventure was only remotely tinged with fear.

There he was again; I saw him from afar leaning against the wall of the house on the corner as I crossed the CORNELIUS Bridge. SCHWEIGERSTRASSE where I lived was only a street-crossing away. I did not hesitate as I reached him.

"What—what do you want?" I asked looking him straight in the eye. That is how Mutti would handle this situation. Never show fear. His eyes were large, night-sky blue and very bright. He smiled. It was a nice smile.

"I like you." He said blushing. "I think you're very pretty. Will you be my girl-friend I—live just round the corner from you." I swallowed and breathed a sigh of relief. "O" He added hastily: "My name is Kurt. What's yours?"

"I—my name is MELLA—but I can't be your girl-friend." I said sadly after a moments' hesitation during which I wondered if such a friendship was possible. "You see Kurt—I'm Jewish."

"So what?" he said defiantly. "I don't mind."

I swallowed again. He didn't mind my being Jewish. What was there to mind? We looked at each other for a few lingering moments each wishing we really could be friends but knowing well enough it was not possible even if neither understood why.

"Anyway," I heard myself tell him almost proudly: "I'm going to England!"

"Oh" he sounded crestfallen. "England, so far away—but until then—and when you get back—we live so near to each other and I like you." The last words were said almost hesitantly, shyly.

I nodded and we shook hands.

"I like you too. Yes, when I get back. So, until then GRUSS GOTT." We shook hands politely and I walked proudly to my apartment building aware of Kurt's eyes following. I had a handsome new admirer who did not mind my being Jewish. And maybe we could be friends when I got back. But when would that be? No-one ever spoke of returning, only of emigrating.

I had not seen Papi or Abi for a couple days. Uncle Oiser (Josef Bienenfeld) his cousin too seemed to have mysteriously disappeared. But I knew Papi had been going to a great many meetings that sometimes lasted until early morning and then Mutti would be terribly anxious and I would creep into her bed to keep her company. The atmosphere at home since our return was as taut as an overstretched clothes-line about to snap at any moment. And now with ho sign of Papi and Abi, the laughter seemed suddenly to have if not died, as Trudel and I never could keep a straight face for too long, but somehow uncalled for. The wireless was forever blaring that horrible, metal-edged voice of the club-footed Dr Goebbels I had seen in person and in news—reels in the cinema the last time Trudel had smuggled us in to see the hilarious DICK UND DOF film. And if not him then the shrieks of Hitler himself that of late, made my hair stand on end though I did not understand a word of what he was screaming about. 'Juden' were rarely left out of his diatribe. Every word, every metal-edged whip he spat out, aimed mercilessly at us?

Mutti's nerves were on knife-edge although she battled with all her everyday tasks with her usual efficiency—with Papi not there to help either. My questions about Papi's and Abi's whereabouts remained unanswered. I continued with my school and Mutti went to the shop in Lindwumstrasse but she had given notice and was selling every single piece still remaining in the shop. She was also making arrangements for a 'LIFT' which she explained meant the shipping across the sea of as many of our belongings and precious furniture that meant so much to my parents, as they could afford. They would be duly delivered or stored in England as soon as there was an address and a reliable date. It was a very expensive transaction but to Mutti it meant that a little of the world they had built up would at least be following them. She knew the people she was dealing with and did not doubt their trustworthiness. They had been recommended by friends and relations.

The morning was cool but not cold. Only Trudel was home. Mutti must have gone early to the shop as there was still so much to do. Maybe Henny had gone with her. At any rate I was quite able to get my own cup of milk and I found a piece of cake which would normally not be a part of my breakfast. But I ate it anyway and dressed in one of my dirndl dresses, always my choice if left to me, with a cardigan slung over my arm. I tidied my hair as best I could. I simply had not yet mastered the art of dressing that unruly mop of hair of mine and had made little effort to improve. My Mutti was always there to see to it for me, wasn't she?

No matter how much I grumbled, deep down both Mutti and I treasured that daily early morning charade.

It could not have been much after seven when I left the building. A little early but I was always eager to get to school even if that did not start till eight and even if I dawdled at snail's pace it would not take me longer than half an hour. But there was nothing to keep me at home a moment longer: everything was so sad. And neither Papi nor Mutti were at home and Trudel was still in bed. I liked meeting friends outside school and chatting. Trudel managed well enough on her own by now with crutches. My poor sister; she was always in some scrap or another. She had been the only one of us who had contracted the dreaded disease diphtheria which we were told could be fatal. But as ever she weathered the storm and I thought she was splendid no matter what she got up to. In fact, there were times I wanted to be just like her as she was never in danger of being a bore.

The streets were remarkably still and silent this morning, with hardly anyone about. But it was early. I walked leisurely through the familiar residential area I could have traversed in my sleep. No shops, just fine old grey brick apartment houses. No one least of all school mates. These back-streets were rarely busy at the best of times but this morning they might have been a grave-yard, the silence was so stark. It was not particularly chilly yet the day was grey as on a bleak winters' day.

I thought I detected a faint smell of burning that became stronger the closer I drew to my school at the main junction leading past the Hotel VIER JAHRESZEIT in the KONIGSTRASSE joining on to the corner of the HERZOGRUDOLFSTRASSE. My eyes were beginning to smart from the smoky atmosphere with bits of grit flying about, darkening the air even more. No vehicles, still not a single pedestrian as I crossed the road to reach the HERZOGRUDOLFSTRASSE with its corner sweet shop that had for years eased even the most reluctant Jewish student's load.

For a moment I stood stock still. I was bewildered more than deterred by the billows of smoke obscuring the latter part of the street where my school was situated.

"What on earth are you doing here?" boomed the familiar voice of the owner from inside the little store. "Go home—this is no place for you to-day!"

The generally genial big Bavarian woman sounded cross as she rushed out and stood on the threshold to face me.

"I—I'm going to my school." I told her tears welling in my eyes as much from the smoke and grit as reaction to her unusual gruffness.

"Ach KLEINCHEN," she said in a softer tone, "don't you know—there won't be any school to-day. Go home as fast as you can. You shouldn't be out. What were your parents thinking of!"

"My Papi isn't here" I began instantly on the defensive as I shook my head. "And Mutti—I want to go to my school."

As I made my way further down the street the crippling stench of burning and smoke all but overwhelmed me. I came to a halt right opposite the school. There was no mistaking it—my school was aflame!

"My school is burning!" I exclaimed to no-one in particular as there was no one close by excepting two brown-shirts further down the road staring straight ahead, entirely ignoring me.

"My school is burning and they are not even trying to put out the flames!" I mumbled with tears in my eyes. But as far as the brown-shirts were concerned I might just as well have been just another piece of grit.

I do not know how long I stood there watching the smoke and flames gorging themselves on the greatest joy and influence of the last three years of my life. It did not occur to me that the main target of this outrage was actually the Synagogue behind our school building, the OHEL JAKOB SYNAGOGUE. As it was not the family Synagogue I had never consciously thought of it as part of my school although in reality it was a portion of the senior school building behind the smaller junior building. Pupils whose parents were not affiliated with the Synagogue were therefore hardly aware of it, especially the youngest. Though The Old Testament was an integral part of the curriculum, religion was not. Our sole required qualification was of course being classified as Jewish. To me until now that had always seemed something to be proud of even if magical occasions like Christmas had to be sacrificed.

I stood a long while alone unable to move, as though my feet were glued to the ground. I do not know for how long as no-one joined me there at any time. Not a single other student. And I do not know just what I felt excepting a searing sense of loss and sadness. I kept shaking my head. I still shake my head at the memory of the scene as real and vivid to-day as then.

At some stage I must have decided to make my way back up the road. I met no-one. When I reached the sweet-shop the woman came running out again.

"Good Lord, are you still here child!" She exclaimed. "I couldn't see you for all the smoke."

"My school is burning and no-one has sent for the fire-brigade." I complained as if she were at fault. She stroked my cheek nodding.

"Please get yourself home as fast as you can. Don't you know what happened last night? I'm really surprised your parents let you come out to-day." She reached for my right hand and deposited a handful of Marzipan potatoes in it. She knew they were my favourites. I shook my head. I didn't want them but she closed my hand into a fist.

"Eat them on your way home." She heaved a sigh. "Auf Wiedersehn!" She called after me without conviction as I walked aimlessly away.

I made my way home through the same deserted streets I had come early that morning. The stench from the smoke had become a part of me. In my clenched fist were the marzipan potatoes beginning to melt. I opened my fist and dropped them one by one into the gutter. I experienced a sensation of misery that gripped my entire being. Shocked I could feel that way I wept very softly the rest of the way.

Chapter Eight

KINDERTRANSPORT (DEEMBER 1938)

Miriam and Josef Hillel Lowy circa 1937

My mother had left at six o'clock the morning after KRISTALLNACHT. It had not occurred to her that my school might be closed or worse. As we lived in a residential district there had been no indication of protracted unrest as in the inner city areas. Friends had phoned to warn her and she needed to check what had happened to the shop. Fear was not in Mutti's vocabulary nor was prevarication. She had no doubt the men had to leave without further ado after the 'POLENABSCHIEBUNG' and worst of all it had to be kept from everyone, including the children. I was therefore unaware of the exact date of Papi and Abi's actual departure, as these were times like none before in my young life, when I had learned instinctively not to ask questions. As it was it was so much better not to know.

The flat had become so bare and lifeless without Papi chanting a Schubert song or the latest Richard TAUBER record or some sad or funny Yiddish songs. As Papi spoke it, Yiddish was a beautiful and full of charm and elegance. But as others spoke it, including Opa and sometimes even Mutti, it turned into angry curses I thought unworthy of my father's treasured 'Mammeloschen.' The family favourite: the song by his childhood friend and fellow poet Mordecai GEBIRTIG who lived in Poland. Each of us could sing along and GEBIRTIG had become a family friend even if we had never met him when we gathered to chant KINDERJOHREN. (Childhood Years) The ambience in the room sufficed to make it special for everyone there.

"ICH MOCHT EINMAL WIEDER VERLIEBT SEIN—(I would like to fall in love again)" Papi had been singing a great deal of late having just learnt the song rendered so romantically by Richard TAUBER, making eyes at Mutti so that we would all burst out laughing in anticipation of Mutti's reaction. And not to disappoint us Nutti had chided good-naturedly: "HOR' DOCH AUF!" (Stop it!")

Papi had liked to chant the 'INTERNATIONALE' until a while ago. In fact he had sung it so often when I was smaller that I had learnt every word of the first verse.

'LEUTE HOHRT DIE SIGNALE

AUF ZUM LETZTEN GEFACHT.

DIE INTERNATIONALE KAMPFT FUR'S VOLKERRECHT'.

Yes, Papi certainly preferred the Communists to the Nazis and I had heard all about the brilliant Leon Trotzky, one of the chief leaders with Lenin and Stalin and a Jew.

From the day I returned home from my burnt-out school, I began to realise the world around us was unsafe, even threatening. So this was what so many of my friends and family were trying to get away from. But was it only here in Germany that people were trying to hurt us? Of course I now knew of KRISTALLNACHT the previous night, when most Jewish owned shops and establishments were vandalised and the windows smashed frequently with terrible consequences for their owners. Our shop had been left unscathed as no-one seemed to have been aware of its Jewish connections. As it was, my parents only rented the ground floor of the old building and the LINDWURMSTRASSE, one of Munich's old streets with little to commend it to smart shoppers, was known mostly for its vicinity to the OKTOBERWIESE (the famous fair—ground.)

Where was Lehrer Berlinger when they incinerated my school? Whenever I hummed a favourite winter ditty he had taught us, I felt the tears well up:

"SCHNEEFLOCKCHEN, WEISSROCKCHEN JETZT KOMMST DU GESCHNEIT,

DU WOHNST IN DEN WOLKEN DEIN WEG IST SO WEIT (Snow-flake, white-skirted one, now you've come a snowing,

You live in the clouds—your journey is so far.)

But Mutti assured me that my dear teacher was safe. When after a few days there was still no sign of Papi or Abi, Mutti finally explained that they had secretly left a few nights earlier with Uncle Oiser, because she felt they were no longer safe here in Germany. They would await the arrival of the visas in Belgium after crossing the Alps on foot. All three were excellent mountaineers and very fit. Mutti was convinced that no Jewish male was safe in Germany now. She did not, however, fear for herself. She had too much to arrange here and anyway they would not hurt women and children surely. There was nothing for it at any rate but to wait until Trudel was fit to travel. But the men folk had to get out of Germany. There was no more time to lose.

I tried to understand. And why was she so insistent that I should go to England on my own with the 'Kindertransport,' rather than await the arrival of visas and travel with her and my two sisters? But Mutti just shook her head. The sooner more of the family were gone from here the better, she attempted to explain. She would see that Henny too would leave the moment the visas arrived, if Trudel was not yet able to travel. My visa would be needed for Oma Lowy. Why all this desperate urgency suddenly—but if I understood nothing else I understood that my mother's Instincts were not something to be ignored, as Papi had told us time and again.

As it was, I was only accepted for the KINDERTRANSPORT at the last moment Mutti having rejected an offer months earlier. But because my school record consistently showed me to be reliable and compliant, they had agreed to fit me in at this last moment. Maybe it had something to do too with my journey to the Polish border too. But I would never know. When I could not hide my absolute dread of going alone to a strange country without any family member, Mutti pointed out how proud she was of me to be thought of so well by the Jewish Council and embraced me, holding me tight for a very long time. It was not something she did often. She threw a sideways look at Trudel which spoke more eloquently than words. As if to say that she doubted if the school's report would have favoured Trudel similarly. The ongoing little battles between my mother and Trudel were an open family secret.

"We will all be together again very soon, darling" She assured me with absolute conviction and no-one ever doubted my Mutti. She herself would remain here with Trudel until the doctor issued the necessary certificate stating her leg had healed sufficiently for her to travel. Jewish doctors were no longer employed but Trudel's doctor appeared to be decent and kind. Henny might have to travel on her own to Belgium if that took longer than anticipated. Mutti was no longer prepared to waste a precious moment or opportunity to get another family member out of Germany as fast as was humanly possible. Much as I tried to see it Mutti's way, I still could not help wondering if she was not making a mountain out of a mole-hill.

"But when am I going?" I asked each day anew. The fearful anticipation was almost worse than the inevitable departure. The trouble was that we did not know. I had been accepted at the last moment only with the understanding that I would be given very short warning depending as it did on a last minute vacancy. As I was one of the younger children they would try to find an older girl who could take me under her wing during the journey. There was also a great deal of bureaucracy to deal with for the department of the Jewish Council: 'DIE JUDISCHE KULTUS GEMEINDE' ascertaining a place upon arrival, for each child in England. They had had so pitifully little time to get the ball rolling and even worse, for such a pitiful few.

A small suitcase was to be at the ready so that I could leave at a moments' notice. I was so confused at what lay ahead that I became morose. This time my sense of adventure was sadly lacking. I had no Papi or Mutti to take my hand and walk with me into the bleak unknown.

Hastily I gathered as many contributions to my treasured autograph book as was still possible. Goethe seemed to have a top spot with adults, shared with God. My father had dedicated a poem to me months earlier in Yiddish. One of the very last was one from Oma Tennenbaum shortly before she and my darling Opa themselves departed for London having received their visas from Auntie Rosel and Uncle Bernhard, with whom they would be staying. The dedication was dated December 18ᵗʰ 1938 in Oms's clear, clean handwriting a trait she had passed on to my own mother. I believe that the Bernstein family with Abi and Hanni were already in Switzerland. Opa in his contribution signed: 'Opuss' and addressed me as his 'MUSCHI'. He could never stop joking and I adored him for it. For the shortest time his light-heartedness made me feel better too.

I had little option but to await notification of the date of my own departure. Mutti made little comment and did not complain. As I was only allowed a minimum of clothing in a tiny cardboard suitcase, I was not consulted as to what I wished to include. But I made sure of one thing and that was my autograph album. In this way I felt I was taking with me all my school-friends and family—everyone I was leaving behind—as well as some who had already left me behind. To have it by me afforded me enormous comfort. It seemed that both Mutti and I had forgotten all about anything as trivial as a doll. Of course it was always possible that Mutti with her admirable memory had simply found no room for a doll in the pitiful list she had been given.

My mother continued to remain outwardly calm; at least that was how I saw it. She was dealing too with the sale of the last mattresses and bedding in the shop as well as making an inventory of the furniture and personal memorabilia that would go in the 'LIFT' finally to be unloaded at an as yet unknown address in Gt. Britain and stored until then.

I do not recall talking to my special friend ZICKEZANGE as I was always most careful not to be overheard and in the flat that would have been difficult. But I did go into my private little hideout in one of the larders where my favourite doll resided much of the time. I changed her dress with my stock of sweet-smelling silver paper in varied colours and told her all manner of secrets.

Mutti sat for hours on end working out the final sums and selling yet more ornaments to cover the mounting expense of the LIFT. It must have cost her a great deal of agony to part with objects she had treasured since her wedding day. We knew that Papi and Abi were somewhere in Italy by now. They were safe and they were well. Details were obviously not forthcoming by mail. Everything had to be carefully and sparsely worded. I took it all in but nothing made sense to me since they burnt down my school. I carried that experience about with me like an invisible, forever haunting grisly ghost.

I played with my 'NEGERPUPPE' (Negro Doll) a great deal in those days of interminable uncertainty, waiting for that pivotal call from the Council. I must have told the doll countless times of my imminent departure. Strangely enough I never thought to pack her. Maybe I was told there would not be room. Mutti had explained there was sadly no room whatever in the minute suit-case for anything but the essential pieces of clothing on a list she had been given. No favourite books of fairy tales. But there were some nice new stockings and vests and knickers, she assured me.

Trudel and I sang songs together and I ambled aimlessly around the flat that now seemed stretched and too large with Papi and Abi no longer there. Sometimes I would pirouette round and round in the spacious hall until I literally flopped down exhausted in front of the open door of what was Maria's and Abi's room in turn, but was now deserted and filled with cases and half-packed objects. As soon as the phone rang my heart missed a beat. And then it came just before Christmas when I had half hoped it would not come at all. I will never know whether it was the 22nd or 23rd of December that I was to catch that train. We had been given exactly twenty-four hours, Mutti did not fuss. WE were ready. Her surely hard come-by stoicism (as deep down she was an emotional woman,) must have cost her a great deal of self-discipline. Had I not for years made every effort to spare her from the knowledge of the slightest injury I might have incurred? Her grit helped now to keep the tears at bay. They would remain ossified that way for far too long.

"You can wear your lovely new coat and sailor hat—she stroked my hair as she brushed and spread her special lotions after the most thorough hair-wash. I almost wished she did not pamper me now as though aware of the terrible void I was soon to experience.

"Remember always to comb and brush your hair and to wash carefully—and to change your clothes often. Make sure you are always clean." She sighed and stopped as she looked into my eyes. Did she realise at that moment that that was one virtue she had neglected to impress upon me—how to take care of myself?

A cold, grey, bleak late December morn with not even snow to brighten it as the taxi deposited Mutti and me in the front of the station after the driver had handed Mutti the suitcase and asked if she needed a porter. Mutti shook her head. The cardboard suitcase was pitifully small and light. Was he being sarcastic? In my hand I clutched a gold box of chocolates of my choice Mutti had bought me. I hung on to it as though it were a precious jewel. Its luscious, chocolaty odours alone brought solace.

My recollection becomes dims the moment we stood before the dreaded train that was to take me away. The 'MUNCHNER BAHNHOF'! Only a short while ago we had boarded the train to the Polish border and returned here the same day. Now I was to board another train into the unknown but no Papi to hold my hand.

Did Mutti kiss and cuddle me? Did she cry and did I not? I'm almost certain she reminded me of the addressed envelopes in my suitcase, one of which I was to hand over to the person in charge for posting upon arrival to let Mutti know I was safe. And she reminded me too that somewhere in my suitcase was a stocking stuffed with emergency money that could be changed into English money. I do remember being seated next to a much older girl who spoke to me and took charge of the suitcase. I thought she was bossy and resented her immediately. Mutti was gone. No fuss, no outward demonstration of pain and heart-ache. No scenes at the station; none whatever. Did I even notice that the train had begun to move and was drawing away? I did not speak to anyone again until we reached The Hook Of Holland en route to Harwich. What I was not to know was that I had also left the old Mella behind for ever.

I know I rejected any and every attempt at approach or communication, let alone friendship and I know several people tried. I refused food and I had no idea why I could and would not speak. It was not a gesture of defiance. I simply could not accept these strangers around me. I thought they were patronising and I felt lost and alone. I wanted to go home. If Henny had at least been here with me I might have accepted her comforting words. But these were not my older sisters. I did not want them around me. I simply could not grasp what was happening to me. I imagined everyone was sorry for me and I wanted none of their pity.

Somehow my suitcase and I were off the train and on the boat in The Hook of Holland to Harwich. I remembered to ask the girl who had elected herself as my minder several times about my suitcase. And here on that Dutch boat, kindly waiters with untroubled, smiling faces serving us, I sat down with the other children at a long table and ate. I was handed the whitest, most fragrant fresh slices of bread and butter and creamy milk I could remember eating. This simple repast served with so much compassion left such a delicious taste, that the horror of the entire ordeal of that day receded, even if I still spoke only in monosyllables. Food had never been of great interest to me and I rarely partook in the squabbles of my siblings over a piece of chicken or some other delicacy. I generally had more than my fill of what I desired and like my father or maybe because of him, quantity was my least concern. But somehow these genuinely warm and gentle strangers speaking in a foreign tongue yet managing to reach me, urging me to eat, smiling bright, insouciant smiles, helped restore my confidence and allay my fear of what lay ahead.

I had not taken off my hat and coat throughout the entire journey even though the collar seemed get in the way of my chin and was beginning to chafe. I began to rub my chin against the collar every so often to ease the discomfort. I continued doing so for the remainder of the trip even when there was no need as though someone had wound me up.

It was dark when we reached Harwich and disembarked. I was taken charge of probably by the same girl who had taken care of me on the train.

"My case—" I remembered to ask. She assured me that it was being unloaded with all the other suitcases. They had all been meticulously labelled by our already distant parents. We boarded a coach. It was very comfortable and the seats were upholstered unlike the ones in Germany.

"Are we in England?" The girl next to me nodded. "yes, we're in England." She sounded very sad.

DOVER COURT

By the time we reached Dover Court Holiday Camp it was pitch dark and the wind blew with an icy ferocity that almost threw me over as I was helped off the coach. It lashed so unremittingly against my face, the only unprotected part of me, as we walked towards the little wooden huts allocated to every three or four KINDER, I felt I was being purposely punished. My teeth chattered—I had never felt so cold. My chin rubbed frantically against my coat. I seemed to have no control over its movements now. In the distance I could just distinguish a fine large building that seemed to belong to another universe whilst we continued along those wooden huts that stood on both sides. I could smell that sharp, fishy, saline odour coming closer with each further step we took. My heart beat. Where were we going?

We walked into this black, ghostly night, a whole bunch of bewildered boys and girls lashed by the icy, merciless wind. The sea only paces distant now roared its disapproval of this motley lot of strangers from a land that did not want them and yet had spat them out agonisingly slowly when they were begging to leave. I felt like Hansel and Gretel lost not in a wood but somewhere far more dangerous, where if I walked only steps further I would be swallowed up. I tried to keep up with the girl who was carrying my suitcase as well as her own. It did not occur to me to see this as a kind gesture. I had lost all sense of reality. But I trailed a few steps behind finding it hard by now to overcome my exhaustion. My fingers had become numb. We had almost reached the last few huts right by the beach when finally one of the girls called out the number of the hut we were just passing.

"That's it—we're here. Our Hut" and she unlocked the door with the key she was holding.

"C'mon" she took my arm and gently propelled me inside. "I've been told to look after you." She informed me matter-of-factly as the door closed behind us. There were four of us, the other three all in their early teens.

Two small bedrooms with a tiny space for sink and toilet led off the narrow corridor. The beds were single and bunk and the light did not work so that the door had to be kept ajar to gain some kind of light from the dim street-light outside the door. The floor was bare and freezing cold. The wind took no time to invade the unheated cabin with its devillish force. My teeth chattered. I had had few words during the entire day and now I had none.

"Your name is Mella, isn't it?" the biggest girl attempted to break my silence as she placed my suitcase on one of the beds.

"Why don't you get your pyjamas out of your suit-case? And have a bit of a wash. But don't undress as we will be going to the main building for supper."

I stared at her as if she stood way down a hill and I could not hear let alone understand her. I hated all the girls' scruffy, pain-filled faces. They smelled of sweat. I wanted none of it; they were intruding in my life. Where was my family, what were they doing at this very moment?

But I nodded and did as I was told. Even the cold water tap in the sink did not function as one of the girls rightly surmised the water was frozen. We would have to go and find a tap outside the huts.

I was still in my coat but I had found a scarf in my suitcase which I tied around my head and fastened under my chin. Carefully I placed my precious sailor hat that had hardly been off my head since the start of my journey in the suitcase, but not before I had located the stuffed sock Mutti had cautioned me about. The girls told me to hurry as they were leaving. I nodded promising to follow.

The freezing cold brought tears to my eyes. We had to walk yet closer to the shore until we found a tap that was not frozen. The water was like ice and I turned from it shivering. I could see the foaming waves and I walked a little further to stand on the pebble beach. I had never seen such a raging ocean. The Adriatic had been like a purring, docile, beautiful creature that accepted my body and carried it gladly. This monster in the black of night threatened to tear me to pieces.

I wanted my bed and refused to follow the others to the main building. One of the girls unlocked the door for me and said she would explain I was too tired. Then they were gone. I found no words with which to describe my feelings that night; I still have not found them. I must have fallen asleep at one stage, undressed only partially as I was too cold to change my clothes. My hair remained uncombed, my face and hands unwashed. I do not know when the other girls returned. I do not even know if I had fallen asleep in the bed allocated to me. But no-one disturbed me.

Shivering I awoke early next morning. Everyone else in the hut was fast asleep. I went to the toilet which did not work. I tried the tap again but it remained frozen. It did not occur to me to put on another dress to the one my mother had put out for me yesterday. I was in my underwear so I slipped the dress over it. The dress was precious—my mother had chosen it. I tied the scarf tightly around my head, having left my hair untouched and put on my coat, stockings and boots and left the hut. I was hungry but the sea, now wailing now screeching, noises I had never heard before, drew me with magnetic force.

Instead of walking towards the main building I walked the few paces to the ocean, stopping by the unfrozen tap we had sought last night, to splash my face and hands with the freezing water. In the bright morning light the foaming waves rolling back and forth held me in their spell. I hated this menacing beast but I also found it intoxicating. I stayed as long as I could bear the cold, hunger and utter confusion. All of this was God's world, the world I had been taught by Lehrer Berlinger he had created in seven days.—I hated it but I also loved it. I tried very hard to make sense of everything that had befallen me in the past days but I could not. I made my way slowly to the big hall. Wasn't God supposed to be with us all the time? I certainly did not feel his presence.

The matronly woman at the door of the enormous hall once I had mounted endless steps, instantly put me at my ease. She was motherly and she spoke a little German. When I gave my name she nodded in relief as if she had been waiting for me. Maybe I even managed a smile. She led me to a small cubicle of which there were a long row on one side and left me with a woman who immediately fell into German.

"Ah, Mella Lowy—we didn't see you last night." I lowered my head afraid she would scold me. "You are very early. Couldn't you sleep?" I shook my head.

"There is no water in the hut at all—not even cold!" I blurted out.

"O' dear, we'll put you down for a bath to-morrow. Meanwhile there is a nice bathroom here where you can wash. Would you like someone to help with your hair?" She eyed the scarf around my head. I was very reluctant but I nodded.

"And—and I have to tell you" I stopped and looked at the kind woman as if asking for help with what I had to say.

"Yes, Mella"

"I must NOT be adopted!" There it was out, the explicit warning my father had given me repeatedly. In fact as I spoke and recalled the horror of what adoption might mean, the tears welled in my eyes.

"No, of course not." She allayed my fears but she had not sounded as emphatic as I would have liked.

I washed in one of the crowded bathrooms and someone came to straighten out my tangled hair—it hurt. Then I was directed to join what to me seemed like an enormous number of mostly older children seated at huge trestle tables. I could not eat what I was told was called 'porridge' but I drank fresh milk and gratefully ate several slices of fresh bread and butter and jam.

After breakfast I was called into another cubicle to answer a great many questions, my answers meticulously recorded on a type-writer.

"O' dear," I said at one stage, "I should have brought one of the addressed envelopes my mother gave me so that you could post it for me. I have money for stamps. But I left it in the hut." I must have looked as troubled as I was.

"That's alright. We have your parents' address. Why don't you sit down and write a letter and give it to me. I will see it gets posted. You can pay me to-morrow."

"But my father isn't in Munich any more. I don't know." The woman smiled warmly.

"You mustn't worry," she said softly, "your mother will be able to tell him of your whereabouts and when he can he will write to you, I'm sure." She sighed as though she had been saying this over and over again. "You really mustn't worry—your father is a writer," she consulted a file she had open.

"O' yes, he is a famous Yiddish poet" I informed her proudly. She nodded.

"You must be proud of him." She said with the warmest smile yet.

Until the Committee lady had told me not to worry about Papi it had not occurred to me to worry about anyone I had left behind. I did not understand their danger. All I could see before me was my own present predicament.

I was handed pencil and paper and I stayed all day in the big hall; it was warm there. I wrote a long letter and handed it in. People were friendly though I answered only when spoken to. I found a few children's books and even a couple of dolls in a box and was told to help myself. I preferred the ladies who spoke only a few broken German words to the officious German speaking young women who had come with the Transport. The English ladies were gentler and more sympathetic. They seemed to understand better how I felt. But then they were not undergoing what my German fellow-travellers were going through.

Lunch consisted of fish with an unaccustomed strong taste and smell accompanied by very watery mashed potatoes. There was also some kind of rice-pudding but none of these dishes tasted remotely like anything I had ever eaten—even the mashed potatoes. I enjoyed the cake for tea and had some soup for supper. I was no longer cold. And we were promised some entertainment after supper. I stayed until my eyes began to droop and someone suggested I might like to get to bed. Reluctantly I made my way back to the hut which I found without difficulty. I had not seen my hut-mates all day or maybe I had simply not recognised them. The hut smelled of stale sweat and it was freezing cold. But the cold water tap in the sink was working. To-morrow I would have a bath.

I awoke very early but more rested and less shivery. It was agony to use the freezing water even for face and hands. But I had been promised a hot bath and I looked forward to that. There was sadly very little empathy between two of the girls and myself. They were probably just as bewildered as I even if they had three or four years on me. The third girl, the eldest, tried her best to engage me in conversation and give me assistance if I needed it. But although I don't think I was ever rude my constant refusal of any help must have seemed to them extremely exasperating.

I was shocked when that long-awaited bath for which I had to wait until after lunch, meant I had to endure the presence of a strange girl to supervise the entire proceeding. I resented her presence bitterly although the poor girl would most likely have been delighted to be anywhere but supervising this proud, spoilt nine-year old.

"I'm nearly ten you know" I continued to point out to her as reluctantly I had to strip in her presence. But when it came to washing my hair I stood my ground valiantly and it was surprisingly easy to dissuade her. Thus my hair would have to stay unwashed a little while longer. Mutti had washed it so thoroughly only a couple of days ago. But another girl came to the rescue and volunteered with great enthusiasm to have a go at my thick head of curls. I think she found the task more arduous than she had anticipated. But was I half expecting Mutti to come soon to wash my hair?

It was Christmas. Some of the local families in Dover had issued invitations to the refugee children to visit their homes. I was chosen by the resident committee with two other children to take tea with two ladies in the town. I had changed into my best and only other winter dress in the suit-case and attempted to comb through the maze that my head of hair had fast become. I had always loved my red velvet dress with the white collar but somehow it felt inadequate now. I was nervous as we had been told that we must make sure to be at our best behaviour at all times, because English people were very polite and had such good manners. It was essential that we refugees made a good impression.

This was the first time I had been inside an English home. Would it be very different to my own in Munich? I was immediately struck by its tired, ancient appearance right down to every stick of furniture. Nothing seemed new or recent. The rooms were small and the wall-paper full of flowers, but the house had two storeys which impressed me especially as it seemed that only our two hostesses, both of whom were elderly, were resident. The garden at the back of the house was beautiful and well-tended even in the height of winter. The front too was full of crocuses and a lovely tall wisteria tree that must have been a hundred years old. I loved all the greenery around the houses in the street. Tall, majestic trees wagged their huge branches in the strong wind and every house had its own private garden. The houses were so large and spacious too, no flats were in sight.

I tried valiantly to eat the piece of Christmas cake and mince pie on my plate. I tried also to drink the cup of tea, my first. I found it a great struggle. Unfortunately I did not understand a word of that was said to me but I hoped I made up for it with smiles and "thank you" and "please" I had picked up from the other two girls. The two ladies seemed as uncomfortable with us as we were with them. We simply could not converse and I realised that it must have been quite an ordeal for them to entertain these uprooted foreign children. The car came to pick us up again not much more than an hour later. I was disappointed; I would have liked to stay just a little longer in that strange old English house and get to know those old ladies better. There was a cosiness here that I longed to savour longer.

By the third day I found I had a new friend. His name was Martin and he seemed to take me under his wing. But unlike any of the bossy girls he had a truly charming way and he made great efforts to draw me out of myself. He actually seemed to enjoy talking to me and there was nothing patronising about his manner. He was sixteen years old and he reminded me very much of my brother Abi.

Now I felt a little less alone at Dover Court. The ocean's never-ending wrath continued to intrigue and frighten me at the same time. I would stand on the beach staring into the white froth of the waves. They said Hitler frothed at the mouth when he was angry it had occurred to me.

It was announced that there would be a farewell concert and anyone willing to contribute should get in touch with the team in charge. They needed more volunteers. They particularly wanted contributions from the youngest Kinder.

I volunteered encouraged by my big friend Martin. I would sing and recite a poem I had frequently performed in Munich for my family and they had always laughed until they cried. And I knew that to be praise indeed. The trouble was I did not know its official title. I called it by its first line: ES SAGT EIN BERLINER (A Berlin man tells this tale.—).

The concert was scheduled for the night before we left. The camp was closing and some children were going to foster homes in London. A few were being adopted, that dreaded word. Some of the older ones had found temporary employment and the others which included me, were being moved to SELSEY Holiday Camp in Essex.

I had actually had one terrifying experience a few days earlier when after breakfast I had been called into one of the cubicles and been introduced to a young English couple who seemed to study me with unusual interest. I understood nothing of what was being said until I heard the word 'adoption' that was too similar to the German for comfort.

I burst out in a most ill-mannered fashion in German, of course:

"No, not adoption—never—my Papi said—! I told the other lady—"and I began to cry in spite of myself. I think it was the first time I had cried in public. The woman from the Committee placed her arm around my shoulders and led me out of the cubicle.

"You will be leaving for Selsey with the others." She said. "Don't worry."

My battered little cardboard case was packed ready to go to our next unknown haven. In truth I had never really unpacked properly as many items like underwear and a couple of dresses were for warmer weather. There really was pitifully little in that suitcase that would normally suffice for more than a month or two. The Jewish Committee in Munich had been specific in typical Germanic fashion in the number of items allowed. Of course it was merely bowing to the command of the higher German powers. To have transgressed a rule that was 'VERBOTEN' was more than even my stalwart mother would have thought of doing. They had all been properly brought up in the German 'KINDERSTUBE'. Only now it was under Nazi supervision.

I had been assured there was no need for further rehearsal on my part. I had sung the lengthy ode to the organiser and they had loved it. I would be the last act with which the evening would close. They showed me where to enter and where to exit. I felt quite at home on the stage as I had often had parts in Abi's plays at home and though this was a real stage, I was certain I could cope. In fact I relished the thought. I had always loved acting and performing in front of the class.

I was a little disappointed when I was told that I did not need a special costume like the older participants and that there was no need for make-up. I thought that make-up was an absolute must as Abi and Trudel had always had great fun painting my eyes and lips. I felt insulted as though I were inferior. It did not occur to me to put it down to my age and the fact that I was only singing and reciting, not acting a part in a play. To me it was one and the same thing and I wanted to belong to the troupe. But I had not even been called for rehearsals.

By the time my turn came it was very late and many people had already left for bed, as everyone would be travelling somewhere early next morning. My eyes burnt with fatigue but I went on, hair scarcely combed; my old dirndl dress hardly eye-catching in Shirley Temple style. And it was undoubtedly Shirley I always set out to be like, if not to imitate, as everyone had compared me to her since I was very little.

I had actually set myself a hard task. The ode told of one Berlin suitor and one from Munich asking for the hand of their respective sweethearts in their own dialects. I was particularly proud of my Bavarian accent and gave it my all. I must have looked and sounded a real little nine-year old ham.

'ES SAGT EIN BERLINER ZU DER SCHONEN MINA "HOLDES MADCHEN ACH ICH LIEBE DIR,

DENN DU BIST JA KLENE, SO WIE DU ES KENE—HABE MITLEID
UND ERBARME DIR." (A Berliner says to his lovely Mina: "precious girl I
love you, 'cos little one, there's none like you—have mercy on me!" And it
continued when in contrast the shoemaker MICHEL from Munich in his
broad Bavarian accent pleads with his love.

It concludes with what must have sounded tragic-comic to the older
audience:

'JA DAS IST ANDERS ALS IN BERLIN

DES IST HALT MUNCHNERICH DA LIEGT WAS DRIN.' (Yes, that sure
is different to Berlin—that's the Munich way with its special charm.) And
it was this last verse I infused with my most heart-felt emotion. It almost
brought tears to my eyes as I spoke of Munich—MY Munich.

The applause was pretty satisfactory but as the audience had thinned out I
felt a little disappointed. I was unsure whether to leave the stage or await an
encore call. One of the actors whispered from behind the curtain to take one
more bow and exit.

My friend Martin came to congratulate me as did several other people. I don't
know what time I returned to my hut deflated. I had looked forward to my
thespian turn. Maybe I just needed for the shortest time to be the centre of
attention again.

Very early next morning I arrived in the main hall with my suitcase. I had
not bonded with the girls in the hut and there were no fond farewells. After
breakfast and having said my good-byes to a few children who were going
elsewhere, I boarded the coach, my suitcase having been safely stacked in
the huge boot together with the other boys' and girls' luggage en route to
Selsey.

I felt sad having realised only now that my friend Martin had not been in the
hall for breakfast and that I would have to leave without a proper farewell. We
had found a moment yesterday for his inscription in my precious autograph
book when I had brought it into the hall for that specific purpose. But we had
not said good bye.

The coach had filled up and my heart sank. I would be leaving without seeing Martin again. And then I saw someone running towards the coach holding a small case. It was Martin. He entered the coach and I ran towards him. We hugged, I with tears in my eyes. And then he handed me the little red cardboard case, about half the size of my one in the boot and even flimsier.

"O' what is it?" I wanted to know excitedly. He smiled, "wait till the bus pulls out. Then you can have a look. I hope you like it." I nodded as I looked one last time at my 'big' friend Martin as he had called himself. He had shown me genuine affection when it was most needed. Quoting Goethe he had written in my book:

"EDEL SEI DER MENSCH

HILFREICH UND GUT (May man be noble, helpful and good)

Holiday Camp 15.01.1939

In Memory of Your Big Friend Martin Nelhans" It was written in German of course.

As soon as I realised that no matter how far I craned my neck Martin was out of sight, I opened the little case that was firmly planted on my lap. And I could hardly believe what confronted me. The case was stuffed with five beautiful dolls! I hugged the case all of that journey to Selsey even before I began to examine the dolls. It had been given me by my new friend and it gave me hope that there might be other new friendships ahead and that I was not destined always to be alone.

Chapter Nine

SELSEY HOLIDAY CAMP & THE SAUNDERS FAMILY

SELSEY was an entirely different Holiday Camp to the one I had just left. To begin with the huts were welcoming, far more modern, warm and spacious. I shared with two other girls and they were older and very kind and friendly. It was an encouraging start and I felt less constrained by home-sickness. This time I accepted the girls' interest and assistance when needed, probably because they were less patronising and even more probably, everyone had got over the first few days of utter misery and confusion and was more adapt at communication.

The Camp was close to the shore but one side was grass-verged so that the houses in the village were clearly visible. And these houses looked homely and friendly. The beach was less alien, the pebbles when I attempted to walk bare-foot on them, less sharp and bitingly cold and the sea far less ferocious. I took a walk that first day with one of the girls after we had unpacked. The sun was shining on the water; there were premature daffodils in the grass-verges and for the first time I began to appreciate the beauty of the English sea-side. I gathered a few sea-shells and decided I would send a couple to Papi when I had his address. Maybe that was when I felt my fist real ties with this new country.

The main building too was more welcoming and bright. The people in charge took me under their wing from the start and by this time I was able to accept help. Perhaps the staff were better trained and I no longer had to control the constant desire to weep somewhere in private. Most wonderful of all there was a letter waiting for me from Mutti. I could not believe that she would have my new address so soon. It was a wonderful start.

A week later came the letter I carried about with me wherever I went. It was from Papi. They had arrived in Belgium and it would not be long now before they could come to England. In my first letter to my darling father I sent three sea-shells and told him that it was beautiful here in England.

I hoped we would always liver here together.

Here in Selsey, in this convivial atmosphere with someone always ready to listen, assist and guide I spent my tenth birthday. I was given a special piece of birthday cake and the children led by adults, made an attempt to sing Happy Birthday. Most like me had never sung the song before and had no idea what it meant. Very few had any knowledge of English. But with genuine smiles, the assistance of a little German translation, I participated gratefully with the thought always at the back of my mind that soon I would be with my family again. Munich could be discarded, my family never could.

The weather was mild and most of February the sun seemed to glisten on the tranquil ocean. We went for regular walks on the shore and I continued to gather small sea shells which when held to the ear like a trumpet, rustled mysteriously. Then the miraculous news arrived that my father and Abi were on their way to England and Henny would follow. As soon as Trudel's leg was healed, Mutti and she would be able to come as it seemed the visas were all now ready. Oma Lowy was already on her way.

I had no idea where any of my family would be staying once they were safely out of Germany and I am not sure if even they knew. The only thing that was apparently of vital importance was that everyone should be out of Germany as soon as possible. So the Germans really were evil.

The weeks spent in Selsey, warmed by sun and children young and older, who had begun to thaw out from the numbing freeze of separation, were made so much more bearable by the anticipation of reunion for everyone there. Martin had made no effort to contact me and I had not expected him to. He had made the worst days in my life bearable with his brotherly friendship and protection. And he had given me something to take with me I would treasure for many a year. Only sixteen years old himself, he had acted with the wisdom and charity of a man twice his age. The strange thing was that I was no longer all that interested in dolls, only the largesse of his loving gesture.

One morning I was called into the office in the main hall.

"We have found you a nice family to stay with, Mella." The lady smiled brightly. My instant reaction was a defensive "But . . ."

"Yes, yes. Don't you worry we know your father will be in England soon. But I doubt if he will be able to find a place where you can stay together for a while yet. You must be patient. As it is you are a very lucky girl."

I smiled as the remark brought to mind Mutti's 'MASELDIG MEIDELE.'

"The family Saunders are a Jewish family with two daughters, one only a year older than you. They are happy to have you stay with them in Ilfor for as long as you need to."

"Ilford—but my father will come to London." "Yes, yes—"again the patient woman smiled kindly. "Ilford is a suburb of London. It is just on the outskirts—"she could see I looked confused. "London is a huge city as you must know and there are many suburbs. It will not be difficult for your father to come and see you by bus or Underground." Her German was adequate and very quaint with her English pronunciation.

I had learnt to eat certain foods like toast and kippers that I had never before eaten. And I had still been unable to accustom myself to the goodness and benefits of porridge. No-one forced me to eat or do anything I found unacceptable. Everyone here was kind, patient and sympathetic at all times. So my time in Selsey passed almost too rapidly. Events overtook each other like a waterfall and there I stood one morning, dressed in my inadequate German winter clothes ready to move on. There was no-one in particular I parted from with a heavy heart as I had from Martin, but on the other hand, everyone came to kiss me goodbye and wish me luck after we had all breakfasted together and I had taken a last stroll by the shore which I had grown to love.

THE SAUNDERS

A small house with two cosy rooms and a kitchen downstairs and three bedrooms upstairs two of which were double and one smaller single, made up my new home at the Saunders family. The street with every house exactly the same was tidy but treeless. But there was a park nearby with swings and slides and to me such parks looked very exciting. The journey to Ilford like my journey to England had passed swiftly and in a mental fog. A coach—ride, something I enjoyed as these coaches with upholstered seats were comfortable and inviting, unlike those in Germany. Then an introduction to two kindly strangers waiting for me and with whom naturally I could not converse, followed by my first ride on the Underground. Those unaccustomed small trains underground were a little frightening; such milling crowds and not a familiar face amongst them.

Then we entered the cosy house and I understood that the two adults were Mr and Mrs Saunders. Conversation was practically impossible those first hours. But as Mr Saunders seemed to know of my father and his work, he managed to communicate a little with me in Yiddish which to my surprise, I understood better now with strenuous effort, than I had realised. At home we had never conversed in Yiddish.

I shared the double bedroom with the younger Saunders daughter and Rita her teenage sister, had a room to herself. Rita was blonde, attractive and very friendly and caring towards me. Her little sister, however, took an instant dislike to me, all the more as everyone fussed over my curly, thick long hair and Rita and Mrs Saunders took enormous trouble to wash and comb it without causing me too much discomfort and even professed to enjoy it.

Fridays was fish and chips night. The chips were home-made and the first ever such fare I had savoured. The entire house seemed marinated in the fishy frying odour which made my mouth water as soon as I caught the first whiff. This was one English dish to which I took with gusto from the very first bite. And to everyone's surprise, the little evacuee who up until then was known for her small appetite could tuck in with remarkable aplomb. And the meal did not end there. For 'afters' there was trifle, another dish I could have eaten every day of the week. A delightful combination of Mutti's pudding filled with sponge cake and bananas. I was always given a very generous helping and the Saunders were obviously delighted to see such a skinny little thing tuck in so heartily, as they would have put it, especially as my appetite was far less robust the rest of the week. I think that was one of the only times I detected genuine pleasure in Mrs. Saunders's plain, tired features as she was so unlike my loquacious mother whose eyes were invariably alight. Mrs Saunders was a quiet woman who seemed to have less to say than any of the other members of her family. She simply dealt with all her endless tasks efficiently and unobtrusively. Although I had never before lived with a strange family, I recognised and admired Mrs. Saunders' unsung accomplishments.

But much as I took to the older sister Rita and it would seem she to me, her younger sister close to my own age (I was never certain of her exact age) made no bones of her resentment of this foreign interloper. I believe it began from day one when the rest of the family made a huge fuss of me surely for no better reason than to make me feel welcome. I wished however, that they had curbed their enthusiasm a little. I craved love and sucked it up like a sponge especially from my peers but her resentment was palpable. She made no attempt to hide it and soon I would reciprocate her antipathy to the extent that I am not even certain whether her name was actually Sandra as I tried to shut her out of my consciousness. (I know I had difficulty pronouncing her name.) Of course it was perfectly natural for her to resent the warmth and interest her family afforded me, thus depriving her of what must hitherto have been hers alone. Sandra was not to know nor was anyone else, that I cried myself to sleep practically nightly and sometimes, when home-sickness struck like a sudden thunder bolt during the day, I would lock myself in the toilet to avoid being seen crying as that would have been churlish, I fully understood. These people went out of their way to make me feel loved. It was not their fault that my own family alone could fill that void.

But if nothing else, nature had been kind in endowing me with a surprising amount of resilience and an ability to adapt like small, lost animals. And so day by day I fitted into the Saunders mould a little less awkwardly. There was always the shimmering expectancy of my reunion with my father and eventually mother and siblings. I was learning as I had never before needed to, to put up with the present so that the future might look all the rosier. My attitude was one of hope and expectancy each day anew. Something good was bound to happen soon. It was the optimism I had inherited from my mother though I was hardly aware of it then.

The first week was almost over when Mr. Saunders sprang the surprise that I would be going to school with Sandra on Monday. Somehow Mr Saunders managed to convert some Yiddish words into a pigeon German I comprehended but not without difficulty. But he seemed pleased with himself and me for making this effort. Mr Saunders was a kind and amiable man with a fatherly face. I for my part was very grateful for his patience and the interest and obvious respect in which he held my father.

And so it was that Mrs Saunders, Sandra and I visited a shoe-shop on Saturday morning. The Saunders's were not observant Jews but they wanted me to know, from what I could make out, that they observed High Holidays. For me it was the first time I had entered a shop on the Sabbath. I was too excited to worry too much about the transgression as I was to have my first pair of English summer sandals. At any rate I had already learned from Papi's rejection of the kosher laws only a short while back, that the sky would not fall in and that maybe God was altogether too busy at this troubled time.

We walked out of the small shoe-shop having found a perfect fit, with the wonderful leathery aroma firmly and delightfully settled in my nostrils. I proudly clutched the box containing my lovely English pair of brown sandals. When upon reaching the house I immediately took them out and with Mrs Saunders' approval put them on, I was happier than I had been since my arrival. I longed to throw out those heavy, ugly little German boots I had not seen a single English child wear. The gesture of the new shoes endeared these people to me as I saw it as proof that they really cared about me. All the more so as they themselves were far from affluent.

That same evening another yet more exciting surprise awaited me. Not only was I to wear my new sandals as the evening was fine, but my best dress and coat. We were all going to the cinema! The family had taken such trouble to make things more understandable and the easiest way to tell me about the treat in store was to show me a magazine with the picture of stars I recognised such as the all-pervading Shirley Temple with great enthusiasm.

I sat next to Mr Saunders and Sandra sat between her parents, Rita beside her mother. In the interval Mr Saunders went out to buy a box of chocolates and handed round the delicious olfactory box for everyone to help themselves. When there was only one chocolate left Mr Saunders handed it to me. I liked him very much indeed and blushed with delight at the compliment.

Early Monday morning Mrs Saunders, her face as ever serious and strained and Rita having spent hours the previous night washing and patiently brushing my stubborn tresses after a hot bath, I was judged fit for school. Was I really to go to school with Sandra when the only words in English I understood and attempted to pronounce were please and thank you? Above all I would have liked to tell my kind hosts about MY school, MY beloved school that I had left behind smouldering with brown-shirted automatons standing there motionless as wax-works. That grisly scene was never to leave me.

A friendly welcome from what I understood to be the headmistress of the junior school after assembly and before I knew what was happening, I found myself seated at a small desk in a mixed class—room full of strange children. Sandra was nowhere in sight. There was a buzz around me more like the hum of a swarm of bees. It buzzed about my ears until I felt like crying out. I could not understand a word anyone tried to address to me and I desperately wanted to escape. Mercifully break-time arrived and someone motioned to me to follow them to the play-ground. Children formed little clusters and soon I stood alone against the wall. Two or three older children came up to me and led me back to the class-room obviously only too aware of my discomfort. I found my desk and was handed a small bottle of milk with a straw. I drank with less thirst than the need of comfort. The milk was rich and creamy.

I was handed a few comics by someone. I turned the pages with some semblance of interest, but as I had never before seen a comic and far less could I comprehend a single word therein, pretence was the best I could offer. The coloured drawings of strange people and animals failed to amuse me. My idea of fun would take far longer to adapt. Then someone called: "change—"I turned round but the comic remained on my desk. Then again "change—change—" obviously addressed to me as the boy came up to my desk and gently replaced my comic with a new one.

"Oh" I said smiling, "change—yes, thank you." It was a word I would never forget, my first English lesson.

I was lost in that vast receptacle of chattering, chuckling children who all knew each other and could converse with each other. O' how I envied them! It was not so much that I wanted to withdraw within myself but that I felt I had no alternative. I did battle on, picking up a few new words each day but without any of the pleasure. I had been uniquely fortunate to enjoy almost every minute in my dear old Jewish school in Munich with Lehrer Berlinger leading his class wherever he chose like the first-rate conductor of an orchestra.

The high-light of the week continued to be the family outing to the cinema as much for the ambience of the beautiful, grand palatial theatre as the pleasant company of Mr Saunders who was too busy week-days to spend much time with me. I never quite understood what his trade was though he tried hard to explain it to me. He went off early in the morning and often returned after our bed-time. I believe he had a small shop in the East End of London. I felt happy when he was home because he made such an effort to converse with me and make me feel part of the family. It must have become obvious to him how much I missed my father.

The cinema with its grandiose organ and fine gilded mirrors and thick crimson carpets was a never-ending wonder. So this was England. It was all very grand when I thought of the dingy, dark little den no more glamorous than a cow-shed, into which Tudel had sneaked us several times and Mutti had taken me to see THE GOOD EARTH just round the corner from our street on the opposite side of the ANLAGE. Even the KARTNER THEATER where I had seen Cinderella was nowhere near as impressive as this cinema in Ilford. And when the organ began to play its tunes of the day which I picked up sooner even than new words in this foreign language and I sat munching Mr Saunders' chocolates, a warm sensation of gratitude filled me.

We had just returned from school. Somehow Sandra and I managed to return home together most days without actually walking home together. Either I walked behind her or she would walk behind me. Rarely did we actually walk side by side as though we had made a secret pact.

I had hung up my coat and entered the living room when the phone rang.

Mrs Saunders came running up to me.

"It's for you" she said with what for her was exceptional emotion.

"Me?" I took the receiver I was handed and from the other end came the voice of my father.

Papi told me during that all too brief conversation that he had just arrived and would be coming to visit that Saturday as Mrs Saunders had invited him for tea. No, I would not yet be going with him as there were far too many matters to attend to, primarily to find lodgings for Mutti and the rest of the family. He would try to explain when he came. He made a point of reiterating how grateful we must be to the Saunders' for taking such good care of me. Somehow he had managed to converse with Mrs Saunders unless Abi had helped out. I did not know whether to cry in disappointment at not being told I would be going with him immediately or simply celebrating the fact that I had actually heard his voice again. I disappeared into the toilet for a short while and cried anyway.

I saw him walk down the street with Mr Saunders who had collected him from the Underground Station. My heart leapt with pride and joy. He was tall, slim as a reed and so handsome and immaculate. Dear Mr Saunders beside him looked squat and insignificant much as I liked him. But I doubt if even Clark Gable or Don Ameche would have stood a chance against my Papi in my eyes that day.

It was an emotional reunion more from my side than his. My father did his best to impress on me and the Saunders' what their warm hospitality and care of me meant to him. He too had few words in English but he could converse with Mr Saunders at some length in Yiddish. I sensed too a certain discomfort in my father at having to accept such largesse from strangers. It was the first time in his life and he was obviously making a huge effort. Where I had expected sympathy for my long deprivation of his love, he must have made a superhuman effort to impress upon me that in these times—unprecedented times—care and charity from strangers was a God-send.

It was a strange afternoon tinged with overpowering emotions of joy and misery. I clung to Papi at parting which must have embarrassed him as well as the kind Saunders.

"It won't be long, darling" Papi had whispered in my ear "but until them you must show gratitude to these wonderful people, they deserve it. Look at your lovely shoes—they are so kind!" as he hugged and kissed me before walking down the road with Mr Saunders in his dignified way. But I could have sworn I spotted tears in his tired eyes.

It was the beginning of March and the daffodils in the Saunders' garden were in full bloom as they had already been earlier in Selsey. Papi had telephoned to say that I would soon be staying with a family called the LICHTIGS who had a large house in London near Stamford Hill. They would be happy to have me stay with them and when Henny arrived any day now, she too would be staying with them. He himself had found a small flat where Mutti and he would be staying. Trudel too would for the time being stay with the Lichtigs. Abi and he were together and he did not mention Uncle Oiser who had come with them on that long trek to England.

"When Papi—when?" I shouted excitedly forgetting my good manners.

"Next Sunday as soon as it is convenient for Mrs Saunders-"

Of course it did not for a moment occur to me to consider the feelings of the people who had put themselves out for a little spoilt refugee child who could not speak a word of English and obviously moped a good deal more than they might have been prepared for. But as ever they were generous when the day of parting came and Papi arrived. I think his obvious gratitude made up for my own lack although I kissed everyone and even managed a brief kiss on Sandra's cheek. Then, after weeks of yearning for that moment, I walked down that tree-less Ilford street for the last time, carrying a large bag while my father carried the suit-case. We were off to London and I would be seeing Papi and soon Mutti too every day.

Chapter Ten

MY SECOND CHILDHOOD

THE LICHTIGS & EVACUATION
TO BEDFORDSHIRE

A beautiful three-storey house in Cazenove Road in Stamford Hill within walking distance of Clissold Park was to be my next home here in England. I had hoped I would be together with my parents and siblings but it was explained to me that the Lichtigs were already giving refuge to several young people and I was very lucky to be offered a place there with Henny who would be helping out generally. Abi and Papi were staying elsewhere for the time being until Papi found a place for Mutti, Trudel, Abi and himself. The hope was that Mutti would be arriving very soon with Trudel, who was now well enough to travel. All that was required was the doctors' certificate stating that she was fit for the journey.

Uncle Oiser, who had crossed the Alps by foot with Papi and Abi and arrived here in England but without apparently, the necessary legal documents, had been interned in the Isle of Man. This did not appear to be the great calamity it sounded to refugees from the Nazis, as Uncle Oiser had already assured my father. Gt. Britain was a haven to these refugees even in restricted freedom which, as it turned out according to dear Uncle Oiser, was far from unpleasant in the company of many highly respected celebrities of every profession. And as Uncle Oiser was an adaptable, amiable chap, he seemed actually to enjoy this unexpected restricted freedom:

"A roof over my head, adequate food and excellent company—it could be worse" as he had assured Papi on the phone.

Oma Lowy too was in England and for the time being, had found a home in Wales with the people for whom my cousin Hilde was working in their dental surgery. Her father, my uncle Stiel however, had remained in Munich whilst her two brothers Louis and Jani, the latter Abi's age and Louis a couple of years older, had left for Nice in the South of France. If I needed any explanation at all of the severity and danger of the situation for Jews remaining in Germany I had only to recall the metallic robots guarding the flames that were licking up my school. But my longing for Munich itself would not be extinguished any more than were those ravaging flames; even if I had begun to comprehend that the world I had just left was fraught with terrifying danger for every Jew. It was that danger that I found difficult to translate into reality. Surely they would not transport everyone to Stadelheim or on a futile train journey to no-man's land—and back?

The Lichtig's house, the entire household was not like anything I had ever come close to experiencing. I had now resided in two holiday camps and a modest, comfortable working class home. This gaping, imposing detached three-storey Victorian residence with beautifully manicured gardens was undeniably grand, but it was not ostentatious. It stood with one other residence in a close shaded by tall, leafy trees, lawns and garages to the side. So much juicy green everywhere!

Once inside the residence, everything was on a large, generous scale and tastefully furnished. The main front salon struck me as of gigantic proportions with a stunning antique, probably Adam fire-place, from which blazed a log—fire distributing warmth that seemed to hug the entire room and its visitors with wide open arms. I had grown fond of the modest open fire in the Saunders' living room, if only because it provided the sole heating. But the magnetism and comfort of such magnanimous warmth was irresistible and hugely comforting.

The rambling vestibule led from one side into the music room with its gleaming grand piano. Music seemed constantly to flow softly into the rest of the house from there, with someone, resident or visitor, tinkling pleasantly on the piano or playing a record or simply the wireless. It was my first introduction to the delightful velvet voice of Bud Flanagan as he warbled the Umbrella Song. I needed little English to comprehend 'Doodle lama lama' and even less to fall in love with his gentle, enveloping tones. I loved every kind of music and my taste thanks to my father's enormously rich and varied repertoire resonating in our home from the day my ears were open to it, was broad and catholic.

The splendid gardens drenched in vivid colour, could be admired from the French doors of the less grand t dining room of two. I never did quite get to explore the entire lay-out of this house. I had no urge to venture into rooms to which I had not first been taken by Mrs Lichtig or Bube (grandma) not merely because I had been brought up not to snoop but equally because I was not a particularly curious child.

From the opposite side, a long, rather dark and mysterious stair-case led down to a huge kitchen whose tempting fragrances of baking flooded the entire area and brought a pang of nostalgia each time I caught a whiff. Further down to a basement wash—room where there was much splashing and chattering and the odour of starch and warm soap-suds was homely and comforting, smothering the exotic baking wafts that still persisted in the background.

The wide staircase with its gleaming mahogany balustrades starting from the hall-way and leading all the way up to the third floor was generously carpeted with deep, soft crimson woollen carpet the likes of which I had previously seen only in Munich's fanciest department store like OBERPOLLINGER, the Jewish store never to reopen after 'KRYSTALLNACHT'.

The vast salon-dining room could hold at least a hundred people and was quite overpowering in its grandeur. Upon our arrival, it was Mrs Lichtig who received us graciously from the heavy, gleaming mahogany front portal. Naturally there was an ornate 'MESUSAH' embellishing the wall beside the door as there had been by our front door in Munich, if less conspicuously. She beamed at my father and immediately kissed me. I was quite overpowered by this tiny, slender lady, so obviously full of good will and charity. And I thought her as glamorous as any film-star in her long, flowing emerald velvet gown in the middle of the day. Her little pale face almost disappeared in the gleaming matching turban she was wearing. But her blue eyes twinkled with warmth and compassion. I loved her immediately and I could sense the esteem in which she held my father and that this extended to his offspring. We had formed an instant bond as I responded to her warmth.

Mr Lichtig joined us after prayers. He was a beaming, amiable man with a thick black beard, well-built and debonair in his gilt satin caftan.

"Ah—"he grinned "so this is our little Mella!" I blushed. Before I had time to reply another member of the Lichtig family emerged with the wise, all-embracing smile I had last seen on my Oma Tennenbaum and Lowy's faces.

"This is Bube" explained Mrs Lichtig "my dear mother and real boss of the house." Mr Lichtig added with a chuckle. Bube was even tinier than the mistress of the house but at least twice her gait and she hardly needed to stoop to kiss me welcome.

I looked around for Abi and Henny but Abi would join us later and Henny was due to arrive any day now from Belgium. I was, however, introduced to and kissed by so many people, that my head spun. There was Rose about Henny's age and Luser with whom I fell instantly in love although he was certainly no younger than my brother and a good few years older than my last friend Martin. Both Luser and Rose were German refugees. I did not quite grasp who stayed in the house permanently and who was there only for meals. Because as we sat down to supper the dining room became fuller and fuller; the vast table seemed to have shrunk. The dining room was of generous proportions as everything in the house but now table and room were filled to bursting as in a popular restaurant. Everyone there was amiable and seemed delighted to be in this uplifting ambience. The room buzzed with uninhibited chatter all about us.

I sat next to Papi. I'm not sure if I ate anything and if so what that first meal consisted of. There was so much to take in and food was the last thing on my mind. My thoughts were taken up with the beautiful house where I would be staying though Papi would not. But at least I would see him daily. For the first time I actually looked forward to being in the company of these lovely warm people who were my hosts. And there was the gentle, handsome Luser to whom I had taken instantly. Seated on the other side of me, he had taken my hand in his, pressed it and promised we would be great friends. The word friend meant so much to me as I had lost all my old ones. I certainly hoped he meant it though I was not entirely oblivious to the fact that Rose, seated next to him, leaned very close to him and held him in conversation. I was particularly fascinated by his slender, long white hands with a web of blue veins that were startlingly visible.

Supper over, with me picking at rather than showing any interest in the food, Papi said he had to leave to go to a meeting with his Yiddish writer colleagues to whom I would soon be introduced. I believe he was staying with one of them temporarily, a Mr Ben A Sochachevsky who was an old childhood writer friend from Krakow. There was a Mr Avram Stenzel and a Mr Lisky too, equally old childhood friends and Mr Stenzel had been to visit us in Munich before I was born. I would soon be introduced to all of them as they were keen to meet me, Papi assured me.

But my Papi seemed very troubled. If I was sad that I did not have my father all to myself more, I resolved not to show it. There was so much to preoccupy me and so many kind people who were taking me under their wings, predominantly BUBE who would be helping Mrs Lichtig to acquaint me with the rest of the house. And there was Mr Lichtig's younger brother Maurice in whom I sensed qualities not unlike those of Papi and who promised to take me on walks to the Park when he had more time. He was always whistling and singing some catchy tunes that greatly appealed to me and which in a short time I would sing with him. Unlike his older brother, he was always dressed informally and certainly revealed little interest in religious matters.

I found the bathroom the ultimate luxury with its gilded taps and a very fine white porcelain tub that was neither marked nor scratched. It appeared to be the only bathroom in the house and was next to the master bedroom on the first floor. Its floor was fully, snugly carpeted unlike our chilly linoleum-covered one in Munich. What luxury! Then there was the exquisite bedroom with balcony which Mrs Lichtig showed me with pride, all golden spreads and velvet matching drapes, more resplendent in size and furnishing than I had ever seen before; more as I imagined a princess' bedroom. And the delightful hostess so very petite and frail, obviously loved children as she told me she could not wait to have a grandchild by her daughter Anne. Anne was I believe, at University at the time but would be home for Pesach (Passover) and possibly before. My genuine oohs and ahs of delighted admiration at almost everything I was shown were very much appreciated by my hostess.

I was to have a small box-room to myself on the top floor. Rose was in the next bedroom and would be sharing her room with Henny. They called it the attic floor. Bube was somewhere on the floor below. There were sinks in most bedrooms and most likely another toilet or two in different parts of the house. It really seemed to sprawl in all directions. My room was tiny with just a bed and a little built-in wardrobe. But a room all to myself—I was thrilled after having had to share with different strangers for weeks and with my sisters all of my past life.

"You are not afraid to be on your own?" Mrs Lichtig asked anxiously. I was quite surprised at the question.

"Afraid—o' no" I hastened to assure her. Her small face lit up and she hugged me.

"You're a lovely little girl. I'm going to bring you some dresses from the factory to-morrow. They will look very nice on you. You can be our model." I nodded wondering what being a model meant. As it was our conversation in broken German and Yiddish did not exactly flow but thanks to our empathy we somehow understood each other well enough. And I was becoming more and more adept at gesturing and attempting to find a word or two in English all the more as I noticed how that pleased Mrs Lichtig.

The Lichtigs owned a children's clothing factory, a fine limousine which might have been a Daimler and a chauffeur. Of course I was entirely mesmerised by such grandeur. All the more so as they behaved unlike any other adults I had ever known, with no sign of hauteur or snobbishness. They appeared very content with their lot in spite of Mrs. Lichtig's mysterious ailment. Religion certainly ruled their lives, Mr Lichtig's more so than his wife's. Many rabbis and bearded men in caftans and black fur hats came to meet with Mr Lichtig in his library and there would be conferences and discussions for many hours. Bube would supervise the teas and plates of sweet honey—cake and plain 'LEKECH' (cake) to be brought upstairs in a kind of troop movement. All these delicacies were baked by Bube who excelled just as my Oma Tennenbaum at the art of baking.

The most stunning room in the house was the library which Mr Lichtig proudly took me to see the following morning. It spread over an entire wing of the first floor and had shelves from top to bottom. There was a tall ladder for the top shelves and the centre of the room was graced by a magnificent antique desk and deep green leather chair. There must have been a thousand books mostly of theological Jewish content. Mr Lichtig was a highly respected sage of great learning in Jewish theology I would later discover. People came from all over to discuss and debate the Talmud with him.

I do not know if Mrs Lichtig shared his enthusiasm to quite the same extent. I know she enjoyed conversing with my far more urbane father enormously. And I was soon to discover that Mr Lichtig's brother Maurice was an atheist, an unwavering Communist and lover of all things Russian, be it music or literature. Not that I understood what an atheist meant but it was pretty obvious to all that Maurice neither dressed like his brother nor was he to be seen at any religious function. Communism, however, was a word I was acquainted with as most of the Yiddish songs I had learnt were of people who had been shut away in Siberia by the Tsar for their Communist activities. And Communism was not a word I had been taught to despise like Nazism. Papi made no secret of the fact that he had Communist leanings though he had never belonged to the BUND. He seemed to get on particularly well with Maurice. But the Lichtig brothers, though one was obviously a capitalist, still remained on close brotherly terms and Maurice, who had few worldly riches, frequently dined with us week-days and enjoyed the fragrant, soothing ambience of the garden and the company of its many visitors as days grew warmer.

That very first 'EREV SHABBATH' Friday night dinner at the Lichtig household, transported me to a theatre where the most rapturous Jewish family play was being enacted. I had been privileged, it was pointed out to me and I saw no reason to dispute it, to share Mrs Lichtig's bath-water in her fine bath tub, was a privilege the little lady I adored reiterated, that was solely mine. It was redolent of her rose-scented bath salts still and I enjoyed my lengthy luxurious wallow all the more as I learnt that no-one else of the refugees was ever thus honoured. They took their baths or 'wash-downs' in the basement.

Then came the turn of my never-ending problem hair: ever since I had left home and the loving care of Mutti, strangers had been battling sometimes more successfully and caringly as in Mrs Saunders' case, but mostly unsuccessfully with it. It had tentatively and very diplomatically been put to me at Selsea if I would not consider a hair—cut. My shocked expression must have sufficed for an answer. Somehow, in my mind, it came under a similar heading as the word 'adoption'.

When Henny came she would be in charge of my hair-washes but this first time Rose volunteered graciously. She herself had lovely raven black shoulder-length hair as smooth and straight as mine never would be. But she was gentle and I even consented graciously to let her trim some ends after which she set about towel-drying and dressing my recalcitrant tresses into some semblance of ringlets. She succeeded to my absolute satisfaction. I felt cleaner and better than I had felt since I had left Munich, especially since as I entered my little bed-room Mrs Lichtig waited there for me to present me with my new frock. It was absolutely beautiful, brand-spanking new with spring flowers you could almost smell sprouting all over the glazed cotton material, hugging me in a perfect fit. Mrs. Lichtig had brought several similar frocks back from her factory earlier that day and they would all be for me. Each was equally gaily coloured with blossoms of red and pink and the cotton simply gleamed in its newness. Impulsively I embraced my benefactress in genuine gratitude and as she returned my embrace I could tell my joy had made her happy too.

Papi was to join us for dinner. What I had not been told was that there would be a constant stream of guests which continued well into the night. I have no idea just how many people attended these Friday night EREV SHABBATH festivities, but to me it seemed there must have been at least thirty and often far more people there. There were times when Bube and a few of the regular residents virtually spilled over into the corridor though the salon used on these occasions was as vast as a small ball-room. Mr & Mrs Lichtig were regal in their Sabbath attire as they welcomed everyone and sat at the head of the table side by side.

I managed to snatch a floor space on the rug by the blazing log fire right from the start. Luser had moved his chair nearby and so did Rose when she was not helping to serve. When Trudel arrived she would squat next to me, affording us the privacy that convinced Trudel she could whisper bawdy wise-cracks in my ear and horror of horror, causing me to explode with laughter. The more I begged her to stop the more she persisted. There were times later on, when I ran out the room in shame. Mutti never attended these Friday night occasions and soon Papi would be missing too. My mother had her own Sabbath candles to light and make blessings over, no matter in what unedifying surroundings. Henny like Rose, was kept busy serving and generally helping out for most of the night. I could tell she felt hard done by but as was her way, she did not openly complain.

That first Friday evening, however, dressed now in my lovely new frock, my freshly-washed black hair adorned with a red velvet ribbon Rose had found for me I was called to the front door. And there stood Papi and Abi both immaculate, both tall and slender and both in my eyes more handsome than any other man in the house—even Luser my new love. I suddenly realised that my nine-teen year-old brother was an adult man and not just a brother and play-mate.

As Mrs Lichtig was a vegetarian, meat was never served at these functions. There was plenty to eat, however and all of it wholesome with countless salads and delicious puddings. I did not learn until much later that Mrs. Lichtig's vegetarianism was not merely choice but necessity as she had been forbidden meat by her doctors and her loyal family followed suit. She was actually a very sick lady but she never breathed a word of complaint in my hearing though I could tell by her frequently pinched, pained expression that all was not well. For me, however, Mrs Lichtig never lost her aura of glamour, no matter how gaunt her face.

The evening began with prayers over the CHALLAH (that delicious sweet Sabbath bread I knew from home) performed by the hostess clad as ever in an elegant long gown, a fabulous silver or golden turban adorning her head. It never occurred to me that these turbans were anything other than part of her dramatic sartorial taste, signifying nothing more sinister, nor that she might not be wearing a 'Sheitel' (wig) as demanded by orthodox religious law. Her little pale face with film-star bright red lipstick added to her glamour. Tiny as she was she walked regally and she behaved invariably with the grace and dignity of a great lady.

The impressive silver candelabra blazed with tall Sabbath candles and the wine glasses of the gentlemen were filled with ruby—red wine. Papi gave me a sip of the potent sweet red liquid as he had always done. My cheeks burnt with pleasure. The meal began with a great deal of rushing about by those I considered lucky to be involved in its functioning and overseen by Bube and Mrs Lichtig. I was far more immersed in the wonder of it all than actually partaking from the platters of raw salads to which one needed to become accustomed. Raw grated carrots were certainly not something I had previously eaten. There was desert and there was cake; so far as I was concerned the meal was a great success although as time went on, I did hear rumblings of discontent by some of the other permanent guests. My dear sister Trudel too, was inclined to whisper one of her inimitable asides in my ear as soon as the usual platters of what she called 'grasses' were served. How I enjoyed my sister's mischievous asides even if I pretended to disapprove in my attempt to prove my loyalty to Mrs. Lichtig.

At first I would look about for Maurice Lichtig but soon I understood that he never attended these functions. But I was more than content as Papi and Abi were there those first few Fridays. Soon Henny had joined the household and one wonderful day my Mutti and Trudel had arrived. Papi and Mutti attempted to rebuild something of a family life for themselves. With great difficulty Papi had finally found a tiny flat nearby but it was not large enough to house even half his family. It had been agreed that Henny like Rose would assist with the endless household chores in a household forever entertaining more and more destitute refugees. Abi, who had resumed his studies at the Jewish Secondary School in Stanford Hill, would have to stay with the parents as did Trudel after the first few nights at the Lichtigs'.

But Friday evening EREV SHABBATH festivities embraced everyone who had been welcomed into their ever-expanding family circle. All were welcome and I suspect that secretly Mrs Lichtig was disappointed at my parents' absence. Mutti attempted from the outset to create a little corner of privacy and togetherness for herself and Papi over the Sabbath. After all the separation and anxiety over her family, those first few weeks must have meant a great deal to my parents though selfishly I would have preferred to have them here at the Lichtig festivities or joined them at their modest rooms. It never occurred to me that sadly there simply might not be enough money for such luxuries.

It was difficult for me to comprehend the enormous need for each other's sole company after all the hazards this devoted couple had had to contend with. It was not something they could share with such a vast gathering of strangers regardless of how much they had in common. Now their family was safe and in particular my mother, a proud woman whose own home had always been a source of pride, needed to begin rebuilding her entire life. Of course I did not understand why she put a stop to their Friday night visits. And of course I took it for granted that it was she and not my father although I never had proof that that was actually the case. Maybe it was because it was obvious that my mother and Mrs Lichtig did not enjoy the empathy that was so evident between Papi and our hostess. Father's charm and charisma had always scored highly with the ladies whereas mother's lack of urbanity and sophistication, was bound to put her at a disadvantage with a woman as sophisticated as Mrs Lichtig. But above all, my mother was proud. She wore no make-up whatever. Her complexion was flawless but her lack of vanity and reliance on nature especially as she took little interest in her clothes those first months and what she wore appeared outdated here, did not do her justice. She had a fine head of thick chestnut hair but her hairstyle was old-fashioned and a hairdresser was out of the question. I would have preferred to be able to glow with pride at her entrance as I did when Papi arrived. It took this little daughter a great many years to appreciate the iron strength of a woman like Marie Miriam Lowy who always considered herself last and who did not know the meaning of vanity.

BOGNOR REGIS AND ANOTHER NEW SCHOOL; CLISSOLD PARK

I knew that after the Passover and Easter festivals, I would be attending the nearest local school. I had been picking up words daily with the help of anyone who had any knowledge of both English and German. As I had already experienced one visit to a school when I did not have a single word of English to come to my rescue, I imagined that this second experience could only be better.

But first I was to accompany Mr and Mrs Lichtig and their daughter Anne to the sea-side in Bognor Regis. More gleaming new frocks had been put on my bed by Mrs Lichtig but as they were all summer frocks I found myself pretending more often than not that I could not have enjoyed them more even though I was bravely freezing in them. The English climate that spring was like porridge and kippers, something it took time to become accustomed to. But I loved the newness and colourful charm of these dresses, so freezing in them seemed a price well worth paying all the more so since everyone fussed over the way I looked in them and no one suggested that maybe a cardigan might come in useful as I did not possess one.

The Lichtigs' limousine, chauffeur-driven, conveyed us regally to a little villa Mrs Lichtig had rented close by the beach. I virtually disappeared in the fine leather upholstery of the lavish space in the most sumptuous motor car I had ever travelled in. And I enjoyed every moment of it and fully appreciated my good fortune to be favoured thus.

Mrs Lichtig herself did not go in the water but the air was very beneficial to her condition and she would sit wrapped up in blankets on a deck-chair enjoying the sun-shine when it chose to make a rare appearance. I too would have enjoyed this sea-side trip far more had I not felt so terribly cold most days and nights. But I showed my gratitude to these lovely people daily and never admitted to feeling anything but comfortable and happy which in truth I was after the nightmarish experiences of the past few months. After all, I had had some first-rate lessons at Dover Court in the endurance of freezing temperatures. Nothing could ever compare to that.

I loved the absolute novelty of the English seaside and Bognor Regis, with its donkey—rides and Punch and Judy Shows on the beach when rain did not put a stop to them. People were invariably friendly and helped me out when I tried to express myself in most likely bizarre fashion. I hugged my little bucket and spade Mrs Lichtig had bought me that first day of arrival as though it had cost a fortune and even though thanks to the weather, I would not be able to use it more than a couple of times. But it had been bought for ME and that meant I was loved and love was what I had had so little of these past few months.

I had finally found my tongue again. There was, however, one thing I was still left with: I could not stop myself from rubbing my chin against my neck-bone. Moreover, I did it surreptitiously hoping that no one would notice and no one ever seemed to. I firmly resolved to stop this ludicrous habit but so far found that impossible.

The Bognor interlude passed all too soon. Rained on as we were most days, it was decided to cut the holiday short. And much as my mouth watered at the tantalising smell of fish and chips, for some reason we did not partake of that delicacy I had so treasured at the Sanders. Perhaps Mrs Lichtig was not allowed to eat fish but it was more likely that as Mr Lichtig adhered so strictly to religious law, fish and chips from a none-kosher restaurant was simply unthinkable.

I felt very sad that this sea-side interlude had come so abruptly to an end although my heart jumped at the prospect of seeing my parents again. I knew too that a new school loomed but there was excitement in the novelty too, tinged with obvious apprehension. Bognor would remain for me a peaceful, small typically benign English sea-side resort, with couples stubbornly braving it out on the beach in deck-chairs in pouring rain or the odd glimpse of sun. Men with kerchiefs tied around the head; ladies with scarves tied under the chin covering their hair in windy weather and clad in dowdy one-piece swimming costumes. The all-pervading odour of fish and chips following right down to the water's edge sprucing up your appetite was as much part of the place as was the pier along which we would take a stroll weather permitting with the furious waves slashing against the cliff rocks below, frequently terrifying me in their ferocity; but no fish and chips.

It now fell to Henny to take care of my hair and a great many other menial chores. She had to help out at the factory some days which she obviously found demeaning. My almost eighteen year old sister, with a successful school career behind her found it hard to conceal her affront although Rose was in a similar position as were hundreds of other refugees. Of course she would later see that she was one of the fortunate few who were given this opportunity but when it came to washing my 'STRUBELPETER' hair as she called it after the famous mop-haired fictitious character, she really took it out on me. Mercifully Rose, who enjoyed working with children, came to my rescue after a lot of squealing and screaming when the horrible soapy shampoo burnt my eyes and Henny accused me of overreacting—who knows maybe I did.

Rose was also given the task of taking me to my new school as she knew the area well by now and Henny was more useful at the factory. I entered the meandering, gloomy grey brick building similar to so many old London school-buildings and Rose, whose English was scarcely more advanced than mine, promptly left. I stood there not knowing which way to turn as there was no—one to guide me let alone receive me. So I wondered gingerly towards the pleasing sounds of communal singing and found myself at the back of a huge hall filled with chanting children. The girls were all in similar uniform consisting of white blouses and black gym slips as I learned to call it. My ears had obviously led me to the right spot and I must have stood out like weed in a perfect garden in my little gaudy cotton frock pretty though it was.

Once the children had marched out into their respective class-rooms I stood alone and forlorn, rooted to the spot. Finally I heard foot-steps behind me.

"Hello, so you are our new pupil from Germany." The smile of the middle-aged woman addressing me was friendly but without warmth. I was unaccustomed to female teachers apart for gymnastics. I had already been taken by surprise in Ilford but my sojourn there had been so short that I had almost forgotten about it. This lady was mature, her grey hair in a tight bun and clad in a brown tweed suit with sensible brown laced shoes. Her blouse was crisp white and buttoned to the neck. And I stood there in my inappropriate summer dress.

I did what I did best: I smiled. I had understood the word Germany and half guessed at what she may have said. I was getting pretty adept at guessing.

"Come" she said as she led me into a class-room filled only with girls. I was surprised. She pointed to an empty desk at the back of the class and I sat down. The form-mistress came to join us. They spoke to me. I must have looked perplexed. I did not understand what they were saying until a few white pages of paper and a pencil were placed in front of me soon followed by some printed pages one of which with sums, the others with writing, none of which made any sense to me.

"See what you can do." The first lady said and left. The form mistress, younger than the other lady, returned to her desk in the front of the class.

My heart beat fast. I wanted to cry.

I looked about me. The rest of the class were obviously engaged in other work and the teacher wrote words on the black-board. I studied the papers before me and felt more and more close to tears. I had never felt so incompetent in my life. But I persevered with some of the sums though they were mostly beyond me too. Most of the girls around me looked older. When the bell went the form-mistress came to collect my paper.

"Name," she said "and age."

"Oh" I said embarrassed, hastily writing my name and as she still waited I finally understood what she meant and put my date of birth. She collected my half-empty paper without a smile.

The milk break as in Ilford was enormously welcome and I still delighted in the creamy richness of the contents of those little gold-topped bottles, the novelty of the straws and the clatter as they were collected. It seemed to me the only thing I was able to share with the other pupils. It was clear from the expression on the teacher's face when she examined my paper that she was disappointed.

As I did not go into the playground during break she came up to me.

"How long have you been in England?"

"Three—nearly four months" I was able to tell her. She nodded.

"We'll have to start from scratch." She sighed. "You're really a year younger than we expected. We thought you were eleven!"

I liked the morning assembly when hymns were sung. I picked up the tunes almost immediately and was able to join in if only humming and mouthing words. I continued to hate break-times as I could converse with no-one and here no-one offered me comics. Besides I stood out because of my unsuitable attire. But I loved coming home, with Rose waiting for me at the gates and walking with her through grey back-streets I was getting to know. So this was London. Bube invariably had some delicacy she had baked that day waiting for me. I adored the little Russian Bube who could converse with me in Yiddish and was always so very motherly whilst my own mother could not be with me. I thought she was at least a hundred years old, far older than either of my grandmothers.

Altogether my time with the Lichtigs held a great many delights from the pretty dresses to the obvious favouritism Bube and Mrs Lichtig afforded me. Then there were the Sundays spent in the music room, with someone tinkling lovely tunes on the piano or records being played on the gramophone. Sometimes we would all sing these songs together. The place was always abuzz with visitors and I learned some new Yiddish songs above all 'A BRIEVALE DER MAMMEN' which always brought tears to my eyes as I knew well enough how excruciating the separation from parents could be. Although I still felt more in need of my father than my mother.

But the most enchanting place for me as the weather grew more clement was the beautiful garden, large enough to hold Mr Lichtig's ample summer house where he entertained and studied with rabbis whilst we sat around little tables munching sweet almond cakes and biscuits when it was time for tea. The intoxicating scent of camellia, lilac and jasmine filled the air, watered and carefully pruned regularly by an industrious gardener. And of course there were the most fecund roses of every hue enhancing every nook and cranny of the garden. Never had I seen or smelled anything like it in Germany. It seemed to me that spring and early summer spent at the Lichtigs was a very blessed existence even though I was not living with my family.

Maurice Lichtig had kept his promise to take me on long walks and he told me about the glories of Soviet Russia. He had recently seen a Russian film and continuously hummed a tune that would stay with me all my life. Finally, nearly seventy years later I discovered it was written by Shostakovich and was called THE SONG OF THE LEGEND, a haunting tune he had written for the Russian film dear Maurice Lichtig had been so excited about in 1939.

One day Papi arrived with something I had only dreamed of but had missed no occasion to gently nudge him whenever I spotted an opening:

"O' Papi, how I wish I could have roller skates like those other children I saw yesterday coming home from school—they simply rolled home." I would begin and would repeat ad finitum. I had not forgotten how to manipulate my darling father. I saw him far too rarely in the week and Mutti even less, as she spent her days looking for accommodation for us all.

There was also the anxiety over the furniture in the LIFT. It needed safe inexpensive storage until a home was found. That precious LIFT contained all that was left of the twenty years my parents had struggled to build a successful existence in Germany. It must have meant so much to her as it contained her bedroom suite and most of our beds as well as Papi's extensive library and Mutti's beloved pictures and ornaments. The piano and beautiful dining room had had to go but there was our family sofa from the living room to look forward to once we had a home of our own again. I think Mutti was the one who felt most affected by the homelessness and utter destitution of the family's situation as she was the one who sought and managed to attain the finer things in life for us all. Papi with his socialist leanings and great respect for Leon Trotsky like Maurice Lichtig, felt that a simple life without all the pomposity and fancy furnishing, was the way to live and he loved the East End of London and seemed to spend a great deal of time there with his writer colleagues, discussing art and politics in the Lyons tea shops.

I have no idea how my father managed to scrimp together the pennies and shillings to buy me this second-hand pair of roller skates, to me the most beautiful gift I had received since my precious suitcase of dolls.

Somehow, miraculously they fitted over my sandals if perilously and I had quite a few tumbles until I mastered the art and imagined I was flying away as I raced through the back-streets, always remaining on the pavements as I had pledged I would. Surprisingly Papi was less anxious of my escapades than Mutti but as he and Abi had only recently crossed the Alps and spent time in both French and Italian jails he was less inclined to be squeamish of late.

I learnt little at the school as no one actually made the slightest effort to teach me the language. But I was good at singing songs which I picked up quicker than most and as ever, I was a fast runner. As far as any other school work was concerned, although I was picking up new words rapidly thanks to the Lichtig household, I might as well have stayed away. I had also made few friends as no one bothered to approach me and as usual, I found it difficult to make the first move. But I was not unhappy either. I accepted it as part of my new life. And I watched the other children chewing bubble gum, something entirely alien to me but that I was secretly dying to try.

The brighter, longer afternoons and early evenings were spent roller skating, going for walks with Papi or Maurice Lichtig and sometimes also with my secret love Luser. He was of course all of eighteen years old, and like Abi, he was continuing his studies. But Luser to me seemed very adult. Not only was he slim, tall and with perfect features and soft, silky brown hair that would fall over a very white, high forehead. His pale hands were remarkably veined for so young a person and he let me play with those veins watching as I pressed gently on them. His expression was invariably serious. I also suspected that Anne Lichtig, a charming university student with a trendy bob, when home, seemed to hold his interest more than poor Rose. I did notice Mrs Lichtig occasionally throwing enigmatic glances their way. Little escaped me where Luser was concerned and deep down I had already decided, not all that happily that Anne and Luser were an item. I was not jealous for myself but for Rose.

The real highlight of those balmy summer afternoons were those, however, spent with Papi and once or twice Mutti also, walking of a Sabbath afternoon in Clissold Park with many other Jewish couples reminiscent I'm sure especially for my parents, of those glorious pre-Hitler days when Jewish couples would walk along the ANLAGE by the river Isar in all their finery after a Sabbath lunch and short siesta. Mutti did a lot of sighing but she never openly complained of anything. Papi was still able to compose silly little rhymes for me to amuse me but I could tell that he was anxious. It was the situation of Jews in Germany that seemed to be on all their minds.

"We are lucky to be in England, aren't we?" I once suggested after listening to my parents discussing the difficulty of finding suitable accommodation for us all with dire lack of funds. The one they were living in at present with Abi and Trudel was infested with mice and worst of all bugs! It was one of the only times I feared Mutti would break down in tears. But she controlled herself as Papi reminded her that there were a great many worse things happening to people. They would find a way. He would ask Mrs Lichtig for advice. But that was really the last straw for Mutti. She would not be shamed before Mrs Lichtig as she saw it.

"Of course," Mutti conceded, "we are enormously blessed to be out of that cursed country. I just wish—"But Papi put his arm about her and we all giggled.

One memorable Sunday afternoon in Clissold Park I begged Papi to hire a little motor boat for half an hour.

"Couldn't we—o' please, please" I knew how to work my poor Papi. His problem was, as I well knew, shortage of money. But somehow after endless badgering that sunny Sunday, he gave in. I think he had actually sold a poem to the YIDDISHE ZEIT, a paper for which he had been contributing for many years but Mr Meyer, the proprietor, had of late been beleaguered with several more refugee poets and journalists and had therefore had to reign in his fees and commissions. But Papi had a few shillings jingling in his pocket and with a little more cajoling from his wily daughter he submitted. In no time we were on that boat floating on glistening, sun-drenched water, Papi steering precariously close to other boats. I yelled with delight—it had been something I had yearned to do for so long. Clissold Park with its fragrant rose-trees and beautifully tended flowers was a little utopian enclave for countless refugees flocking there at week-ends from their dingy rooms. But I felt especially blessed as I was sailing in a boat with my Papi even though we nearly capsized several times.

Suddenly there was talk of war. Papi looked distraught much of the time and spent less time at the Lichtigs. He was in touch with many foreign sources and the news out of Germany was grimmer from day to day. And then there was another new word for me to grapple with. I had enjoyed the summer holidays not having to go to a school I had no empathy with. I could still feel connected with only one school, one teacher.

I was told that all London school-children were to be evacuated. To be evacuated meant in one word: leaving. Yes, but where to, with whom, alone again? I did not panic because I firmly intended to stay here with the Liuchtigs. But Papi soon clarified the situation and though it was far from ideal, I understood that if all London's school children had to leave or be evacuated as they called it, I had little option but to go too without much fuss. But I would not have to leave with my new school. Instead, as Abi was a student at the JEWISH SECONDARY SCHOOL (a free school) in Stoke Newington, it was agreed that Trudel and I would join the children of that school. I was growing accustomed to being a stranger among strangers.

September 1st. 1939 very early in the morning, Henny, Bube, Mrs. Lichtig and Rose kissed me good-bye as Papi and I stepped into the limousine the Lichtigs had kindly put at my disposal to convey Papi and me the short stretch up a few roads, little suitcase filled with summer frocks packed by Henny. Trudel and Abi would be waiting at the school with all the other children assembled there.

Papi kissed me before handing me over to some lady at the school and left too soon. I had promised not to cry. Mutti was nowhere to be seen as most likely the parents were asked to arrive singly. Or maybe she had not yet quite got over our brief parting at the Munich station. I saw Trudel from afar talking to some girls her own age. There were lots of buses waiting in the street. It reminded me vaguely of something I did not wish to recall.

A handsome man by the name of Dr. Schoenfeld made a speech and added a few words in Yiddish. "KINDERLECH" he called us. I liked him. Papi was gone, the Lichtigs car was gone, my suitcase had been taken care of; someone had placed it somewhere on the bus I was boarding with the other children. This time there was much excited chatter, some in English but quite a lot in German and yet it seemed as though it was not my language any longer. I did not see Trudel or Abi for the entire journey to Bedfordshire. I was off again into the unknown and as before most of the journey went by in a haze. But as the bus left the grey London streets and sped along green lanes with fields on either side glowing yellow with ripe corn and even cattle and little lambs became visible, my heart suddenly lifted. The bucolic scene unfolding outside my window was new and enchanting and made me feel less lonely.

BOOK TWO

1939–1947

Chapter Eleven

MY NEW WORLD MY NEW SCHOOL

STOTFOLD, SHEFFORD & CLIFTON

That second journey into the unknown on Friday the first of September 1939–how long did it take? I do not know but it hardly mattered as I took little notice of what went on inside the bus, magnetically drawn by the varied sights we passed as I sat glued to my window-seat. Green gleaming everywhere in the bright sunlight! Tiny village—houses and narrow streets frequently caused the wide bus to drive on the pavement and occasionally even stop to allow a herd of cattle to pass. I could see some of the herd's faces, their huge, sad eyes seemingly staring right back at me, bidding me welcome. My heart beat with excitement—it was not like anything I had ever seen before. Live animals, so many of them apparently content, munching on the long, fecund grass or simply relaxing in the warm sun. I knew absolutely nothing of farming, had never even been near a real farm. I had seen some chickens in the villages in Germany outside Munich and had always felt sad for them. These creatures whose gaze had somehow mutely spoken to me—I felt an uncanny bond with them.-

Right then I felt closer to these animals than to anyone inside the bus. I would be sharing their world and that was an exciting thought. Silently I told them they were my friends and I loved them. I made up little rhymes. Their closeness gave me comfort as we approached the village by the name of Shefford, supposedly our destination. But we were told to remain seated until our names were called. Abi had not been on my bus but Trudel was somewhere in the back. Maybe the boys were separated from the girls as I saw no boys on our bus.

The few glimpses I had of Shefford were discouraging. Very dark old, sad, stooped buildings: more ancient than any I had ever been close to before. Though there were gargoyle fountains and all manner of ancient monuments in Munich, the residential buildings I was familiar with did not look this antiquated or forbidding. The ones here looked spooky, gloomy and hunched. I knew nothing of Elizabethan times let alone architecture, or I might have been excited as some of the older students on the bus appeared to be. So far as I could see Shefford on this sunny day, our bus parked outside endless small grey cottages no jollier than their grandparent buildings, was a bleak sight that caused my heart to sink once more. To add to my misery, here in the main street I could not detect any animals either. I am not quite certain when exactly I had come to the conclusion that I preferred animals to humans.

So much German chatter all about me; Trudel seemed to have made friends with a lovely girl by the name of Martha Haftel. She came to say hello to me and her sunny, dimpled smile and dulcet voice instantly enchanted me. Her chestnut hair was long and fell over her shoulders in soft, silky waves. I thought her very beautiful as I did my sister, only in an entirely different way.

"I'm Martha—Martha Haftel" her bright smile was a ray of sunshine. "We're all going to be good friends, aren't we?" She assured me in her lilting Viennese German. I nodded sleepily, readily returning her smile.

I must have dozed off as the next thing I knew Trudel and Martha gently roused me and informed me that we had arrived. Arrived where? No-one actually knew the answer to that until it was announced that the village we were now in was STOTFOLD and in a short while we would be taken to our new billets. There were several ladies standing outside the coach with long lists from which they began reading out names. By now it was growing dark but I could see pretty cottages and the coach had stopped by a huge patch of green which was actually called 'THE GREEN'. There were trees and beyond them I could see traces of fields. I liked what I saw. I was certain there would be animals here too.

Anxious rumblings about the lateness of the hour were audible throughout the coach, with the Sabbath only minutes away. Would we be forgiven under the circumstances for breaking the Sabbath laws? Would God understand? Neither Trudel nor I were troubled by such scruples as Papi had bred in us a far more relaxed attitude to our faith, whether he was aware of it or not.

Someone helped lift me off the coach as Trudel went to collect our luggage and we were asked to follow a woman across the road to a charming detached house virtually opposite The Green. I had great difficulty to keep my eyes open and it had now grown dark. I saw no animals but endless rows of wooden sties and a very strong fetid whiff of what to me was an unfamiliar malodorous stench. Trdel and I looked briefly at each other, wrinkled our noses and smiled.

The huge lady standing on the porch of the house taking up almost all of its width, bade us welcome, stretching out her hand to Trudel and then me. She introduced herself as Mrs Oliver, our landlady. Neither Trudel nor I understood much of what was being said but the woman from the committee spoke some German and explained that we would be staying with the family Oliver who had kindly agreed to put us up for the time being. This was to be our 'billet'.

We were directed to the back of the house via a huge, muddy backyard and through the kitchen door. I was shivering in my treasured summer frock as Mrs. Oliver led us into the living room where to my delight a huge coal fire blazed its welcome. She told me to sit down by the fire and get warm while Trudel and the other woman would see to everything. I smiled at her tearfully as by now I felt weary and lost again, even though my sister was nearby. I think Trudel too felt depressed although we liked the house well enough with its huge kitchen sink taking up most of the front wall and an equally large black stove the adjoining one. It was all so strange. The floor in the kitchen was of very cold stone but everything was clean and tidy if, permeated by a blend of unfamiliar strong odours not so much unpleasant as entirely alien.

As I leaned back in the arm-chair Mrs Oliver had guided me to, a huge ginger cat jumped on my lap. I yelped in delight and kissed and cuddled the animal as though she was my long lost friend. The warm feel of that first feline friend whose name was Whiskey, was the greatest comfort I could have been given at that particular moment. Everyone in the room stopped to look and broke into broad, approving grins, especially the substantially built lady of the house.

A tall, equally generously built, but imposing young woman had joined us, accompanied by a startlingly lean elderly man clad in working clothes. We were introduced to Olive the daughter, about four years older than Trudel and Mr Oliver, the man of the house. After Trudel and Mrs Oliver went upstairs to the bedroom we would be sharing, Olive and Mr Oliver bade me sit at the table with them but not before Mr Oliver had gone into the kitchen where I could hear him splash about until he returned, certainly looking spruced up. Though I found it so hard to keep awake, I made a huge effort when I saw freshly cut white buttered bread, cheese and ham in the centre of the table and I was asked to partake in the friendliest way.

Olive and I got on from the start. She was obviously fond of children and I took to her kind, protective attitude when so many times previously I had rejected it from fellow refugees. She was a large girl in every sense with a lovely, glowing complexion. Her contented disposition shone from every feature of her attractive face. She made friends with Trudel too though conversation was inevitably limited.

I gladly accepted the fresh bread and butter and a tall glass of particularly tasty, creamy milk but I refused the ham much to their surprise. I had no way of explaining to them that I was not allowed to eat none kosher meat even if at the time I could not differentiate pig's meat from any other I recognised it as meat. I hoped that at some stage the people in charge of billeting would explain as I did not wish to offend my new hosts. But I gladly accepted the biscuits that were passed round with my milk as well as some unaccustomed fruit cake I finished once begun but hardly to my taste as it was very far removed from Mutti's or even Bube's cakes. Mr Oliver sat there quietly, watching me in silence. I was grateful for that because it was an enormous effort for me especially as I was so tired, to squeeze out some comprehensible English phrases I had picked up. But I did my best to give him a grateful smile every time he offered me another biscuit. As it was I was to learn that it was not done to speak at table.

By the time Trudel rejoined us, my eyes were barely open and Mrs Oliver, taking one look at me, insisted I go upstairs while Trudel had some supper.

Olive, her arm about my shoulders, softly assured me she would show me upstairs and I warmed even more to her. Mrs Oliver in all her kindness was overpowering because she was so excessively big. Mr Oliver, in striking contrast, sparse and very serious, politely but with the fewest words bade me good night. Trudel whispered something to me in German but I could see the disapproval on Mr Oliver's face at the sound of the foreign words and I did not respond.

The entire upstairs was surprisingly cramped, as though someone had run out of building material. Two bedrooms one side and another opposite; in the middle was a bathroom but it was explained to us that it was not yet functioning as there was no plumbing for water hot or cold. We would have to use the toilet outside or in an emergency a chamber pot under the bed. And we would wash in the kitchen sink where there was no running hot water. It was a huge leap from the Lichtigs but we accepted instinctively that we had arrived in a different world—the English countryside.

Our bedroom consisted of a remarkably small double bed and a chest of drawers. At least we were assured it was a double bed though it was hardly as large as our old beds in Munich. From the one window we could see the back yard. Yet the bed looked inviting, with its cover off ready for me and the room clean and friendly with its floral wall-paper. Sharing a bed with my sister was the closest I had come in months to living with a member of my family. I thought fleetingly and achingly of Papi and Mutti before, after pulling off my dress and washing hands and face in the bowl of water I spotted atop a small stand by the side of the bed, I fell into bed in my underwear. I must have fallen asleep almost immediately because the next thing I was aware of was bright daylight bursting through the window and the insistent crowing of what sounded like a cavalry of cockerels. I jumped excitedly out of bed to the window which was within touching distance from my side of the bed.

What I beheld was too exciting to keep to myself no matter what the time:

"Trudel, Trudel" I had sufficient sense to keep my voice down in case I woke the Olivers, but I could hear much movement downstairs and smell a frying odour both immensely tantalising and at the same time nauseating. I would never again confuse it with any other: the smell of frying bacon.

My sleepy sister told me in no uncertain manner to shut up. But I simply had to share the wonders outside the window with her and not all that graciously, she stumbled out of bed to stand next to me

"Ugh—" Trudel wrinkled her nose, "what a terrible stink!"

"Yes, yes, but don't you see, all those rows and rows of wooden huts—there are little pigs in them!" I simply could not conceal my excitement. "And there—there can you see over there, all those chickens walking about—o' and little ducks too! Isn't it simply wonderful?"

Trudel looked at me with sleepy eyes and put her arm round me.

"It stinks to high heaven." She laughed. "But there's a lovely cooking smell coming from downstairs. Do you suppose we will get some cooked breakfast? And by the way, those tiny little creatures just down there are baby ducklings."

"O' ducklings, aren't they delightful" But I don't really like that cooking smell. I wonder what it is. Anyway, it's 'Shabbes'.(Sabbath)" But Trudel was back in bed and fast asleep for another half hour until Mrs Oliver knocked on our door and told us we could wash in the kitchen sink now that Olive had gone to work and Mr Oliver had had his breakfast and resumed work on the farm. Breakfast was on the table. As Trudel had been in England a shorter time and had as yet had little occasion to pick up the language, I had become the official translator and afforded due respect, probably much to dear Trudel's understandable aggravation.

Downstairs I was greeted by Whiskey and what seemed like at least half a dozen of her siblings of varying sizes and colours, one more delightful than the next and each friendlier and more hungry for attention than the other. But Whiskey had already assured her place of honour though a little black and white kitten was very hard to resist. They all seemed to need my love and I certainly responded generously: I needed theirs too.

Conversation with the kindly Mrs Oliver was very restricted but I tried whereas Trudel had by then no more than a dozen words and we found ourselves giggling a great deal which did not seem to please Mr Oliver, especially when we giggled at table. I tried really hard but just as at the Lichtigs, Trudel knew just where to hit my funny bone and off I'd go while she sat there with a straight face. Fortunately only Mr Oliver seemed to mind, whilst the ladies were faintly amused as well as bemused by these two foreign siblings and took no offence at Trudel's impish ways, as she was otherwise unfailingly charming and attractive.

The first day was one of exploring the village and meeting for the mid-day meal at the LIBERAL CLUB HALL in the High Street. It was easy to find one's way around Stotfold, It was a small, ancient village with few streets and endless sprawling fields pock-marked with hay-stacks, green meadows in which cows and sheep grazed as though they had an agreement with the farmers never to harm them. And that is precisely what I believed in my delight at their sweet faces and the farmers' apparent non-aggressive hostelry.

Some of the tiny thatched cottages near The Green were so unlike anything we had ever seen that I did not know whether to admire or feel intimidated by their antiquity. But in all, I loved the village at first sight; it was cosy and unlike that first gloomy glimpse of Shefford, with its dark Elizabethan buildings (as I discovered much later), it was bright and colourful and chock full of animals of every kind but pigs, though not visible in the open, seemed to be in the majority, with sties on almost every farm. An abundance of verdure and golden fields encircled the village like a silk ribbon.

The gathering of all the children who had come to Stotfold in the Liberal Hall, was for me the kind of ordeal I had hoped to put aside for ever. I hated having constantly to meet new people and make an effort to befriend total strangers. I had left behind all the friends and teacher I was ever really prepared to accept deep down and yet here was just one more excruciating torment after another. Even the handsome young Dr. Schoenfeld failed to impress me when he came to address us after lunch. But I believe judging from Trudel's and Martha's comments later, that he had made quite an impression on them, as he really had film-star looks.

The names of children under twelve, all girls it seemed, were called out and we were told to assemble in one corner of this huge, bare, freezing cold hall. There were not that many of us, maybe ten or twelve and we found chairs and sat there at first staring at each other and gradually beginning to chat. One particularly jolly girl maybe a year older than me though she was shorter, with a head of dark thick, frizzy hair, rosy apple cheeks and eyes round and bright as marbles, began imitating and making fun of some of the older women at the far end. Somehow it broke the tense atmosphere and we all began to giggle. Her name was Ilse Herzberg but she leaned over to me and told me I could call her 'ILLE' that's what her friends called her although she confided that the landlady here called her Topsy for no reason she could think of. She had been in England longer than I and could converse in English but her strong accent was unmistakably German. Everything seemed to amuse her and her high spirits were infectious stimulating even me.

Ille noticed I was shivering. The large wooden hall furnished only with a few chairs and trestle tables was unheated our end, with a few paraffin stoves scattered where the older evacuees were gathered.

"Typical, "she sneered in her comical way, her cheerful little face pulled into a grimace. "They WOULD get all the heat." She spoke loudly enough for one of the women in charge whom I took to be a teacher, to come over with one of the heaters. Ille had become the undisputed heroine and leader of our pathetic group.

There were several speeches and some prayers after a lunch of sandwiches and some horrible soup. Dr Schoenfeld took his leave with several young women in toe. I could scarcely take in anything of what had been said and hoped that Trudel, part of the oldest group with her new friend Martha, would explain things to me later. I felt drained and sad although I had made my first friend in Ille or Topsy.

Ille and I promised to meet the following day when we would all be returning to the LIBERAL Hall. Ille's foster-home lay in the opposite direction near the cinema, but Trudel's friend Martha walked back with us as it happened that she was staying in the grand Manor House just down the road from us. Apparently it was a magnificent old residence, the kind you see in films and she was delighted to be staying there but like our parents, both hers lived in London's Stamford Hill and she missed her mother and rabbi father.

That first evening at my new home when hopefully we would be sharing their supper and I would be reunited with Whiskey and all the other cats, was something I really looked forward to; all the more so as I knew there would be a lovely fire blazing in the grate. And I hoped we could hear some cheerful songs on the radio although that was kept in the parlour but with the door open leading into the adjoining living room. As it was, we were not allowed into the parlour which looked very grand with its red plush three—piece suite and walnut gramophone not unlike my grandfather's; o' yes and the parlour was carpeted! But I could only catch glimpses of this Oliver oasis through the open door. However, as I never saw a fire burning in the grate it appeared to me far less desirable than the living room. There we could also enjoy the company of the cats on comfy, well-worn armchairs even if they were covered in cats' hairs and emitted their very own pungent odours.

To our surprise, the Olivers were in the front parlour listening to the wireless when we returned. Mrs Oliver came out briefly to greet us and told us to help ourselves to bread and butter, cheese and pickles. A plate of ham was on the table too. Trudel grumbled to me at the meagre fare but I did not really mind. I drank the fresh milk and enjoyed the bread and butter. I could not eat the cheddar cheese and even less the pickles. But there was some cake left for us and as it was Madeira and not that funny fruit cake I enjoyed that too. Soon I was in the arm-chair by the fire as none of the adults were in the room. Trudel sat opposite me in the other arm-chair. A cat a piece on our laps we could hear much talking on the wireless without, of course, understanding any of it. The atmosphere in the house was surprisingly taut, even gloomy with not even Olive to talk to us. Something was wrong. Was it our fault?

But Trudel soon dispelled that fear as she reasoned that it must have something to do with the news. Eventually Olive and her boyfriend joined us soon to be followed by Mr and Mrs Oliver. I jumped up from my chair but Mrs Oliver gave me to understand that as it was almost bed-time I could remain there a little longer while she made tea. Olive accompanied by a pleasant looking tall, young man to whom we were briefly introduced, left with him soon after. To my regret there was no music as the wireless had been turned off.

The following morning that same agreeable smell of frying greeted us as we came down to breakfast. But as it was Sunday we were offered a fried egg without what we now recognised as bacon. With the egg came fried bread. It was the tastiest breakfast I had ever had, oblivious as I was to the fact that the whole meal had been fried together with bacon and in bacon fat. (I still had no notion that bacon was part of the animal I grew to be so fascinated by in their smelly sties,) hence that very special flavour. Trudel ate heartily too but did not let on that she knew full well what made our breakfast taste so special. And it was then that it suddenly dawned on me the reason my friend Topsy enjoyed her food at her billets was simply that she ate everything put before her. She had never said as much but had confided in me that her parents had not been at all observant.

Rudely we left the table without helping to wash up although we did help clear our dishes and take them into the kitchen before we rushed off as we were late for the meeting in the Liberal Hall. But I did remember to say "thank you very much for good breakfast—"which was about all I could offer. At any rate, the Olivers rushed off to their church, only a few doors from our meeting place. It would certainly have been hard to get lost in Stotfold, even for an alien 'Munchner Kindl' like myself.

Sunday 3rd. of September dawned: a perfectly clement, unexceptional day in our new domicile. With our double-barrelled tag of 'refugee evacuees', we were easy to distinguish. We looked different, we were clumsily unsuitably dressed and above all we spoke if at all with a terrible accent and ludicrous lack of grammar. Worst of all, some of us had the audacity to speak in our foreign tongue in the street.

Now a small bunch of very young to teenage girls were assembled here in Stotfold's Liberal Hall, only a few paces from the Oliver's METHODIST CHURCH. The boys it seemed, had all been billeted in Shefford and surrounding villages the night we arrived as had most of the girls. We were the overflow. The charismatic young Dr Schoenfeld had stayed in Stotfold until the end of Sabbath and had then joined the headmaster and temporary headmistress of the JSS (Jewish Secondary School) in Shefford before returning to London with his small entourage. There was an aura around him that even a ten year old could sense—princely and mesmerising.

The atmosphere in the hall was tense much like at the Olivers the night before and there was far less laughter and chatter than previously. The word 'KRIEG' and war was like a constant echo. I knew of course what it meant from Lehrer Berlinger's sad songs and I even knew the Yiddish word 'MILCHOME' from my father's equally tragic tales and poems. But did I understand its true meaning—how could I? How could any of us in that hall from the youngest to the oldest?

Older children and teachers were densely pressed around an old wireless set; the bigger girls with three or four teachers closest and the younger ones wherever they could find space to squeeze as close as possible. As soon as Ille or Topsy caught sight of me she called out my name. Trudel had already spotted Martha and both girls stood as far back as possible. They must have decided that as they could not understand what was being said, there was little sense in crowding around the wireless set already swamped by too many anxious listeners.

My new friend came towards me and we decided to remain at the far end of the hall not far from Trudel and Martha and a couple of other bigger girls. But no-one dared speak louder than in whispers as they would immediately be shushed.

Finally the women in charge of our food remembered to serve some kind of stew in metallic, unbreakable bowls on the long trestle table. Some of us sat down to eat whilst others ignored the food entirely most likely having enjoyed a full breakfast with their foster parents or caught a whiff of the unpalatable stew. Ille wrinkled her snub-nose and pushed her plate away as soon as the stew was placed in front of her. I did likewise. I loved the way Ille mumbled her disdain in no uncertain manner. She could cheer me up within seconds. She displayed her independence proudly and openly, it would take me a while yet to replicate.

And then it happened.

"Quiet!" The command rang through the hall. Dropped cutlery clanged on plates.

"It's Mr Chamberlain the Prime Minister!"

Ille looked at me and shrugged. We listened to the solemn words we did not understand delivered in a curiously phlegmatic nasal voice. Neville Chamberlain had said we were at war with Germany. War meant soldiers fighting. We had seen enough of soldiers in jack-boots to understand that they were terrifying. Now they would be attacking the lovely English people. And they weren't even Jews! I tried to dismiss my dark thoughts but I suddenly missed my parents more than I had these last few bewildering days. I wanted to be with them. And Abi was in Shefford. Why couldn't he be with us at least? Were the Germans coming here?

.For a few moments the hall was Rapt in stunned silence. Then the word war echoed throughout like a dirge, interspersed with the German KRIEG. Some of the older girls began to weep. Their parents were still in Germany. Ille's parents too were in Hamburg but like me, she could not grasp the full significance of Neville Chamberlain's announcement.

Very few of us that afternoon touched the food before us. We were told that to-morrow we would be supplied with some kind of masks—gas-masks. What did that mean? I looked over at my sister but she was wholly engaged in quiet conversation with Martha and another girl called Steffy. Soon after we were told we could return to our billets or remain here longer if we preferred.

It was very strange. I could not decide whether I preferred to go back to the Olivers or remain here with Ille. It seemed to make little difference. Neither was home. But either way I was told by one of the teachers I must wait for Trudel. If I had not been ashamed I would have cried because I realised that I belonged nowhere. Back at the Oliver's the atmosphere was very sombre. I still felt like crying and did not really understand why. Trudel had said I must go in whilst she went for a stroll with Martha and would be back soon.

Mr Oliver was out tending to the pigs and his other animals. Olive was out too with what I learned was the man she was going to marry at Christmas. They had gone to his parents for tea. I was alone with Mrs Oliver and Whisky. She seemed to be Mrs Oliver's favourite too.

I was invited to sit by the fire and play with the cat to my heart's content whilst Mrs Oliver was busy in the kitchen. I avoided using the outside toilet religiously as there was an indoor one or what amounted to almost indoor, at the LIBERAL HALL. I had already trained myself at Dover Court and before that even at STADELHEIM jail in Munich. I could hold back longer than anyone I knew.

The following day we were each handed a gas-mask and there was a demonstration on how to apply them. Ille found it all very amusing but I hated them and resolved never to use mine no matter what. The rubber smelled abominably and the entire contraption frightened me. We were informed that we would be having lessons in English each day for several hours in the morning. And we, the youngest, would be ascribed older girls who would be our kind of supervisors. Mine was to be the girl Trudel had already made friends with, Steffy. I instantly bridled at the idea although I was told that she had chosen me and I should be flattered. But I could not understand why if at all, it could not be Martha who would supervise me.

Steffy wanted to help me write a letter to the parents. I rejected her assistance. I had managed well enough without her previously. She wanted to discuss my problems. I told her I had none to discuss. I thought her a sixteen year old busybody and hated her. She was short and buxom and looked years older than Trudel and Martha. Maybe she was very clever but I did not want her interfering in my life. I would have been happy to talk to Martha but Martha it appeared, had not volunteered for this make-shift child-care; only Steffy and a couple of other girls. It was something they were planning to take up professionally later on, I believe.

It was soon obvious that Steffy and I were not getting anywhere and I believe poor girl, she gave up too. I saw no reason for anyone's intrusion in my personal feelings or psyche. There was my sister whom I loved although we fought a great deal much to the Olivers' dismay. There was Ille with whom I began to spend more and more time roaming in the wheat fields and climbing huge haystacks at which Ille seemed expert. WE were both extremely agile and athletic. Once she even defecated on the tip of a particularly high haystack much to my bemused amazement and yes, admiration. We laughed all the way home. She had become my friend and my heart felt that little bit lighter.

Lessons at the LIBERAL HALL were not all that successful. In fact they were a disaster as the handful of teachers left behind from the main school in Shefford, were inexperienced and worst of all, spoke little German. We youngsters on the other hand, were far from appreciative of their undoubted efforts and the whole thing was for us rowdy insubordinates, more of a joke and for them a trial. Ille and I decided to give these sessions a miss as soon as we realised that there was no-one to force us to do otherwise, two truants enjoying every moment of this sudden freedom.

Ille seemed to have come up trumps with her landlady as she shared every meal with her whereas I still had to go for my mid-day meal to the hall with Trudel. But as time drew on, we both gave these lunches a miss too and Trudel, Martha and I, and frequently a few of their older pals too, boys who had come from Shefford to see Trudel and Martha, roamed the fields and meadows with some shared bars of MARSETTS or MARS bars.

The Shefford visitors consisted mainly of my brother Abi as much to see the lovely Martha as his sisters, as well as a handsome, serious Czech young man called Imre Szarkani billeted with Abi in Shefford, who seemed to have taken an interest in my pretty sister. We would rest in the hay and Martha Haftel would be urged to sing. In her captivating voice she gave her very own rendition of songs she had recently picked up from Deanna Durbin films or Paul Robson records; it seemed to brighten the entire day. There was one song that particularly brought tears to my eyes as I began to understand the words: "O' Lord You Made the Night Too Long!" Or as if by magic she could change the mood of everyone when she began "I like to whistle—"when we would all join in: "cos it makes me merry, makes me feel so very—"and then came the huge communal whistle "Tralalalalalala!"

I wrote regularly to my parents and grew hugely excited when a letter came from London even though addressed to us both. Trudel's name had somehow become Trudy and Ille's was now Topsy as everyone said it suited her so well with her wild mane of dark negroid hair just like the heroine Topsy of an American novel. My dear friend seemed well pleased with her new nickname. But then she was so good-natured and happy-go-lucky that she would have acquiesced to any name. Her brother and sister were here in England too but her parents had remained in Germany and of course, no-one understood the ins and outs of these sudden family break-ups at the time, least of al we youngsters.

The days grew shorter and very cold. We were told we had to help pick potatoes in the fields for a few hours. As I suffered from the cold ever since Dover Court, this particular task was extremely trying. I had few warm clothes and no suitable Wellingtons, only my little German leather boots which were too small for me and pinched my feet atrociously. What was worse they let in water. By the time I returned to my billet my feet felt dead and my hands entirely numb. There was no Papi to bring them back to life and I ran upstairs and cried on the bed. But I did not want anyone to know. And in my own way I felt I was doing my 'bit' for the war effort, as we were told to.

As I grew more used to the discomforts I began to enjoy potato-picking with my friends. As ever we laughed more than we picked potatoes. And we were muddier than we had a right to be at the end of our morning. It did not take long before we were relieved of our tasks, especially as there was no bathroom in most of the houses and it was realised that we often remained less than properly scrubbed after our outings to the grimy, muddy fields.

One night I made a disparaging remark about the unpleasant smell in our bedroom. I told Trudy that the bed smelled of pig. I thought that that would make her laugh. Instead she took it very badly and slapped me hard. Taken aback I hit her back and before long we were really bashing at each other wherever possible. I hit back as hard as I could as I simply could not understand what had brought on this fight. The trouble was that Trudy was a strapping fifteen year old and I was a scrawny ten years old and she hit me so hard on the head that I literally saw stars. I ran downstairs bawling, frightened by this sudden blow.

I don't know what Mrs Oliver said to Trudy but she bade me sit down and comforted me. The real trouble was that I had no idea what could possibly have brought on this unaccustomed fury in my sister. The odour I found so revolting had come from Trudy's underwear.

Soon it would be Christmas and Trudy was to leave after Christmas with Martha and the other older girls. Most were returning to London but Trudy would go to Shefford so that she could have some English lessons. I was to stay with the Olivers. I was very unhappy at the thought of being separated from my sister. So far as I was concerned the fight was a thing of the past. But it seemed the Olivers were not prepared to forget it and Trudy was no longer welcome.

Olive would be getting married at the METHODIST CHURCH the Saturday after Christmas. She had asked me to be one of her bridesmaids. As I had no decent winter dress the Committee for REFUGEES were prepared to find me a couple of dresses that had been donated by Jewish families in London. As it was, I desperately needed some warm clothing. I was allowed to choose a dress from a suitcase filled with worn clothing and I chose a wine coloured little velvet dress. It covered about half my thighs as I had long legs, was of a heavy cloth but certainly warm and pretty. I liked the way I looked in it as it also had a fancy little white collar. They found me a pair of black shoes with buckles too. Olive was not to be a white bride as it was war-time but she spent a lot of time at the dress-makers', a friend of the family, who was making her a smart, light blue suit until it fitted to perfection. As she was a tall, buxom young woman it took more fittings than average. A pink silk blouse and a little blue hat matching her suit, shoes and gloves would perfect her wedding outfit. She had travelled to Bedford on the bus to find her elegant blouse and accessories at ROSES', the most up-market store in the entire area. Over her hat a little gossamer half-veil would cover her face.

I was anxious about the part I had been accorded. I could still speak only fractured English and as it was, I dreaded meeting more strangers. But it was not something I could refuse to do either. And as everyone tried to impress upon me, it was after all a huge compliment.

Christmas here as in Germany, was something I always anticipated with mixed feeling. I wanted to be part of this warm, cosy celebration but I knew though did not comprehend why, that I really could not be. Now so many people were affected by the war and Olive's husband to be would soon be stationed elsewhere when he joined the army straight after the wedding. An air of sadness seemed to hang over the hitherto insouciant village. Food-wise it was very different to German fare and I did not enjoy Christmas cake or mince pies. In fact, I could hardly get them down they were so alien in taste. But Trudel and I were each given little presents of chocolate and a pink satin pouch with three embroidered hankies. I showed my appreciation by kissing Mrs Oliver and Olive but not Mr Oliver who simply was not the kind of person one could kiss. Besides he always reeked of a mixture of pipe tobacco and farm-yard though he washed meticulously daily before every meal at the huge, wide stone kitchen sink.

Topsy and I had become inseparable. We roamed the fields and climbed up the highest haystacks, jumping down covered in hay which we shook off in a fit of glee. The hay was clean and smelled fresh: somehow it smelled of freedom; the higher the stack the better. Topsy was only one year older but to me she seemed far more adult and less inhibited than any girl our age I'd ever met. In spite of both her parents still in Hamburg and her older brother and sister in London, she seemed remarkably unaffected by all the upheaval. Her irrepressible high spirits and infectious laugh were contagious even at the ripe old age of eleven. She also had the most infectious giggle and bright red apple cheeks that went so well with her plump little person and endeared her to everyone. Her eyes were round and shiny like brown marbles and her full mouth was almost as African as her frizzy mop of hair. For me, entirely unfamiliar with the looks of the different races, she was simply that rare person who stood out from the crowd thanks to her delightfully different appearance and her obvious attachment to me. I realised even then that we were the exact opposites and that that was what perversely drew us to each other.

The Saturday of the wedding was damp and cold. I shivered in the unheated first church I had ever entered and felt uncomfortable. Trudy sat somewhere in the back. I alone with another two older girls far more grandly and warmly attired would walk behind my landlady's daughter, a modest bouquet of assorted blooms in our hands, under the gaze of the entire congregation. My hair was washed and as carefully dressed as a friend of Olive's had managed. I believe Trudel too assisted but I was far too nervous to be a reliable witness by then. I longed for it to be over and was only anxious not to spoil the proceedings as I really had no idea what else was expected of me. I tried hard to look happy. Olive wanted me there and there I would be.

Mercifully I was guided by the other two eager, self-assured bridesmaids and after some pleasant communal singing accompanied by a lady on the organ, the brief ceremony took place. I tried hard to see Olive's face but of course her back was to us. My back was to the congregation so I could actually see only the vicar's face. I knew that Mr Oliver was at Olive's side and Mrs Oliver nearby. I had to be prodded by my two bridal colleagues to move with Olive when it was over as I had understood not a word and copied the other two as though sleep-walking.

We left the main hall to partake of the modest wedding fare, not before I remembered to hand over the flowers. Unfortunately the food consisted yet again of mince pies and wedding cake which tasted exactly like the Christmas cake and both of which I would not grow accustomed to for a long time. The sandwiches were filled with ham and the sausage rolls too, were not even offered to us as by now everyone knew that we were forbidden meat products not killed according to Jewish law.

If I had expected festive singing or even dancing in that small reception room above the church hall, I was to be sadly disappointed. People's faces were anxious; the young bride-groom would be leaving to go to war within days. And even if I did not understand, the country was now at war with a deadly enemy. The day ended as it had begun, in a sombre atmosphere. But the young couple looked radiant and Olive gave me a kiss and hugged me warmly.

Those first cold winter days after Christmas we were left to our own devices and to my horror, suddenly Topsy was gone. Most likely she was reunited with her sister Clare who was older than she, but I had no idea where. Trudy's friend Martha never minded my tagging along with them, especially as Abi now mysteriously managed to come to Stotfold far more frequently too. I could never get enough of Martha's singing. It was from her that I had learned of the fine black singer Paul Robson whom she idolised and whose songs she had learned.

"O' my baby, my curly-headed baby," she sang,

"Your Daddy's in the cotton fields etc." And these songs fired my imagination just as my father's always did.

But Martha too was talking of returning to London. She saw no sense in being shut away in the country whilst her parents and all her artist friends were back in the city. She was determined to make her way as a singer and anyone who met her and heard her was equally convinced that she would succeed. To us even at the age of sixteen, Martha Haftel was a star.

AN UNSCHEDULED STOP AT THE SLAUGHTERHOUSE

As Trudy was in need of some schooling, it was decided that a place should be found for her in Shefford where school had been resumed in several church halls. It was decided the Olivers could not look after me without Trudy and Olive there. A new billet was found for me a few streets away, in a tiny terraced cottage with a newly wed couple who were very keen to take in an evacuee.

The little cottage did have an indoor toilet but again no bathroom. However, there was a tiny room with a single bed all for me. It was all I needed especially as I was promised a weekly bath in a tin tub in front of the living room fire which was more than I had ever had at the Olivers. The couple were very pleasant, especially the young husband. They both could hardly have been more than twenty or twenty-one. The young husband spoilt me and brought me little treats when he arrived home from work. I never knew their name or maybe with all the new people I continuously came across their names simply remained unregistered as my stay proved so brief.

To my enormous delight, just as at the Saunders in Ilford, Saturday nights with this couple meant cinema night and I was taken along when they thought suitable. And that is where I first saw 'Huckleberry Finn' With Mickey Rooney; I was mesmerised by this Mark Twain masterpiece and the whole evening was almost as good as it would have been spent with Papi, as my new friends rode to the cinema on their bikes and I rode on the back of my host's. And just as at the Saunders, I shared sweets and chocolate with this nice, loving couple.

It was obvious that my new landlord loved children and longed for a child of his own. His attractive young wife occasionally grew impatient with him when he put a couple of extra slices of tinned peaches on my plate because he noticed how I relished that desert and I was even treated to a dollop of condensed milk on the top. Bath-time was less enjoyable as I was embarrassed to have to bathe in front of my landlady, a tin bath having first been filled with boiling hot water from kettles by her husband who would then graciously disappear until his wife said he could return. But at least it was a regular weekly wash which was something I had missed since leaving London. I could start the week well cleansed, smelling unmistakably of a terrible soap that was supposed to protect you from all threatening germs.

On one particularly delightful occasion my landlord took me saddle-back to visit his mother in her tiny cottage outside Biggleswade. It seemed a very long ride on a cold day but I loved every minute of it. I was grateful to be so well liked and I was fascinated by this absolutely ancient little cottage where virtually everything appeared to be happening in the one front room. There was a huge black hearth which took up all of one side, upon which stood assorted pots and pans, throwing out welcoming heat that thawed out my frozen fingers and toes.

An unfamiliar smell of all manner of ingredients hit my ever alert olfactory senses immediately. The cramped room was modestly furnished with table and chairs that had seen endless use but I felt comfortable and at home in the friendly atmosphere. I could still not converse as fluently as I would have liked, but at least I understood much of what was being said. Everyone else seemed to think I was making excellent strides but I was impatient with myself.

I watched the old lady remove a steaming bundle wrapped in white muslin from a pot she had taken off the hearth. There was my answer to the strange odour. A combination of steaming wet cloth, dough and some other meaty ingredients. Her handsome son beamed as his mother handed him the entire culinary feat to be taken outside and placed in his saddle bag, sauce pan and all.

"That's what you call a steak and kidney pudding—thanks Mum."

"ope you enjoy it tonight for yer dinner." She turned to me smiling.

"O' I can't eat anything with meat in." I informed her tactlessly even though she may have detected a note of regret.

"Goodness gracious—poor child, n o wonder there's nothin' of yer!""

After a biscuit and a warm glass of milk whilst the adults drank tea, we commenced our icy return journey. By now much of the ground was hard and frozen. But my landlord was a first-rate cyclist. Frozen fingers and toes maybe, but I had enjoyed every minute of the outing. Cold weather was something a child from far-distant Munich was well accustomed to.

With most of my new acquaintances once more gone, I was virtually left on my own to roam about Stotfold at will. I knew I would soon be joining the rest of the school in Shefford or Clifton, another nearby village, where I would finally attend classes with the JEWISH SECONDARY SCHOOL.

Maybe it was due to my constantly being outdoors in the freezing cold or perhaps I was not eating properly but suddenly I was gripped by a terrible bout of diarrhoea. One night as I tried to reach the toilet from my room across the tiny hall, I was unable to control it and my pyjama trousers were soiled. For a moment I was lame with misery and shame. I had told no-one of my problem so far and I could not bear the thought of having to call my landlady. I found a clean pair of knickers and as the toilet paper consisted of newspaper anyway, I took a few pieces and wrapped the soiled, stinking pyjama pants in the paper.

At the crack of dawn next morning I tip-toed out of the house, my pitiful bundle under my arm. There was a meadow a short walk from the cottage and mercifully it was covered with a shallow carpet of snow. Not a soul in sight—it could not have been more than six o'clock on this freezing morn. My hard-working landlord left before six each morning on his bike. I found a spot by a bush and buried the fetid bundle with my hands until I could scarcely feel my fingers for the cold. I heaved a sigh of relief. It was done. Now I would return and wash in the kitchen as best I could. There was nowhere else to wash until I had my bath on Friday, three days away. But no-one ever discovered my mortifying secret. I had one other pair of pyjamas and I alternated the trousers. Most nights I slept only in the pyjama top.

On one of my lonesome meanderings I straddled along the length of the entire High Street which was backed by fields. I had never gone quite that far before. But now I was drawn by an appalling stench far more intense than any I had yet experienced. As I drew ever nearer the stench intensified and was accompanied by squeals that made my hair stand on end. I stood rooted to the spot as I noticed rivulets of blood at the entrance of a cavernous building.

What I witnessed that day was never to leave me. Men were unloading lorries upon lorries of pigs which were driven inside the building by the dozen with sticks, lined up as though queuing to be served. I stood aside squashed against the wall, with no-one taking any notice of me and I watched and watched undisturbed.

I watched as pig after pig was driven through a barrier where men stood with electric contraptions they used to give an electric shot to each ear as the animal squealed and was perfectly able to see what was now happening to the pig in front. Screaming, squealing unbearably as it was pushed towards waiting men who held the struggling animal far from sedated and slit its stomach wide open with an enormous knife, not waiting a second before it was hauled by its feet into a steaming cauldron of boiling water. Minutes later it was hanging on a hook with countless other unfortunates ready to be skinned by yet another team of men. All the while the queuing doomed, were waiting to be dealt with similarly, squealing and wriggling wildly after that first dose of sedation, nowhere near unconscious.

I stood and watched unable to move. Not a soul had even attempted to move me or taken the slightest notice of me. My eyes glazed with horror, travelled from the waiting line if victims along to the next in line for torture. It was nothing less. I kept shaking my head but my lips were glued. Not a sound came out of my mouth. I don't know exactly how long I remained in that slaughter—house, certainly over an hour, maybe even two. When I walked or stumbled away finally, I knew beyond all doubt that one day, as soon as I had complete command of my food, I would not eat a slaughtered animal again no matter what. "This is wrong "I kept mumbling to myself. "This is so wrong!" In my ignorance I still did not connect the nice farmers like my former landlord Mr Oliver with this massacre. Yet I had often wondered where those lovely little pigs were being taken in similar lorries to the ones I had just seen.

Only a week or two later the few remaining children here in Stotfold were informed that places had been found for them in Clifton and Shefford. I would be joining an older girl on a farm in Clifton, the village adjoining Shefford. It was good-bye again but my brother and sister were still in Shefford and after the slaughterhouse experience I was not sad to leave Stotfold though it would always remain my first and lasting impression of a green, sleepy rural England.

Chapter Twelve

SCHOOLDAYS IN CLIFTON AND SHEFFORD

Our bus stopped in front of the dilapidated old house that must once have been white. I recognised it immediately from our original arrival from London. Old Shefford looked just as drab and miserable to me as that first time. There were very few shops in this High Street, but at least no slaughter house. I spotted a bakers a few houses down and that cheered me as I loved the smell of newly baked bread and buns. The Inn on the opposite side, a crumpled, antediluvian edifice, forbidding in its aura of a bygone time, looked like a picture of a historic building I had seen in one of Papi's Dickens novels. A kind of darkness lay over the little town because its ancientness was so stark. The lady who had overseen our move now explained that she would be taking me to my new billet in the company of another girl waiting for us inside.

The three of us walked all the way across Shefford to Clifton Road, the start of the village of Clifton. Now we were surrounded by fields and meadows and mooing cows on all sides. This was a good omen. I was quite tired, having had to carry my meagre belongings all the way; but the sight of open country and animals once more as in Stotfold, helped perk me up.

I dragged my suitcase down the dirt drive, endless fields to both sides, sheep just visible further down and the now familiar whiff of pig-swill and dirt. I had become so accustomed to the smell of manure and all the other bucolic odours that they felt like home from home. The girl who had come with us was older and we were a little shy of each other though she made an effort to put me at my ease.

"I'm Henny," she said as we reached the old farm-house at the end of what seemed like an endless muddy drive. I could see the outside toilet in the yard opposite the back of the house and sighed inwardly. It was something I found hard to get used to. It was the inescapable stifling stink I dreaded each and every time. It seemed to intrude into one's senses long after one had left and was somehow more offensive than all the other smells, maybe because it was of human excrement and I was not ready to make allowance for it as I was for animals.

"Oh" I eyed the attractive young girl with new interest. "My sister's name is also Henny. She's my older sister."

"I'm Henny Sokal—I haven't any family here in England. Have you?" She sighed. We were conversing in German as the woman who accompanied us walked slightly ahead, most likely to give us a chance to get acquainted.

"Yes, all my family are in London." But I sighed too.

"Really—"she looked at me in wonder with her enormous velvet brown eyes. "Do you know how lucky you are?" Her question took me by surprise as I saw little difference in having left my family behind in London to hers left behind in Germany, like my friend Topsy.

We did not enter 'DORCAS', the ancient farmhouse, by the front door. Instead, Mrs. Cooper stood ready to welcome us by the back-door, a sunny smile on her rotund face. She was a short, chubby woman with a most friendly, bubbly personality which surprised and cheered me from the first moment we greeted reach other with a kiss on the cheek. Her strong Scotch accent too, was more musical and attractive than the country accents I was used to hearing. She studied me momentarily then gave me another hug.

"Ai—"she said, "You're a bonny wee lass." And she greeted Henny Sokal with equal warmth and enthusiasm. I knew instinctively that her words were complementary.

The woman who had brought us left soon after having a short chat with Mrs. Cooper and we were promised a little tour of the house after we had had some tea, a most welcome suggestion as even I found myself longing for food after a confusing day with no proper meal. I had become anglicised enough to understand that 'tea' thankfully stood for more than the simple liquid I found hard to drink.

I had bidden good-bye for the fourth time to people who had befriended me and given me a home. Where to next and to whom? This new place looked promising if only because Mrs. Cooper was such a sparkling lady and also because my new companion Henny promised to be less bossy than my sister and there was nothing to dislike about her: she spoke little and when she did it was in a gentle, modest voice.

We were told to leave our cardboard cases and miscellaneous paper bundles in the flag-stoned kitchen-larder that led directly into a small stone-floored morning room, empty save an old wooden table and some wooden chairs. The window was open and the dust from the yard had settled on the floor—as well as the smell. The narrowest, darkest staircase I had ever seen, led off the morning room directly upstairs into the bedrooms off it. The ceilings were so low that even I could only just walk upright without crouching. I don't think I was more than four foot eight and Henny Sokal was not much taller though her body was of a well-developed young woman. We looked at each other and grinned—A very new, rather exciting experience.

First, however, we were finally led into that holy of holies: the front parlour and from there straight into the dining room. The door that led from the morning room into the front of the house was covered with what to me looked like a thick blanket. And now we saw that the parlour's door to the front was actually the front door through which we had not entered. To its side was another door leading into the dining room. The stone floors of both rooms were partially covered with generous if dusty multicoloured rugs and the parlour sported a velvet settee and arm chairs in some indefinable red shade it was too dark in the room to discern, with the tiny windows heavily shuttered. It was all very reminiscent of the Oliver's parlour excepting for the remarkably low ceilings everywhere, the staircase and other—worldly aura so that even I could tell that this little house was weary with age. Even though I knew nothing of English history I felt I was stepping into another era. What was more, I found it all very exciting. But why no lights; it was growing dark outside and darker still inside the house; could it be haunted?

"The light—"I said, "may we see this nice room—can we switch on the light, please?" Mrs. Cooper smiled.

"Just a wee moment," she said as she reached for some matches from a container on a side table. It was only then that I noticed two strange lamps on the wall, at least they resembled lamps but there were no light switches anywhere I could see. Then Mrs. Cooper struck a match and ignited one of the lamps. I clapped in delight. It was so unexpected and dramatic. She then ignited the second lamp.

"That's just for now," she explained. "We're not going to need these lights when we're in the dining room. We'll light the ones in there."

I was enchanted by this quaint form of lighting. The parlour took on a dream-like ambience as though someone had thrown a gossamer net over it. I thought it was beautiful as in a fairy-tale. Henny Sokal made no comment but she looked thoroughly nonplussed. It was clear she too had never come across anything quite like this old house.

We were led into the adjoining dining room, a larger, brighter room once Mrs Cooper had lit two little lamps on one wall in similar fashion and had extinguished the lights in the parlour.

"Gas light—"Henny whispered hoarsely to me. "No electricity." Henny's tone implied anything but enchantment now.

The table was already laid with plenty of fresh white bread, butter and the usual large chunk of Cheddar cheese. It was not a cheese I took to maybe because of all the smelly cheeses we were accustomed to in Munich, cheddar was not one of them, being a uniquely English cheese with it's unique, strong flavour. There was a jug of milk on the table too and tomatoes, cucumber and pickles.

"Help yerselves—"Mrs Cooper told us." I'll be right back with yer eggs."

And true to her word she returned soon after with plates of scrambled eggs that tasted remarkably like the eggs we so enjoyed at the Olivers. We ate with ravenous appetites and much appreciation.

Suddenly a huge girl appeared at the door her large head ducked so as to avoid the low door-post"

Ah, there she is—here's our Peg'!" beamed Mrs. Cooper. Peggy was only two years older than Henny as we were soon informed, but she was a head taller and at least double her size. Her face was large as her body and her cheeks round and ruddy as two over-ripe apples. It was a friendly, rotund face full of fun and little else. The big girl was to be our room and bed-mate.

The three bedrooms upstairs consisted of two rooms big enough to hold modest double beds and one tiny room with a single bed known as a box room. We were shown into the second smaller of the two double bedrooms, furnished with a bed against one wall and directly opposite the window, which was inches from the bed. There was a chair squeezed between window and bed, little else. To me it all looked cosy and friendly enough even if the bed looked like an egg squeezed too tightly into an egg-cup. What was visible of wall-paper was floral and jolly.

But cosy it certainly was. I was elected to sleep in between the two older, bigger girls. I liked the idea well enough as I thought both girls very nice. The only trouble was that each had their own peculiar odours, particularly Peggy. But she made up for this drawback by being invariably cheerful, giggly and silly and above all affectionate. She would fall asleep with her arms about me. We soon became great friends as she was just about on my own or below my age level most of the time. She would pinch me where it did not hurt and teach me all manner of rude rhymes I did not understand until much later. She always made me laugh often so late at night, that Mrs Cooper would come in and hit out at her daughter who was hiding under the bedclothes in a fit of giggles with the two of us. Peggy was dependant on her mother in most of what she did, from the moment she was practically dragged out of bed to go to the Spirella Corset Factory in Letchworth, to the moment she went to bed. She loved her mother and took everything in the best of spirits, obviously aware that she needed her mother even if her mother did seem to clout her more than I liked. But Peggy laughed it all off and so I joined in her amusement. There were, however, the rare times when Mrs. Cooper would hit her on the head too hard and Peggy burst out crying. Such occasions brought tears to my own eyes—but they were rare and soon forgotten by all concerned.

Our bed-room had neither lighting nor heating but while the weather was warm and the sun draped the bed early in the morning, the three of us had little to complain. At any rate it was often too warm on a hot night. We would come downstairs after Peggy had had her breakfast earlier and caught the bus up the road to Letchworth Garden City. We could smell the remnants of her breakfast but ours was naturally a far more humble affair of a little Corn Flakes and bread and butter. Fried eggs were left for Sundays and festive days with the accompanying fried bread I loved all crispy and tasting of forbidden ingredients I did not want to know about.

But now began an entirely new phase in my life: real school. I would walk daily to the Clifton Church Hall at the end of the village, where the youngest of us were assembled to be taught by Mr Ganser and Dr. Jacobson whose own children were at the school in Shefford. The only native English teacher was Mr Russell who was to write in my precious autograph album filled with all my old friends' dedications: SILENCE IS GOLDEN. This was written at the end of term in July 1940. Yes, by the age of eleven I had found my tongue again. But I was less than pleased at his inscription, only too aware of the irony.

We were a motley, noisy, 'chutzpadig' (cheeky) bunch and mostly we had more fun than lessons much to Mr Ganser's aggravation. But we had realised early on that this tall, thin man was extremely good-natured and extremely slow in all he did. Dr. Jacobson was an entirely different matter. He was deadly serious, a German refugee and in contrast to Mr Ganser to be feared as the poor man was easily enraged and would throw anything that came to hand at the offending pupil, sometimes with unfortunate consequences. I was once struck quite unexpectedly by a wooden pencil box belonging to my neighbour and presumably aimed at him. It hit my forehead and caused quite a bruise. But there was another side to Dr Jacobson, this very European-looking, swarthy-complexioned man of medium height and dark hair with a strangely menacing look. He was a wonderful teacher of song and music whose task at this stage was also to drum a little arithmetic into our disorderly brains. I learned more from him about English folk and traditional music in a short time than from anyone else. He taught us youngsters in Clifton against all the odds, having left behind who knew what illustrious teaching institutions. His wife taught French in Shefford to the older children. I was not to become acquainted with Mrs Jacobson, Lotte and Heinz Jacobson until later on in

Shefford. For now Dr Jacobson would have to drag himself to Clifton from Shefford where he lived with his family, several times a week.

But no-one would at this stage describe me as a quiet, reticent little girl any longer. I had mastered the basics of my new language and now there was little holding me. I was cheeky enough to crawl under desks in Mr Ganser's classes together with a few other reprobates and even munch a piece of his sandwich my naughty neighbour had dared me eat. I had also been christened by Mrs Cooper as her little Spitfire which I took to be a compliment especially as I did not know what that meant.

We were not long in Clifton Church Hall and by the end of the summer term we were informed that all schooling would henceforth be in Shefford, in another church hall again at the end of that village. But we would be united with the older pupils in what was now officially called THE WHITE HOUSE, the little dilapidated house having had a white brush up. There we would have religious and music tuition as well as receive our kosher midday meals one of whose chief purveyors was the unfortunate Mrs Finklestone.

A disappointingly modest farewell celebration was held that last day in Clifton Church Hall. One of the older boys had written a special song in honour of Mr. Ganser:

"Mr Ganser, we present you this lovely gift

To make you schneller (faster)

We present you this propeller."

And after our united rendition of the ditty, someone handed our kind Mr Ganser who was leaving to return to London, a home-made paper propeller. He took it in the best of sprits. He was that kind of teacher and most likely glad to see the back of this rowdy little lot of refugee ragamuffins who had only just thawed out. I may have thawed out with the rest of the refugee children, but like them I was still very confused about the world about me deep down.

I would compose little ditties whilst sitting on the top deck of a bus to Hitchin or Bedford:

"I hate you

I hate them

I hate everybody

But I love nature!" was one I sang to my own melody over and over.

Hardly the composition of a happy little girl; rather that of a confused one seeking comfort and invariably finding it in open fields or the silky touch of a cat's fur.

SOLLY AND HELGA

The walk to the Shefford Church Hall from where I lived on the edge of Clifton was much further than that to the Clifton Church Hall, but that was only yards from the communal White House. What was more, now our class would be joined by more boys and girls of similar age and hopefully standard. We would begin serious schooling and I would be meeting new fellow classmates. I was quite accustomed to walking long distances in all weathers and it never occurred to me that there must be children who had to do a lot less walking each day and above all, were better equipped clothing wise. I liked the freedom of rambling at my own pace through the verdant countryside, whether alone of with a friend. There were all those ever-changing fragrances depending on the seasons. And the vibrant colours all about me be they green and gold in summer or crunchy white in winter.

But yet again I was confronted with the dreaded task of making new friends as it seemed the Clifton pupils most of whom had been a little older, would be joining a different class or had left the area. As for the Stotfold ones, of whom there had never been more than a few handfuls and mostly of Trudy and Martha's age, they had dispersed to various places or like my dear friend Topsy, had been found new homes with relatives in other parts of England.

Was I in Form Three or Four—I had no idea. Dr Jacobson would still give us music lessons at The White House and his daughter Lotte had joined our group. We had a new English master by the name of Mr Kahn, a very tall, darkish man with a most agreeably deep baritone voice and a pipe that hung perpetually from his mouth and scented the class-room with an instantly recognisable aroma that I liked. He spoke beautifully and clearly. Mr Kahn was to teach us English and history. I hung on his every word and he gave me every opportunity to answer his questions. As he gave us compositions to write frequently, I definitely gained his favour. I loved writing stories. I suppose it was the next step from conversing with ZICKEZANGE and no matter what the subject set, I dived into it enthusiastically. Mr Kahn liked what I wrote and frequently read out my work to the class, a class with most of whom I would be spending the next four years for better or worse. My English was naturally far from perfect but then neither was virtually any other fellow student's there. In fact, some of them still spoke extremely comical English and by now I could distinguish the fact. But there was an English girl amongst us to begin with, by the name of Lillian Weinberger whose younger brother had written me my first love note in England. Lillian was charming and very elegantly dressed. It was she who first introduced me to the wonders of SELFRIDGES in Oxford Street, vicariously that is. As I had no idea where Oxford Street was in relation to any other location in London, Selfridges merely seemed like an oasis which I might one day be privileged to visit. But it was obvious that Lillian's parents were well-to-do and to my regret, Lillian and her brother soon left us.

Helga Schonhorn chose to sit next to me and would continue to do so whenever she had the choice. She was a lovely brunette with straight raven hair to her shoulders, fine full remarkably red lips and altogether perfect features enhanced by her dark eyes and slightly olive complexion. She was my height and slim but somehow at this stage looked older and more developed. She was quiet, unassuming and extremely clever. And of course she was popular from day one. I was very pleased that she had chosen to sit next to me as there was little one could dislike about Helga.

Esher Spitzer, daughter of a well-known rabbi from Germany, was much taller and bulkier than most of the girls and she was also an expert bully. Her younger, far meeker and shorter brother was a nice boy with a sunny face and an enviable talent for maths which soon became apparent. He seemed to like me almost as much as Esther did not and always complimented me on my essays. Where English language, spelling and grammar were concerned I soon skipped ahead faster than most of my class-mates. I also had a far less prominent accent than most including Helga. There was, however, little skipping ahead for me once simple arithmetic transmogrified into the ogres of Geometry, Trigonometry and to a lesser degree to Algebra.

And then there was Solly. Solly Bornstein was also the son of a rabbi but emanating from Poland. He and his sister Esther had come with the school whilst his father and presumably his mother had remained in London. Solly was probably half a year older than I and at that stage quite short and stocky. He had a cheeky, turned up nose, twinkling blue eyes, a wide mouth and somehow his features looked as though they had been thrown together in a great rush, to even themselves out as he went along. He was never untidy, with brown hair worn short, but like most of the boys and girls his clothing could have done with a little more care. I had been taken to see the film of Mark Twain's HUCKLEBERRY FYNN with Mickey Rooney, when I stayed with the young couple in Stotfold. I loved the film and Solly reminded me in looks of the young Mickey Rooney.

Now Solly and I had a strange relationship. He would pick a fight with me at the slightest opportunity and physically attack me until we were locked in battle somewhere in the street, sometimes to stand there for the shortest time clutching at each other, his face red, until I managed to tear myself away. We would both retreat out of breath, with flushed faces unable to make out what had caused these clashes. They were never anything but amiable and nether of us quite understood how they had begun or why Solly's face was invariably so beetroot red.

Sadly Mr Kahn left to return to London and his position was filled by Mrs Klein, a very pleasant woman but for me it was a disappointment. As it was, the following term we would all be moved up to the next form and would be tutored in English and English Literature by the headmaster of the school, the beautifully spoken, highly skilled' goatee-bearded Dr Levine, who resided in a very modest flat annexed to the ASHBY HALL. And this was where from then on our schooling would be taking place. The ASHBY HALL was only a short walk from the Cooper's house. But much was to happen before then.

My brother Abi, meanwhile, shared billets with his friend Imre Sarkany, the Czech student who had taken a liking to Trudy, enthusiastically reciprocated by her. Abi and Imre lived only a few houses away from the little church hall our lessons were held in. Abi had written a play about Spartacus, the great freedom fighter and it was to be performed in yet another church hall at the borders of Clifton village. I was promised a small walk-on part as actually there was not a single child in the cast. I could busy myself back-stage, Abi promised and at curtain call, I could take a bow with the rest of the cast. Trudy too, helped back-stage and had a small speaking part.

"We do not fear the blood-hounds—"sang the slaves,

"We do not fear their teeth.

We fight for our freedom

Until we cease to breathe!" Trudy had, I believe, composed the melody to go with the poem. And Abi had worked for months with dictionaries and Thesauruses to perfect his still wobbly grammar and vocabulary. We all thought it was magnificent.

It all went very well and I was so proud of my brother and sister. I did not doubt that one day Abi would be a famous playwright. Trudy had also accompanied the song backstage with her treasured accordion that had travelled with her from Germany. But Abi would soon be going to London to join up. Imre too would be leaving. And as he hoped to become a doctor he would go to University as soon as he passed the necessary exams. Abi had hoped to take his Intermediate Exam (Inter BSC) but that would have to wait until after the war now. Everything had changed. Even I understood that things would never be the same again. Munich belonged with people who, as I saw it, had betrayed us. I longed desperately to be with my parents and they in turn, were very keen to leave London and come to the country to be near us.

It seemed impossible for my parents to find suitable accommodation for the entire family as Oma Lowy too wanted very much to be reunited with her son. She was seventy-six years old now and though independent as ever, without a word of English, she needed to be with her family.

Suddenly I received a letter from my parents that they had rented a little house in Harefield, Middlesex—a whole house to themselves! Oma was with them already and so was Henny. There were three bedrooms and most importantly an Anderson Air Raid Shelter in the garden, as the situation in London was growing more and more dangerous and Harefield was only a stone's throw out of London. I could come for a short time and attend the local school but would then return as The Jewish Secondary School was a first-rate institution and Bedfordshire was much further from the capital and therefore far safer.

It was wonderful to have this brief interlude with my beloved parents and grandmother who seemed to have grown even smaller. When the air-raid sirens sounded she exclaimed: "a BEWED, a BEWED!" obviously meaning air-raid and rushed into the garden to take her place in the shelter. We found it all hugely amusing but my dear parents' English was not much better, especially Papi's, though with his sense of humour, he was inclined to make fun of the foreign words rather than simply mispronouncing them. I loved his sense of humour as I loved everything about my father though I would correct him sternly, showing off my own superior knowledge. Papi was as ever immersed in his work and his poetry would never be written in any other language but Yiddish.

I visited the local school a couple of times but since I would soon be returning to Bedfordshire, I was excused from further visits though the children here were very friendly. Maybe also, as I could now converse with them, there was no longer that huge gulf between us. Apart from being with my family in a pleasant, modern little house with indoor plumbing, I was hugely impressed that Harefield was close to the famous Film Studios in Elstree as I had already become a film buff.

One other momentous occurrence: I had my first taste of real KELLOGS Corn Flakes with fresh sweet cream! Once or twice I had been given some kind of cereal, but mostly porridge which I hated. This, however, was a taste of heaven and I could not get my fill. My darling father, as ever too acquiescent where I was concerned, especially at this bewildering time, allowed me to gobble down three platefuls to the hue and cry of the rest. And for my part, I shall never forget that blissful taste of fresh, crunchy KELLOGS flakes with plenty of cream. They would never taste like that again. Maybe it had something to do also with my father seated opposite me, watching me with a beatific smile on his beloved face as I went on gobbling my breakfast.

Helga Schonhorn and I had forged a close friendship much as I had done with Ilse Herzberg though Helga could not have been more different from the gamine Topsy. She was easily the most popular girl in the class and as unassuming and quiet as I was loquacious. Helga would remain a steadying influence. She did not as I did, resent the strict religious rules nor the frequent lectures delivered mainly by the 'Queen' Dr Judith Grunfeld.

Solly Bornstein, what is there to say about a boy who was highly intelligent, always friendly, good at sports and football and particularly delighted at beating me at ping pong, no matter how hard and determined a fight I put up? He, like Helga, was very popular because he had such a pleasant nature. He seemed to have grown taller and slimmer within weeks; his puckish, far from handsome face with its turned up nose and intense blue eyes somehow appealed to me for no reason I could think of, especially as I had only recently fallen head over heels in love with the inimitable, beautiful Errol Flynn. And yet for all that, Solly could make my heart beat faster.

Esther Spitzer and her brother, who seemed at some time to have admitted to liking me to some of the other boys, a truly courageous step in our buttoned-up class atmosphere, were like chalk and cheese. He was short, quiet and brilliant; she was very tall and heavily built. I believe she was at least a year older than most of us and she certainly lacked her brother's intelligence. But worst of all was her bullying. She missed no opportunity to assemble a few of her cronies to taunt me. Why me—who knew. Had it not been for Helga constantly at my side, my life could easily have been made miserable. She tried quite openly to separate Helga and me. But as it was, it hardly touched me as I soon found a few more older friends like Jochwed Heidenstein, Klara Schiffman, Katie Welcher and more as time went on. Eventually Esther joined her family back in London whereas her brother stayed throughout to take his Matriculation Exams with the rest of us and would excel in mathematics as had been more than predictable from the outset. The class-room was a brighter, happier place once she was gone.

Helga's parents had not been able to emigrate and it had soon become obvious that like all Jews trapped in Germany, they were in great peril. Helga spoke less and less of them. The same was true of the majority of my classmates. I knew I was fortunate as was Solly, the Spitzers and Jacobsons. We were the lucky ones. Jochewed Heidenstein, Jock as she was known, was not. But every one of us was engrossed in our new life here in Bedfordshire; that much we all had in common plus the fact that most of the younger ones like me, had come with a 'Kindertransport' and had thus shared that trauma.

The Jewish Secondary School run by Dr Schonfeld in London was a strictly orthodox establishment which may have accounted for the increasingly inedible kosher meat so scarce and hard to come by. It would of course have been far kinder to man and beast not to serve it at all. As for refrigeration—there was none which was probably why fish was never served to my knowledge. But what the reason was for the accompanying vegetables and even deserts to be so grossly inedible, smelly amd rancid, would remain an enigma. Maybe the fact that they had to make do with a handful of ingredients for far too many hungry mouths and had thus augmented it with water. But I for one could rarely get a morsel down and became even scrawnier.

The school's official Headmaster was a Dr Levine whom I had yet to meet. He was a highly qualified Doctor of Philosophy who taught the upper classes in London. But soon he was due to come to Shefford with his wife. Meanwhile Dr Judith Grunfeld had taken over as head and so far as I knew, never quite relinquished that position although apart from her superb knowledge of Jewish History and Jewish laws and edict and her commanding manner could hardly hold a candle to Dr Levine. She was a handsome woman, ultra orthodox with a turban instead of a 'Sheitel' (wig) and clad perpetually in dark suits that flattered her trim figure. She drove a small car that might have been an Ausin, which impressed everyone. There were few ladies to be seen driving their own cars. But she was intimidating and it took a very brave youngster to hold his own when in the presence of THE QUEEN as she soon became known throughout the school. Children either adored her or were terrified of her. Either way, she was a great disciplinarian. Darling Trudy fell against her sword early on and was duly expelled. As it was, Trudy was now too old to begin serious tuition and she was happy at her release. I stood my own later on but in those early days she managed to intimidate me as much as most everyone else. Unlike most, however, I never quite succumbed to either her intimidation or her sometimes quite unexpected charm offensive.

Sugar, butter, sweets and eggs were rationed but as I had no idea what that meant and at any rate, our landladies were naturally in charge of Ration Books, it was up to them to see that we received our fair share. I was very happy at the Coopers and never gave food a thought. I doubt, however, if I ever had butter on my bread but I did have an egg on Sundays and I was treated with affection. In fact, as German air attacks on London increased, I began to fret and asked Mrs Cooper if she could help find a place where my parents and Oma could stay.

Mrs Cooper's eldest daughter Ella was married to a very prosperous farmer who owned a great deal of land and life-stock in Clifton. They lived in a beautiful old beamed residence even I could appreciate—and it did have indoor plumbing. I had been taken there several times for afternoon-tea in their lovely, fragrant gardens and had played with her little daughter Rosemary. No smell of cattle or pigs as they were kept well away from the residence.

Ella Hale was a serious, no-nonsense lady, prim, kind and exceptionally unostentatious for a woman of her status. Her husband too was informal and sometimes took me for a ride in his Jaguar with Peggy and Henny Sokal. He was a pleasant looking man and certainly did not smell like the other male farmers I had met. He was also invariably well dressed and well scrubbed, the perfect squire.

It was to these kind people, into their beautiful home that my mother and father and Henny would be made welcome until other accommodation could be found. As for Oma, she would be staying with us at the Coopers in the little room opposite our bedroom. The steep, narrow and unlit staircase she would have to climb was a minor hindrance under the circumstances hardly taken into consideration. She would also have to be brought food from Shefford as the walk was too far and she would touch nothing that was not kosher. But my father would take care of his mother's needs. All that mattered was that they would all be out of the city and close to each other. My cousin Hilde too was found accommodation in Shefford and would keep her grandmother company in the day-time.

DORCAS was soon full to bursting but during the day Peggy, Henny Sokal and I were out so that Oma would be left sitting in an old arm-chair in the dusty breakfast room holding her prayer book or looking out of the grimy window where she would see endless pig-sties and smell the poor creatures' odour until it became part and parcel of life. And invariably she would smile her heartrending, bitter-sweet smile at anyone who addressed her and to her relatives she would respond with 'leb' lange' as she always had done. The Coopers called her BUBA and adored the undemanding, modest, pious old lady who never grumbled or complained though her life must have been one of great hardship. But so long as she had her 'SIDDUR' (prayer book) and was left undisturbed, she seemed content.

She would ask me to sweep the floor covered in dust with one of those huge brooms whose heads were made of thick straw. I obeyed before I left for school, often before my cousin Hilde arrived.

But one morning my father came early and saw what I was doing. He took the broom from me and confronted his mother with uncharacteristic severity.

"Mother, couldn't you have waited till Hilde arrived?" He asked with ill disguised anger. "Can't you see how thin and undernourished the child is? I don't want her breathing in all that dust!" He admonished his mother though he never raised his voice.

At the time I saw it as just another token of Papi's love for me, unaware that I really had a bad colour, was very thin and as it turned out the constant itch I experienced all over was diagnosed as scabies, a most unpleasant skin infection. But my grand-mother I now realise, adored her dearest deceased daughter's child Hilde and certainly favoured her above any of her other grandchildren. It is not so difficult to understand to-day. At the time it scarcely troubled me, but it must have offended my father greatly.

For me, my existence at Dorcas, indeed at Clifton and Shefford, was exciting and slightly unreal. My parents were now close by as were my siblings; I had made at least a few new friends and above all, there were sweet animals and wonderful vegetation all about me. If I scratched a great deal it only amused Peggy and thus set us both off giggling. I was certainly less troubled than I had been since I left London.

Chapter Thirteen

ASHBY HALL, MY DEVOUT OMA; SOLLY'S UNFORTUNATE OUTBURST.

The Reverent Ashby had donated his building, a historic church hall, to the Jewish school. This philanthropic, remarkable Christian, obviously moved by parentless refugee evacuees, had from the goodness of his heart given over the lovely old building for prayer and tuition to the Jewish school. I like to think he may have been impressed too, by Dr. Levine's stature, his fine proud bearing though his clothes were far from immaculate and often frayed and he was even mocked by some ignorant, impudent pupils. He was his own man as was his artist wife who obviously did not give a fig for outward appearance and was herself a surprisingly unprepossessing lady. But as soon as her erudite tall, goatee-bearded husband opened his mouth you knew you were confronted by a totally different teacher to any other in the school. His wife kept to herself and was rarely seen even at High Holidays. Religious practice was obviously of little interest to her though her husband never failed to do his duty leading services and welcoming the congregation.

Dr Levine would be our English and English Literature master in our final years and take us through to Matriculation. But at this stage all I knew of Dr. Levine was that he resided in the tiny flat that came with the somewhat dilapidated building with his artist wife. And I would see him only at services held there for High Holidays and which it was mandatory to attend. I was overawed by his biblical appearance in those days and when he smiled and made some cryptic remark, all I could do was blush and remain silent. It was he who pointed out to me right at the start, that I must be proud of my name Mella and live up to it as it came from the Latin and meant honey. The reminder stayed with me and has done throughout my life, because I liked being thought of as sweet as honey, even if I knew that to be far from the truth more often than not.

Oma would have had only a short walk to the Ashby Hall as it was literally minutes up the road from DORCAS, the Coopers' house. And I believe she did attend until the weather became more inclement and she herself weaker. For my part I could not wait to be schooled at the Ashby Hall, so close to where I lived. But I knew I would still have a long wait.

Without much warning and to my huge disappointment, Mr Kahn bade us farewell one day and left for London and his family the next. Mrs. Klein took his place within weeks. She was short, slightly plump with a friendly face and a nice smile—and miracle of miracles, she actually wore lipstick! She was also English whereas so many of the other teachers had like us been torn from their homes and often family too. Naturally she taught us English and English History. We got on well but I had preferred the laconic, pipe-smoking Mr. Kahn who had also been English and had been so nicely spoken. Maybe it was simply that never to be erased adoration from way back of Lehrer Berlinger, who was still very much on my mind.

Most of my class-mates were billeted in Shefford. So if I was quite often late, at least I had the excuse that I lived a great deal further from the Church Hall at the far end of Shefford, even beyond the White House where we took meals and went for religious tuition and Jewish History lessons (SHIURIM as they were called) given by Dr Grunfeld—far from coveted by me.

It was also at the White House we assembled for all too rare music lessons and song. As there was no piano that task was made all the more difficult for Dr Jacobson. But he persisted against all odds and though it may not have become apparent to me for many years later, he taught us a wealth of English song repertoire that would last a life-time, not omitting even the words to Handel's "See the conquering hero come" from his Messiah, though our English was so poor and some of us like myself were not yet twelve years old. At the time, those words sounded comical and it was difficult to suppress the urge to chuckle, especially if I caught Solly's or Helga's eye.

"Drink to me only with thine Eyes" would be chanted with faces strained to capacity to keep straight, until the final words; until it glows and smells I swear not of itself but thee!' at which the entire class would simply explode and poor Dr. Jacobson was defeated. On the other hand Barbara Allen's cruelty and subsequent come uppance, wouls bring tears to my eyes and I was often called out to sing the song of the vainglorious beauty's fate.

It was on a sweltering Sunday afternoon that we found ourselves assembled for a walk to the Letchworth villa of the Sassoon family, in response to their gracious tea-invitation. The walk entailed trudging through Shefford, parts of Clifton and much of endless, wild, bedraggled Arlesey, until mercifully w we reached the town of a more civilised Letchworth and a villa not unlike that of the Lichtigs. By that time most of us were not unlike coach horses that had not been fed and watered throughout a tedious journey. In fact upon our arrival as we were ushered straight into the vast gardens, presumably to save the residence from an invasion of miserable urchins, I sank down on the grass and refused the sardine paste sandwiches, gulping down some watery lemonade as though it were my last and only chance of survival.

It was not long before we had to line up and one by one thank our far from gracious hosts an Indian Jewish couple of great renown and wealth, for their gracious hospitality. I must admit I was shocked by the lack of anything close to what I had expected like some delicious delicacy normally out of our reach. I felt personally affronted at this discourteous treatment, even if we were poor refugee children and they great benefactors of some kind as had been hammered into our heads for days. I bitterly resented Dr. Grunfeld's insistence on our attendance. We might be no more than children, but humiliation was something every refugee was familiar with.

By the time I reached home, I felt degraded and humiliated and found I had tears in my eyes. I do not know how the others felt as I was too tired and hungry to discuss the matter. Maybe those who were able to stomach the sardine paste sandwiches did not feel quite so bad. I did not see Solly or Helga there as many of the boys were in Shefford practising on the football ground beyond the railway lines. And girls could be excused if they were unwell, a pardon not to be in my grasp for another year and a half. I had trundled along on that awful, hot walk to Letchworth, expecting a pleasant reception from people I had heard spoken of with veneration. And our dismissive treatment had felt like a personal slight as I was made to feel inferior as none of our foster parents had ever made me feel: I was a poor, ill-clad, scruffy, unimportant little refuge with whom these great, wealthy people wanted as little contact as possible. Why had they invited us in the first place?

THE FAREWELL MARCH

It was difficult for me to like Dr Jacobson because you really never knew where you stood with him: he was so eccentric. At least that was what I was led to believe. In other words he was a laughing matter, someone to make jokes about. Besides we were afraid of him as he lost his temper without warning. And yet I loved these often far too short music lessons, eagerly soaked them up never to let them go. He was very nice to me during those music lessons, appreciating my interest and my quick uptake of the tunes and words.

Of course the teachers would have known that Dr Jacobson's unpredictable outbursts were not mere eccentricity. And there were times of late when his unpredictability was dangerous. He resided with his wife and Lotte and Heinz somewhere in or near Shefford. His appearance became increasingly disturbing; his face looked darker, his eyes even under glasses, truly menacing—but that was far from always. When we all sang together to his perfect guidance and satisfaction, the man was what he must have been in Germany, the perfect teacher with an unlimited love of his subject and pupils.

These treasured music lessons became fewer and fewer much to my disappointment. And one day the rumour spread like wildfire that Dr Jacobson was mad. What was worse, that he had been admitted to the ARLESEY LUNATIC ASYLUM. Arlesey was a small, unkempt and overgrown village between Letchworth Garden City, Clifton and Shefford, with almost more public houses than visible family residences apart from a few cottages. It was undoubtedly the least prepossessing, most uninviting village in the entire neighbourhood. On the other side lay the far prettier village of Shillington. And Clifton, with its ancient church and beautiful, far-reaching open country-side had its very special charm. But Arlesey was a forbidding, unpleasant little village which, by dint of its feared hospital, its wild, overgrown hedges and trees, was a place best avoided. All of these villages were within touching distance of each other and could, in fact had to be reached on foot as there was hardly any transportation.

It was inevitable that we would all be tempted, goaded on by the seniors, to make jokes about a lunatic asylum all the more as we scarcely understood what exactly it meant. When Lotte was in class, no-one spoke of her father, however. I never told her how much his musical instructions meant to me for the simple reason that it would take many years before I realised it myself.

One morning Dr. Grunfeld entered the large room upstairs in the Church Hall where our lessons were in progress. We rose as one as we were taught to do. I cannot recall the words but they were few and terse: Dr. Jacobson had passed away! We would be going there that afternoon to pay our respects—the entire class. Suddenly, to our intense consternation, there was an outburst of laughter right behind me. I did not need to look round to know where it came from. Solly was unceremoniously sent outside still rocking with laughter. I felt terribly sorry for him—the strange thing was that it felt as if my own hair was standing on end at the sound of this uncontrollable laughter that seemed to follow him all the way outside the class-room and beyond. It was quite obvious that he had no control over the hysterical sounds that were emanating from him. I saw him only briefly as we all left the building; his face was red and blotchy. He spoke to no-one.

That walk to the Arlesey Asylum took well over an hour each way as we struggled, most of us bare-legged, with overgrown, unkempt woodland, thorns, wild bushes and stinging nettles finally to catch sight of the huge, austere monster of a building in dark, hostile, untended grounds so vast that it was difficult even for the few teachers sent with us on the march, to find the entrance. With beating hearts we stood in silence waiting. I shivered. Would we be seeing our dead teacher? Would we have to walk through that cavernous building about which such awful stories had circulated? I was devoid of sympathy, consumed only with dread. The day was so bleak and everywhere around us was dark and eerie. The black heads of gigantic trees in this grey mist added to the haunting desolation as we stood motionless shivering, waiting for our teachers' orders to proceed. Soon we might be facing our dead master and I knew one thing—I did not want to take a step further.

Finally it was decided that this, the youngest class need not proceed. We had paid our respects. A sigh of relief must have been audible as we began our trudge back cold, hungry and apprehensive. I thought only of my own discomfort and dread instead of my teacher whose all too brief months of fine tuition must have inspired many more for the rest of their lives. I thought little about the man of such high degrees of learning, torn from who knew what exalted position in Germany, driven to madness by the Nazi beast, now lying in this God-forsaken hell-hole, destroyed in the prime of life.

The service at the Ashby Hall that Sabbath was attended to bursting and Dr Levine, in his modest way, shook everyone's hand at the door after the service. I could detect several food spots on the black jacket he wore each Sabbath and put it down to his wife's failings. She was a strange looking bird-like woman and we were all inclined to make fun of her. I did not think she did him justice.

I cannot say whether he gave the sermon or whether Dr Schonfeld had purposely come from London for this sad occasion. I had already sneaked out as soon as possible. I hated these services but this time remained until the main service was over as leaving earlier would have been noticed and been considered a grave lack of respect. But at that age all death meant to me was something ghostly, threatening and unknown. It did not directly connect with the person who had died; instead it seemed a horrible force that might grab a hold of me.

Papi had come to the service and I would be accompanying him back to share the parents' lunch, preferable to that at the White House. Abi, Henny, Trudy and I all assembled in the Hale kitchen to partake of tinned salmon, boiled eggs, tomatoes, lettuce and cucumber. Mrs Hale had kindly made her huge kitchen available to us for this shared repast. For me the most edible part of the meal was the custard that invariably followed. Oma Lowy was unable to walk such distances and Abi and Papi had brought food on Friday as Oma would not eat food that had been carried on the Sabbath. Hilde stayed with her most Saturdays but on occasion she was able to join us at the Hales. Somehow walking with Papi dispelled any thought of death that sad week-end of Dr. Jacobson's Memorial Service. We walked hand in hand that long walk through the ever colourful, fragrant country-lanes, chickens, cows and geese audible every which way we turned, their cacophony never failing to sound like an indictment to my ears; but how I loved the ambience of the lovely little village.

OMA'S SWOLLEN FEET

I was suffering from scabies still and had to have a fetid ointment, strongly smelling of every unpleasant thing I could think of, rubbed into my skin. The reason for my affliction was evidently lack of hygiene and regular baths. In fact at the Coopers as at the Olivers, there was no hot water let alone bathroom. I had to go to the White House where with many other children, I would have to take my turn in the bath lottery as there were a mere three bathrooms for the countless unwashed.

My grandmother simply never complained though life must have been fraught with nothing but hardships for her. She rarely went outside. It was a swampy back-yard for her little boots to have to trudge through even just to reach the stinking hole that was our bog. Let alone steer clear of the pig-sties and general mayhem of a farm-yard she never could have dreamed she would be residing by. Yet somehow she kept herself immaculate as though she was able to float over everything. And she never failed to thank the Almighty for his mercies.

The Coopers adored her and thought 'Buba' was nothing short of a saint as she sat praying, eating so little that I hardly ever saw her taking her food. Her small frame was always clad in clean long black skirts and dark blouses. On High Holidays she might wear a treasured silk blouse. I had no idea whether she had more than one because they always looked the same: immaculate shiny, silk-satin with ruffled collar buttoned to the neck and long sleeves with cuffs. Nothing was ever soiled. How she kept herself so clean was obviously something I took little interest in at the time. But it was little wonder that the adults around her admired this brave little woman who had come from a different world and never lost her dignity.

Did I love this tiny lady so beset with inner grief yet so stoic outwardly? Could I love this dour woman poured over her prayer book by the grime-encrusted window in the breakfast room, mumbling her prayers? I wondered often what she could be praying all day and I had begun to wonder quite a bit about God too. If I asked her she would simply reply: "leb' lange, Meidele—"as she always did; as she always had done. It was no reply really as she wished everyone a long life. Sadly at the time I could not feel close to her as I did to my maternal Tennenbaum grandparents who could be funny and happy, laugh and sing. They possessed warmth Oma Lowy seemed to lack. This grandmother prayed. Had I been older and wiser I might have admired her for it as it really seemed she was praying for the whole Jewish people at this terrifying time, in its never-ending struggle to survive. But was that what she spoke to God of in her prayers? Maybe that was what puzzled her son too.

My father's love for his mother was less overt than it was for his wife and children. Papi would dedicate his highly successful book of poetry (MEIN TATE DER SEUFER) in a few years' time to his father and he had written poems about his mother too. But it was obvious to whom he had given his life-long affection and devotion. It was simply not easy to get close to Oma Lowy yet my cousin Hilde certainly had found a path through her deceased mother, whose death Oma had never ceased to mourn. As for me, I was too rapt up in my new existence here in Clifton and Shefford to give my grandmother the attention I wish I had done.

From Form Three in Clifton Church Hall with Mr Russell and dear old Mr Ganser, to Lower Four in Shefford Church Hall with Mr Kahn and the music lessons with Dr Jacobson; my life drew on. Endless walking that could never be avoided, in bad weather, cold wet, snow and ice. Then Oma caught cold. The nights were freezing cold and we had practically no heating at the Coopers. A small paraffin stove had been put in the breakfast room for Oma. It was smelly and gave off fumes that made everyone cough, including Oma.

Meanwhile my cousin Berni, Auntie Ida's son, had come on a brief visit. He was a Captain in the Royal Air-Force and looked terrific in his spanking new blue uniform, jaunty officer's cap and fetching moustache. He was very young and very handsome and to top it all, he took me for a brief ride on his motor cycle around Shefford and Clifton. My heart simply swelled with pride and adoration.

Abi was to join the Army Intelligence Corps and had decided to postpone his Inter BSC exams until war's end. There was more urgent business to be done now. Trudy waited eagerly to hear if she would be accepted in the WAAF (Women's Auxiliary Air Force) as soon as she reached the required age and her English passed the interviews she was asked to attend. She could not wait to get away especially since my father had been informed by Dr. Grunfeld that she was no longer welcome at the school. Moreover he was warned that she was a disrupting influence—in particular on me.

Trudy had been fighting her own private battle with the omnipotent 'Queen' from day one. The two were never meant to meet and I for one wholly applauded my sister's brave stance as I too, had I had Trudy's advantage in years and general devil may care attitude, might have confronted this headmistress, who I felt had usurped Dr Levine's rightful position. I disliked her turban with never a hair showing; I disliked her strict adherence to every word written in the Thora though I would not have found the words at the time to voice this. Above all, I disliked her overt self-confidence and expectance of total subservience. Never was the name 'Queen' more apt. What Trudy had done or probably said, I never discovered. At any rate she would look wonderful in a WAAF uniform as she had recently grown tall and slim and many a soldier had whistled after her when we walked along the wild country-lanes picking black-berries. Her complexion was fine and clear and she had grown her hair and curled and combed it into a page boy.

But I was soon to discover the reason for Mutti's scarcely disguised disapproval of my cheeky sister at that time. It appears that at being stopped at the first frontier upon finally leaving Germany and having to open their suitcases for inspection, my fifteen years old sister told one of the guards that being subjected to such treatment was absolute chicanery. Somehow Mutti managed to appease the furious young guard when she explained about her daughter's long stay in hospital as he was about to send them back to Germany. As Mutti told it she trembled every time she thought of it since. How easily they might not have made it out of Germany!

Henny and Hilde, though both determined to work in London eventually, had taken on war-work in a hastily converted barn in Clifton, where they were producing war materials for the forces. I had peeped in at the door once or twice, as no outsider was allowed there officially all war-work being secret. It seemed very jolly to me, with a wireless constantly blaring, much to my envy. I could hear Vera Lynn, Gracie Fields trilling 'Sally' and Anne Shelton, whose voice I particularly loved.

I missed the music from the wireless which had introduced me to the lovely English and American tunes of the day. It had been plentiful at the Lichtigs but since then, apart from the Olivers, there had been none. Mrs Cooper was a religious Chapel lady who with her husband and Peggy walked up the road to the Chapel each Sunday morning. There was no wireless—at least if there was, it was not tuned to music. I had learned many tunes of the day from those brief fond moments and thanks to the lovely Martha I had also learnt a few Deanna Durbin songs, so well suited to Martha's voice.

"I like to whistle

'Cause it makes me merry

Makes me feel so very

Tra, la, la, la, la, la, la" And I too would whistle the last verse as I was pretty proficient at whistling.

Henny Sokal had left. I believe after inspection of our billet, it was decided that the bed the three of us shared and which was no more than a large single, was not suitable for three especially as Peggy was a large, strapping sixteen years old. I am not sure if other lack of amenities were also taken into consideration. I know it was decided that I was to stay and Henny would leave. She returned to London soon after as she did not wish to remain with the school. I was sad—but not for long.

The doctor's visits to Oma seemed to become more frequent as her cough did not improve and the word pneumonia cropped up ever more frequently. Yet the days had grown warmer and longer and soon the early spring would turn into summer. But if anything, Oma's condition deteriorated and for the first time she would take to her bed in the day-time, in the tiny room just across from our bedroom. I detected the chamber pot under the bed but as that was standard and there was one in Mr and Mrs Coopers' bedroom too, it was obviously de rigueur. There was one under our bed too but Peggy and I would only laugh when it peeked out from under the bed. There were enough pungent odours already. Now, however, I frequently saw Hilde or Papi carry the covered pot surreptitiously down those narrow, steep stairs.

Papi came more frequently to Dorcas too so that he could see the doctor. His English was very poor but either Hilde or I would help out and it was easy enough to see that Oma was very ill. She, however, said little, even less than usual. Her prayer book was in constant use but she slept a good deal more and ate even less though hot soup was provided for her from the White House and laboriously carried all the way through Shefford, by Abi, Henny, Hilde but mostly Papi. As I was at school I could only help occasionally, but I was not allowed to carry plates.

The days were warm and sunny and soon it would be the Jewish New Year and still Oma was no better. The doctor came and went. There were hushed discussions with Papi and Abi as he could translate and converse with the doctor. Papi looked distraught and Mutti came as often as it was thought proper without imposing on the Coopers even more.

I would look in on Oma every morning before school. To br honest as she looked more and more drawn and wan I began to be afraid. Was she going to die? I had heard the whispers and felt Papi's mounting apprehension. Oma had pneumonia and although the doctor obviously did his best, there seemed little improvement. No-one spoke of her going to hospital Maybe Oma herself would not hear of it but several strange elderly ladies, apparently nurses, came to the house and attended to her whilst I was away during the day. I saw these nurses rarely.

Though the days were fine and the evenings bright beyond our bed-time, Dorcas, which had always been a dark house with scarcely any lighting, now seemed to have grown even gloomier as I walked up the stairs towards the bedrooms. In the summer the smells of human sweat, urine plus the never-ending manure stench, became far more oppressive. My own pet hate was sweat. Peggy had her own smell and though I was used to it, I was never able to ignore it. No matter where one went, at bus stops, in the little shops or bakeries, everyone seemed to smell of sweat. Perhaps I smelled too. I took as much care as was possible, but the amenities were sadly lacking. Some of our more mature class-mates were also beginning to be unpleasant to sit next to. Helga and I rushed to find seats next to one another whenever possible. Next term we would be having our lessons at the Ashby Hall. We were determined not to be parted.

These last few weeks there had been much movement at the house and Papi or Abi had sometimes stayed with Oma all night. Meanwhile, as ROSH

HASHANAH was drawing so near it was obvious that I had absolutely nothing to wear. In fact I had grown out of most of the few clothes I had been given by the Jewish Board for Refugees. Mutti, who had begun to buy little trinkets in Hitchin with the few pounds still at her disposal, had managed to sell them in London and make who knew how small a profit. Now to my delight, we were to take the bus to Bedford to find a little summer dress for me as there was a large Woolworth in the town. Bedford was also richly endowed with cinemas—four in all—and I hoped we might stop to see a film but I did not want to push my luck so decided to say nothing.

It was Mutti's intention to find a basic cottage here for the whole family and remain in Bedfordshire until war's end as I needed to remain with this first-rate Grammar school and my parents would not leave me behind again if at all possible.

It was July and I was on holiday. The day was very warm as Mutti and I caught the bus from the Clifton bus stop outside the bakers' who baked such tantalisingly sweet-smelling buns. Of course my darling mother could not deny my pleading looks as we absorbed the olfactory delights of the bakery. Armed with a bag of warm buns safely stored in Mutti's bag, we boarded the green double-decker when finally it drew to a halt. I loved sitting upstairs so I could observe the lovely countryside as the bus rolled along and Mutti kindly obliged.

It turned out to be a momentous afternoon. I found the dress of my dreams not, naturally, at Roses the fancy department store of which I could only dream—but at Woolworth! I loved it at once. It was blue and of a gleaming, satiny material. The dress was exactly my size and there was a matching bolero to go with it. My heart leapt with delight. Mutti was not sure if she had quite enough money but when it was explained to us that there was a reduction and Mutti worked it all out, with added coaxing from me, the dress was mine. I did not think that there was a finer dress in all the world as we left the Bedford Woolworth, my parcel clutched tightly, proudly, my head in the clouds.

But the wonders of that momentous day were far from over. We walked over to THE GRANADA Cinema, the grandest and most modern in the town. And it was there that I was to start a life-long love-affair with the most beautiful film-star ever: Errol Flynn. The film was Robin Hood and a strange thing happened. Yes, the star held me spell-bound but so did the music. That day was doubly blessed as not only was I to harbour a life-long infatuation with the incomparable Errol & with the music of Erich WOLFGANG KORNGOLD, whose name I would learn to revere only decades later but whose music became precious to me from then on. One day perhaps, Mutti and I might walk that short stretch to the fancy KADOMA CAFÉ for hot chocolate and cake as we had done so often in Munich—but right now my cup was more than full.

Buns devoured in the cinema; Mutti had bought two and had insisted they were for me. Dress clutched possessively in the large Woolworth bag, we dismounted almost in the front of Dorcas as Mutti wanted to see Oma though she lived in Clifton, I, of course ran in to try on the dress. It was a little large just as Mutti had hoped and everyone thought it was magnificent. Mrs Cooper said I looked bonny in her loveable Scottish twang and I could not wait to show Peggy too.

It was the last day in July 1942. The night was very warm. Oma's door was wide open and I thought I would say good night if she was not asleep.

"May I come in Oma?" I asked.

"Come MEIDELE—"she replied in an almost inaudible whisper.

I crept in shyly, but remained standing by the door.

"Come and sit on the bed." She invited.

She had only a thin blanket over her tiny frame on this hot night. The room as ever was dark but her little face was lit up by the half—moon outside the soiled, small closed window. I approached gingerly

"Oma, aren't you hot? Do you want the window open?" I asked avoiding looking directly at her. Her face was so pinched and white and by the slurred speech I knew she was not wearing her teeth though they were not visible on the chair beside her. She was always so tidy. But she was not wearing her

'SHEITEL' (wig) and it was the first time I had ever seen her snow-white head of short-cut hair. I felt terribly uncomfortable and tried not to stare.

"How are you feeling—"I managed to stutter at length.

"May I bring you something—a cup of tea?" But I knew full well that she would not drink from a cup from Mrs Cooper's kitchen. "I—I can take your cup down and—"I added hastily as I noticed an empty cup on the floor.

"No, no, Mellale—"she said taking my hand in her clammy bony one. "Look, look at my feet—"she went on pointing at her uncovered feet.

"Yes, Oma"

"Can't you see Meidele—can't you see how swollen they are? I can't get any shoes on—not even slippers!"

"I—they'll get better—"

But my tiny grandmother shook her head vehemently.

"It's no good—Melleschi—it's very bad!" She told me in the most resigned whisper I would ever hear. I shook my head, tears in my eyes and I bent over her pillow to kiss her parched lips.

Next morning as I went across from our bedroom to see her, there were several people at the door, including the doctor. I was told I could not come in. By evening it was either Peggy or Mrs Cooper who told me she was dying. Papi and Abi were with her but I was not allowed in her room. I do not think I wanted to go in at any rate. I was gripped more with fear than any other emotion just as I had been in Arlesey.

I awoke in the night and heard foot-steps and talking. But I crept under the bedclothes. Death—my grandmother was dying! I did not realise that we were losing her for ever. I was simply terrified of the word death and the darkness and whispers all about me with strangers rushing to and fro. I did not see my father or Abi.

Channa, Henne Lowy died on the 2nd. Of August 1942 and was buried at East Ham Jewish Cemetery. At that time orthodox Jewish women did not attend funerals, let alone little girls. I spent all day with friends at the White House, confused and devoid of any emotion I could understand. By the time I returned to Dorcas after supper-time, the house felt empty and sinister. Passing Oma's deserted room would be not only painful but eerie the rest of the time I remained at the Coopers. Death was an enigma I did not seek to unravel. I would push Oma to the back of my mind until I was ready to revive or make sense of my real emotions.

Chapter Fourteen

TOGETHER AT LAST

Oma was gone. Chana Henne Bienenfeld had had a fine education in Poland, spoken French and was well read. Most likely she had been lovely in her youth: petite and with deep, dark saucer eyes. But there were no photos of her when young and if ever a woman lacked vanity it was certainly she to her dying day. Then she had married Israel Dov Halevi, the famed Scribe who had given her a son and a daughter. As the grand-daughter and great grand-daughter of celebrated rabbis her own of Bienenfeld, had been a venerated family name. Undoubtedly it was an arranged marriage in keeping with the tradition of such families and love would not have been spoken of. But two great families had merged and there would have been rejoicing of the elders.

All the love she had to give seemed to have been drained from her on the death of her beautiful daughter Malka, mother of four young children. I never understood her bitterness towards her son-in-law as it was never discussed in our presence. But even we had heard whispers of Oma's estrangement from her son-in-law. They were not on speaking terms. Perhaps too her heart had never been in the match in the first place. Chaim Joachim Stiel was wealthy but far from prepossessing. He was as expected, a very religious man. Was the rift connected with Malka's final care or lack thereof and his being less than generous with doctor's expenses? Had he been a less than caring husband? Again it was never discussed—certainly not in our presence.

Papi was such an emotional, artistic and certainly far worldlier person that at times, it was quite difficult for me to connect Oma with my urbane Papi. But he was a loyal, devoted son who had obtained a visa for her as he had for the rest of his family-members. Yet I could never sense the warmth and adoration he displayed for his diseased father. It seemed that even he could not get close to his mother. Or simply that they could not get close to each other as he was so different, maybe even a disappointment to her.

She had been unassuming in life and taken up less space than anyone else around her. She had made less noise than anyone else; she had been less vociferous than anyone else. She had been the least egotistical or vain woman I was ever to meet. Now her absence was equally unobtrusive. No-one spoke of it as though it was somehow unseemly. Maybe it was simply that every member of the family had their own private way of grieving and words could only diminish these emotions. It was a strange, a terrible time for Jews in particular.

There was hardly a day when Papi did not bring back more grim news he had received from Poland. Grim news beyond comprehension and he was in mourning and would have to say KADISCH (the prayer for the dead) at least once each day trudging to Shefford as there had to be a MINYUN, the sufficient number of men required to say the prayer for the dead. He had to make sure these were available each day anew, preferably twice a day. Occasionally he would travel to the East End in London and meet up with his friends in one of the numerous synagogues there. They had of course all been at his side at the funeral.

He was a slender man at the best of times and now he had to walk from one village to the next twice a day as he attended both morning and evening services. It was his duty, I understood, to honour his mother in the way she would have wished. He was also supposed to remain unshaven and he honoured that obligation, I believe, for the first three months. He simply did not look like my lovely Papi during that time and I disliked the smell of his beard as well as the obvious fact that he had lost weight and had that tormented look I recognised from our time in Stadelheim Jail and the ensuing journey to the Polish border. He looked to his adoring daughter as though he carried the weight of the Jewish people on his shoulders with his hands tied behind his back.

My enterprising mother meanwhile had set herself the task of finding us a temporary home here in Bedfordshire. She felt too, that she could not continue to impose on the kind Hales. Mother and father had built up a beautiful home and business together in Munich, but she had always been the lynchpin and she was determined not to sit idly by and let the world crumble entirely beneath her feet. Her husband continued writing poetry, he always would; she needed now to summon all her seemingly inexhaustible energy to pull her family together once more. As it was, my parents were well aware of the favouritism providence had shown them already. I did not see it that way at the time. I did, however, sense Mutti's strength and determination, close to infallibility. I thrived on Papi's gentleness and romanticism but I needed Mutti's realism and determination just as much—even if it took me far longer to understand why.

The 'LIFT' delivering our furniture had long since arrived at its port of call in London and the parents had been paying storage which could now be used for rent. There was talk of a dilapidated stone shed or barn that was being turned into some kind of basic dwelling. The shed had been used only for storage of hay and it was part of the land belonging to the aristocratic owners of Clifton Manor, the grandest house in Clifton with acres of meadows and fields surrounding it. The only resident was a very old lady who resided there with her small entourage. Somehow Mutti had been advised that there might be a possibility of turning it into a rental accommodation and not losing a moment more as was her way, we went to see it just before the new school term.

Clifton Manor was tucked away beyond the edge of the village, around the corner of the beautiful old church and cemetery, paces from the Church Hall where Abi had performed his play and our school had frequently been permitted use for similar functions. A little further down the tree-studded lane towards Shefford and beyond to Southfield, blackberry bushes to one side, a gleaming green meadow with a spindly silver stream squeezed in between, on the other, lay the winding, hushed private drive to the Manor House. Invisible for three quarters of the gravel drive, entirely obscured by gigantic chestnut, fir, pine and poplar trees, interspersed with wagging weeping willows, so tall and sinister at night, that they looked like threatening phantoms and suddenly to one's relief, there stood the old crone of a building.

You could be forgiven for believing you had stepped into a Dickens novel like Great Expectations that I had recently begun reading. Had I been familiar with Bleak House I might have been reminded of that. The Manor itself was a dilapidated, grey beast, almost brought to heel but still powerful.

The grounds around it were wild and neglected but spacious and there was a copious bungalow to one side of the stone shed we had come to see. Somehow I instantly took to these hidden, secret surroundings so shut off from the outside world, surrounded only by wonderful rustic fragrances.

But as we explored further we could see to the back lay stretches of meadow—land inhabited by herds of cows and bulls belonging to the local farmers. I delighted in the discovery of these free-roaming, contentedly mooing herds. But my heart soon sank when the owner of the bungalow, a Mr Swingler, unlocked the door for us at the back of the shed instead of the front as I had expected. As yet there was no front door he explained in his shy but accommodating way. Mutti was silent as I acted as interpreter but she seemed far less perturbed than I. In fact it seemed nothing could ruffle her, her animated expression and unaccustomed gleam in her eyes speaking for her.

The back door leading into what we would soon discover was the kitchen, was solid enough and had obviously been installed recently. Mr Swingler pointed to a small stone structure just behind the shed with a door similar to that of the shed. I went to open it and found myself in a respectable toilet with normal seat and wonder of wonders—a chain with which to flush! Yes, it was outside, but for me this appeared the height of luxury after the seemingly never-ending confrontation with fetid holes in the ground.

Mr Swingler explained that it would fall to him to decorate the little house newly turned into human habitation and continue improving it wherever possible. It was L shaped and we were now led straight into what he called the kitchen. It housed a white stone sink and a tiny, ancient gas stove. Bathroom—the good man shook his head with another self-conscious smile; hot water also regrettably none.

To the right of the kitchen was a spacious, bright room with a wide, black iron hearth and grate taking up half of one wall: the living room. It was front-facing and was graced with obviously newly-installed windows allowing for ample sun-light and the view of lovely tall pine and chestnut trees. A very nice room, I thought and Mutti was already secretly calculating where she would place some of our furniture. Yes, there might just be enough space for the huge wardrobe from her bedroom-suite which she treasured, with the other few pieces that had once been a part of our lovely Munich home. For my part I too could hardly wait to be reunited with these leftovers of my stolen German childhood though I had a strange premonition that somehow they would have lost their charm in these surroundings.

Along the L shaped corridor three rooms had been constructed, one after the other with their own doors and electric light—bulbs hanging from the ceiling—we hardly uttered a word. Electricity in potential three bedrooms! Mutti's face was flushed with pleasure. Yes, o' yes, this would do very nicely—she could make a home for us here. No bathroom—we would get hold of one of those tin baths you filled with boiling water with which I was already well acquainted; dear Mr Swingler and his wife would see to that too. This would be our first home in England. How much luckier can an escaped Jewish family from Hitler's Germany be, in a Europe ever more in awe of the German monster. Somehow these kindly, sympathetic people so eager to assist us, made us feel less pathetic and despised. They did not treat us like miserable refugees; instead they treated us with respect.

My mother had picked up some English, more than my father who continued writing his Yiddish poetry and had far less contact with local people. He met his writer friends regularly in White Chapel, a part of London with which he had fallen in love for all its unpretentious Jewish ambience and they would converse in Yiddish. But it was obvious that anyone he met held him in great esteem. He had not lost his unaffected charisma and he was never anything but immaculate, no matter what the occasion. His clothes might not be in the height of fashion and they were anything but new, yet father looked in the eyes of the perceptive English, the gentleman he would never cease to be.

Mother on the other hand, had got on very well with Mrs Hale from the outset and was able to make some kind of linguistic contact, no matter how basic or more often hilarious, to everyone's amusement. An unassuming, modest woman at the best of times even if she hugged her pride to herself like a hidden jewel, she somehow managed to make herself understood and equally respected. She would be the first to laugh at her mistakes. She had been through German schooling from the age of seven and had learnt to adapt as now I was learning to do.

Where would we find the rent for this undreamed of haven? Papi was only earning pennies, but Mutti was confident that even if the few pounds still left were gone, she would find a way. An added bonus was a sizable patch of garden at the back near the toilet. The Swinglers grew their own vegetables. Mutti had made up her mind: she would learn to grow vegetables too. I do not know how much the monthly rent was but it was all settled a few days later, with a rent book and the assurance that both Mr and Mrs Swingler would always be ready to give a hand and advice. Their surprisingly extensive bungalow was impressive in its size as well as their huge, beautifully tended vegetable and fruit garden. It was explained that the Swingler's were in the employment of the lady of the Manor and that the bungalow and all its proceeds were part of the Manor. There were several Swingler children, one no more than a toddler and one and all were welcoming and helpful as though they were just as delighted as we were to be here. There were cats galore too. My heart leapt with joy. Maybe, just maybe I could adopt one for my own? And there was talk of chickens. Chickens—I did not understand why Mutti kept talking of chickens to Papi and Abi. I could not see how these dear little noisy, talkative creatures would appeal to my mother as pets.

CLIFTON MANOR, ASHBY HALL

My excitement was such at being reunited with my family just before the new term at Ashby Hall, that I scarcely gave leaving the Coopers a thought. At any rate, I was only going down the road so to speak. Even if it was a long, dreamy walk down the wild, winding dirt—road called Pedley Lane. And though Mrs Cooper had been nothing but kind even if we never saw a spot of butter or sugar from our rations, I had also outgrown the somewhat feeble, oversized, smelly bed-mate Peggy. She had taught me some rude rhymes it took me many more years to comprehend, but I would continue to think of her as my pal and Mrs Cooper, who had dubbed me her little Spitfire, as a kind of auntie I loved. But moving from pillar to post had become part of my young existence and it persists to this day. No, I was not sorry to leave DORCAS—the house had become twinned with a terrible sadness since my grandmother's death. The dark, narrow staircase leading to the bedrooms would figure in many a spooky dream for years whereas my pious Oma rarely did.

The fact that I was actually a member of a first-rate Secondary School with an excellent tutorial reputation only became clearer to me as my education there progressed. Yes, it was war-time and allowances had also to be made for the fact that many of us were not merely German Jewish refugees but like myself, had never spoken a word of English before arrival in this country. My friend Helga had arrived on a 'Kindertransport' only a little while before me and there was Jochewed Heidenstein, a year older but like several other class-mates, also in our form because of language difficulties. I never did quite comprehend the class-system as I seemed to glide from Form Two to Form Three and in a flash I was in Form Four. Five B would be the top class in preparation for the dreaded Matriculation Exam. Not that I dreaded it as much as the older students for the simple reason that I did not comprehend its significance and neither did my parents. I would actually be permitted to go in for it half a year early as a special war-time concession; that and my refugee status. Gt. Britain was kind to me' not that I appreciated this particular favour.

So I would in fact soon be in the top class once the older pupils had taken their exams. But the students above us were years older with some of the boys and girls seventeen or beyond. What I did not then understand was that these refugees had been torn from their schools at a time when they, like Abi, were ready to take their 'ABITUR' and had now to learn to take their exams in a foreign language, even if most of them had had some English tuition. Recently a boy by the name of Kurt Bader, reputedly the best mathematician of his class, had failed his Matriculation Exam because his knowledge of English had been so poor. When he retook it he passed with distinction. If that could happen to someone as clever as Bader, what chance did I stand? But unfortunately or fortunately, anxiety where school-work was concerned, found no home in my psyche.

From the outset Jock as we called her, was a sobering, even motherly influence and we got on well. It was nice too, to have our wits pitted against the boys, especially Solly Bornstein who seemed to have grown taller in the holidays and for some awful reason made me blush every time we spoke. I realised almost subconsciously that I had missed his teasing and generally turning up at unexpected moments. We were still sparring but occasionally we would become less adolescent, particularly he, discussing school-work during break. He admired my English work, especially my essays. I was becoming increasingly frustrated by Mrs. Jacobson who now taught us French, as she obviously picked on me. She had taken an indisputable dislike to me, even accusing me of using rouge on my cheeks as I had begun to thrive since I lived with my parents and my complexion had changed from pallid to a healthy peachy glow. This could not have been a more terrible slur on one's character in a school with such high principles and unbending moral laws. It was akin to being branded a flirt in front of everyone! It hurt even more because it was such a fabrication.

How Solly had matured so rapidly with the perspicacity of a person twice his age, would go on puzzling me. Where I was head-strong, impulsive, truly deserving of Mrs Cooper's pet name of 'Spitfire' and simply too impulsive by far, Solly would counsel patience and reflection. Yet he was hardly the most studious or obedient of students either or I would not have felt drawn to him. He had a gentle sense of humour but maybe because his father was a rabbi, he was not as overtly recalcitrant as I could be. Or he simply had more common sense than most of us; although that like so much else, is something I would only recognise many years later. I really think I owe him my excellent results in the French Matriculation exam as I had almost given up on the subject with Mrs Jacobson's constant badgering and had begun missing her classes. My English, English Literature and of course German that I planned to take, were invariably in the top two or three, but my Maths was weak and without French I would fail even though it was obvious that I was gifted for languages since I had made such strides in English and my German, unlike most of my class-mates' was perfect. I had begun devouring novels from my father's library as soon as they had arrived in Clifton. And would continue to do so until I had almost exhausted my teen-age curiosity for books I had long heard discussed at home by authors of every nationality, all translated into German.

Savouring every delicious bite of still warm buns bought from the bakers next door to the Ashby Hall and squatting by a rare blazing fire Solly had stoked back to life after classes, the bakers' expenses shared, we squatted by it—but never too closely—discussing various subjects. And on that rare occasion we were actually entirely alone in that vast, imposing gabled church hall. It was not often that I did not hasten home from the freezing building; rarer still to enjoy the soporific comfort of a log fire.

Generally we would begin with a puerile squabble that gradually settled down to a more sensible discussion. But as we had already had a snow-ball fight earlier that day with Solly daringly stuffing snow-balls down my neck, it was here that he now brought up the subject of my absence in French class. I explained that I had had my fill of Mrs Jacobson and I would have to give up French and if need be, forget about Matriculation altogether as I really wanted to be an actress.

Solly eyed me with those perceptive, soulful blue eyes that seemed disconcertingly to read what I could not say out loud:

"So are you really going to let her ruin your life?" He asked in utmost seriousness, never taking his eyes off mine. His voice had recently become husky and our eyes locked for a very long moment. His words like his eyes dug deep into me.

But just then his actual words were less significant than the way for the shortest time, we had eyed each other as though never wanting to let go. I did not understand what I felt any more than I understood Emma Bovary's mad longings. But a little later on, the significance of the words themselves would impact on me equally.

A HOME OF OUR OWN

The few days it took to arrange and supervise the entire move to our new home at Clifton Manor, as we tended to quote our address rather euphemistically, it was arranged I would visit my Auntie Rosel and my cousin Abi at their new flat in Riverside Drive, Golders Green, a lavish new building, the finest in the area. Uncle Bernhard sadly died not long previously from stomach cancer. He had only been in his late forties.

Hanni, Abi's sister had married Max Rosenthal, a budding solicitor whose wedding I had graced with yet another brief role as bridesmaid in a less than satisfactory outfit and felt decidedly like Cinderella as the guests there were obviously prosperous to judge by their clothing; I was, however, not the best judge of prosperity as anyone in a reasonably fashionable dress and well-heeled pair of shoes looked prosperous to me at the time. But Hanni and Auntie Rosel had wanted me there and there I had to be with Mutti and Papi with whom I returned to Clifton on the Birch Bus that same day. The other bridesmaid was Max's beautiful teenage sister Ruth Rosenthal. I suffered my third appearance as bridesmaid as I had done the two previous ones and secretly resolved that that was it, basta. There was not the slightest advantage in being a bridesmaid as the only present I received was a box of chocolates when I had hoped this time to be treated to a new frock and shoes. I had secretly yearned also for those gorgeous silk stockings instead of my terrible thick woollen stockings in a murky brown. The bride, my perpetually sweet-smiling, glowing cousin Hanni, was in a fashionable navy-blue suit and white satin blouse I believe, but to be honest, I was too overcome by my unwelcome task, to take in much detail. I did, however, take a liking to her new solicitor husband, the tall, handsome Max, who had an authoritative bearing and an impressively noble manner. I liked handsome men and Max Rosenthal was decidedly handsome.

Hanni herself had grown into a pretty, elegant young woman in her early twenties, tall and buxom with a velvety smooth complexion. Like her new husband there was about her an air of impressive gentility. They were both very orthodox and Hanni would be wearing a 'Sheitel' (wig) much to my regret. I had a fierce dislike of these unshakable religious demands even then. But as she was a highly fashionable young woman, a pretty turban would do as often as not, just like my headmistress's Dr, Grunfeld and the glamorous Mrs. Lichtig. With a romantic lace veil over a charming pink creation perched jauntily on her head, my happy cousin looked radiant and so obviously in love. With my own hair in a frizzy mop thanks to the dearth of hot water at home and Mutti's rush to get ready, I felt distinctly dowdy but was received with affection by my auntie Rosel and fussed over by my dear Oma and Opa Tennenbaum who were staying with Auntie Rosel.

Although I had spent only minutes in Auntie Rosel's new flat in the stunning, ultra-modern apartment building, across a main road from Brent leading to Hendon Central and apparently an architectural modern masterpiece not without its detractors—I was certainly enchanted. It was the most stunning building I had set eyes on with its reflecting glass-fronted balconies and every block of a warm milky colour. The interior with its stylish mirrored lifts and thickly carpeted stairways in ruby-red, fully complimented the exterior. Naturally there were porters in smart uniform with one standing right outside the gleaming glass front portals. As in Leipzig, my auntie resided once again in a palace!

The flat itself seemed to invite the sun and was bright no matter where you chanced to be, from the generous, stunningly furnished sitting room, to the dining room and ultra modern kitchen not unlike the one I had seen in the palatial Leipzig flat. And the bathroom, all marble tiles and a snow-white bath tub, a matching sink and that miraculous innovation of constant running hot and cold water! I had almost to be prised out from there when it was time to accompany the bride to the nearby synagogue. I was promised a longer stay there soon by my handsome, forever humming cousin Abi, when he promised to take me to the nearby Lido Cinema. He himself was madly in love with Carmen Miranda at the time, I recall. Abi had thick, black frizzy hair not unlike my own but it was shiny with brilliantine like a newly-tarred pavement. How I wished someone had taken pity on my long unruly tresses and smothered them in something—anything to make them look more groomed!

And soon now I would be paying a visit on my own for a whole week-end. I would ride once more on one of those new trolley-buses I had scarcely wanted to leave. The ride was smooth as gliding on air and the trolley purred like a sated cat as it started off. Much as I loved the country-side and all those noisy, smelly, suffering animals, I wished we could live here in London in spite of air raids. No one seemed afraid. I was sure I would not be either. People sheltered in Underground Stations so why couldn't we? But it was explained to me that even discounting the danger, we could not afford to live anywhere near here and that I was particularly fortunate in belonging to the excellent Jewish Secondary School (JSS.) And of course, although I would not admit it just then even to myself, I had formed a bond with the country-side that would never be broken.

That week-end in Riverside Drive with my gracious aunt, forever elegant and lady-like, would have been perfection had I not suffered from an upset stomach. But both my cousin Abi and Auntie Rosel were so thoughtful and kind that it was almost an added pleasure to be a semi-invalid when I was so fussed over. And with a beckoning bathroom close by, it seemed more of a bonus to be unwell, as I was allowed not just one but two delicious, sweetly fragranced wallows in plenty of warm water.

I assured him I was well enough when Abi wondered if he should take me with him to the Lido Cinema half a block away, where LADY HAMILTON was showing with Vivien Leigh and Laurence Olivier. I won the day and had found a new idol in the breathtakingly beautiful Vivien Leigh whom I vowed I would one day resemble, if I could not look like my first idol Hedy Lamarr. The story moved me to tears though I did not quite understand why Lady Hamilton had met with such an awful end. I was far more interested in the beautiful Emma Hamilton's fate than that of Horatio Nelson. At any rate it took me quite a few years to comprehend the unfortunate Emma's final fate in a French brothel.

By the time our move was complete and I could come and join my parents in Clifton Manor, the London Blitz was at its height. Yet more momentous so far as I was concerned, was the sight of that beige gem of a bakelite wireless-set perched saucily on the little table to one side of our living room as I opened the door. Immersed in my own little world, the blitz simply did not impinge on it but music: Anne Shelton, Vera Lynn, Bing Crosby, Deanna Durbin, Paul Robson, Gracie Fields, wonderful Bud Flanagan and my introduction to the unique strings of the Glen Miller orchestra with their unforgettable rhythms and beat—that became part of my world and could carry me away to wherever my dreams longed to land.

I had heard rumours that Glenn Miller would be coming to Bedfordshire and somehow it brought America closer. If you passed by the GOLDEN LION public house in Clifton's Church Street you would be treated to a plethora of the latest records blaring through doors and windows via the nickelodeon. Somehow the unique beat and sonorous arrangements of the Glen Miller band made you want to dance and sing with them, their rhythm was so infectious. America must be a magical country!

War-time tunes, particularly the new ones by Irving Berlin ("this is the Army Mr Brown") and Jerome Kern, simply clung and would not let go. They accompanied me wherever I went, including to school where they had no place. 'The Yanks are coming', 'Johnny Zero Is a Hero To-day', "Say a Prayer for The Boys over there" Deanna Durbin sang in her movie. 'I'll Be Seeing You In all The Old Familiar Places', 'Comin' in On a Wing and a Prayer—though there's One motor gone we can still Carry on—'and soon the early and best Sinatra and Dinah Shore was added to the list. I loved

Anne Shelton's lyrical presentation and her naturally lovely voice. Those perky Andrews Sisters who even sang 'Everybody loves Saturday night in Yiddish—Yiddish on the wireless! Or they would ask 'Mamma if they could go out dancing.' And of course there was always Vera Lynn and 'I'll be seeing you' and the 'White Cliffs of Dover until I felt they played too much of' The 'Forces Sweetheart' and too little of my other favourite Anne Shelton. And there was the ever-recurring "hanging out the washing on the Sigfried Line" or the good old 'Lambeth Walk', as English as the 'cuppa'.

How and where my mother had found the little bakelite gem or how much it cost I never was to discover. It was certainly second-hand but spotless. My father fractured English or no, would sit by the little beige apparatus as soon as the news came on and if Winston Churchill spoke, no-one dared utter a sound even if every word had later to be translated to both my parents. For my part Churchill's voice was as comforting as Hitler's had been spine-chilling. And I loved his bullish portraits. But I also found Stalin's portraits inspiring and loved recordings of The Russian Army Choir. 'Uncle Joe' as we called Stalin, was an avuncular figure and no-one at the time sought to dispel that fantasy. After all, the Russians were not murdering Jews; they were fighting incredible valiant battles and helping to destroy the German beast. The Russian soldiers were heroes just like our own and the American boys. And their music was so beautiful.

Papi still received reliable news from Yiddish newspapers sent to him regularly from Argentina, Brazil, Canada and the States. The news from these papers was not merely up to the minute but almost always superseded English papers including the Jewish Chronicle in details where the fate of the Jews of Europe was concerned.

At the time I am ashamed to admit that because Papi made a point of sharing much of this news with me, it showed me up as the insolent, unfeeling adolescent I could be. To be fair, what my young ears beheld was simply not credible. How could he believe such fallacies I would demand—deliberately thrusting from me what I did not, could not believe; as though my poor father had no right to credit these atrocities. He sat there in silence, pale and stricken having just related the details of the fate of Jews hounded from all over Europe into Polish ghettos and from there taken to extermination camps. There had even been the first details of how people had to undress and go into the showers naked to die. Perhaps Papi had hoped for me to fall weeping into his arms and thus find some comfort himself. But no, I would not accept any of it, thrusting it from me like excrement. And Papi did not persist. Deep down maybe, he hoped that my reaction might have some justification.

I actually raised my voice to my heart-broken father. It was not possible; the Germans simply would not do such things. No human being would do that to another. Papi's moist blue eyes looked away and he said nothing. There was neither rebuke nor any further discussion. He understood that it was simply not something I could credit. He understood because he too felt it almost impossible to credit the incredible. Countless of Papi's friends and relations had been dragged from their homes into the Warsaw, Vilna and Lodz ghettos—and now this.

My father had never been a Zionist. Ever since I was tiny I recall him being deep in discussion with his Zionist friends like the Teitels and Konigsbergs, arguing that there would be too much blood-shed in Palestine as the Arabs could not simply be forced out of territory they had occupied for centuries. As for the religious belief that God gave the land to the Jews, that was never on my father's agenda. Yet as he related these horror stories I wondered if now he too saw Palestine as the sole sanctuary for the stricken Jews as this was where the fortunate few had set up home and were rebuilding and irrigating the desert.

For me it was a strange, an in-between time. The books had arrived with the Lift. Much of my father's salvaged library—hundreds of them. And somehow they were housed, some in the living room, others in the bedrooms on second-hand pine or damaged old wooden stands or cases picked up in Hitchin, that ancient market town abounding with second—hand and antique shops. Mutti was a dab hand at such matters and when Abi was around he would have to cart these objects on and off buses to the raised eyebrows but never objections of bemused bus conductors.

Another new world lay before me. This time I had merely to flick the pages to be transported to different countries with their individual trials and tribulations but also their smouldering romances. No one now supervised my choice of reading and I pulled out indiscriminately every single novel I had heard spoken of for years (all in German, of course). I would be sprawled over long week-ends on our dear old couch that had travelled so far across the waters and now graced one half of the wall of the living room still miraculously redolent of those unforgettable Munich odours. I was at liberty to devour ravenously the world's greatest literature. I decided to omit translations of English books into German, wisely I think. Child Herald which my father revered, some Shakespeare and even Goethe and Schiller in their original, did not draw me. I attacked instead Maupassant, Balzac, Zola whom I particularly enjoyed especially Germinal being the daughter of a left-wing father. Victor Hugo's Les Miserables and The Hunchback of Notre Dame conveyed me into the depth of a past world though not fraught with the horrors of the one we had just escaped, was still bleak and cruel. The Trial by Franz Kafka would go on puzzling me longer than most as I found it so difficult to comprehend.

A little later I immersed myself in Strindberg and Ibsen. I liked Peer Gynt, its poetry attracted me and besides, it brought me closer to Papi. He loved Peer Gynt, the original and the musical version by Edvard Grieg. Did I even come close to understanding let alone sympathising with my tortured father in those heinous years of slaughter? I don't think so.

I dived into the mountainous Dostoevsky works like a parched fish: The Brothers Karamazov, The Gambler and Crime and Punishment opened my eyes to a style of literature that I would never outgrow only marvel at more and more. I realised very early on that here I was in the company of incomparable genius. That he was also profoundly Christian and thus anti-Semitic hardly dawned. Tolsoy's War and Peace was equally greedily devoured. I fell in love with Prince Andrew as well as the kindly Pierre and thought Natasha lucky to be so adored. I wept over Anna Karenina but could not sympathise with her the way I sympathised with Emma Bovary whom I associated with the exquisite Lady Hamilton. (Vivienne Leigh)

By the age of fifteen I had read practically half of my father's erstwhile forbidden literature. Novels by Thomas and Heinrich Mann, Leon Feuctwanger and Jakob Wasserman now so unfashionable: Jew Suss and The Gooseman, Gogol and Gorky. Flaubert's Madame Bovary and Zola's Germinal remained still in adulthood amongst my favourite novels as did Mann's Magic Mountain. But each novel had left indelible marks. They were not wasted on a mind too young perhaps to grasp the darker, more profound messages. It was a time when I could imbibe far more readily than at any time later on when I was caught up in romance and study—regrettably far more in the former than the latter. It was a time I lay sprawled on our dear Munich couch, sometimes racked with pain that I did not understand but simply endured. The more stomach and back pain I endured, the more I lay on that couch enveloped by world literature. And no-one explained why I was suffering, not even Mutti though the suggestion of appendicitis was mooted from time to time.

ERROL FLYNN, HEDY LAMARR, GENE KELLY—ESCAPE TO BEDFORD.

It was a deadly serious time for all of Europe; a devastating time for its Jews. More and more blood-curdling accounts of the Jews' plight became known. But they were never main-stream enough for the British national papers to make the headlines. Of course 'there was war on' as the hackneyed phrase went and people were concerned with their own problems. It appeared that the Jews herded into ghettos and then onward to the extermination camps did not really come under that category. In fact it was guarded like a dirty secret. I still did not really comprehend—nor if truth were told, believe it in my heart of hearts. It was just too abhorrent. But I now kept my mouth tightly shut and if I was still able to console myself that maybe accounts were exaggerated, I had more sense than to upset my permanently distressed father any further. What I should have given him was comfort and understanding as he stood helplessly by watching the world he loved, the people he loved being destroyed. But instead it was he who understood that he was asking too much of me too soon. Mutti spoke far less of the horrors. Her brother, my uncle David and his entire family were in one of the ghettos. We knew no more. But it was not Mutti's way to speak of such things. Perhaps like me, she too still found it impossible to credit.

The world around me in the tiny, bucolic village of Clifton, buzzed with a life of its own. Apart from the seemingly ever-burgeoning animal population, suddenly tall young men in smart uniforms could be seen coming in and out of the local pubs in the centre of the village—the Yanks had arrived 'over here'. American music streamed out of the open doors of the pubs. Now Glenn Miller's orchestra resounded as soon as the pubs opened. For me the most exciting thing about the new arrivals was their accent. They all sounded like the film-stars that took over my dreams. And some of them even looked like film-stars they were so tall and spruce.

A bus ride from Clifton to Bedford took about forty minutes once the bus would finally reach its destination. Back was equally unreliable though at least one could wait at the terminal where there were benches. The fare was affordable if one was fortunate enough to have any money at all. It cost a little less to Hitchin in Hertfordshire in the opposite direction. But only one of its two cinemas, the newer one in Hermitage Road, screened new films whilst the other in Bankroft, was no more than a dark flea-pit showing films so ancient that even we would only visit there as a last resort. And Bedford was a bright town with a posh KADOMA restaurant and uniformed waitress service entirely out of the reach of our pockets, of course. But there was also a much more affordable Lyons right on the opposite corner of my adored Rose Department Store where the mannequins in the enormous windows resembled Ginger Rogers or Rita Hayworth and held my attention for dream-laden minutes on end. Of course even they could not rival my goddess Hecy Lamarr.

Sometimes with the few saved coppers it was possible to buy a small portion of chips on a plate as opposed to the usual ones on newspaper from the fish and chippie. Naturally the treasured portion had to be shared between Trudy and me. For it was with her that I occasionally set forth in my holidays, while she was awaiting news from the Women's Auxiliary Air Force she hoped soon to be joining. This was not an uncomplicated matter as she was both an alien and had not yet reached eighteen. But she spoke a foreign language and had picked up enough English to get by very well.

How Trudy and I, both absolutely penniless, found the necessary wherewithal for cinema and on the blessed occasion, a plate of chips, was a closely guarded secret of my very own device. I suppose I revealed early signs of Mutti's innovative talents, but fortunately she was unaware of it. It really turned out to be less difficult than it seemed at first and I became quite a dab hand at it. And it was all perfectly legal and respectable.

There was a long row of second-hand shops along the road leading away from the bus terminal on the side of the fine old church opposite. All you had to do was walk along that road to come upon an absolute swarm of these little shops almost next to each other, displaying the most disturbing array of dross it was possible to imagine: odd socks, gloves, panties, trousers, knickers of every dimension; nightdresses and pyjamas, minute babies' shoes and dresses; ragged old hand-bags as well as pots and pans and any and every other conceivable bit of rubbish imaginable-all of it used, if one could employ that euphemism.

I had walked along this rather dilapidated street several times with my sister when a thought struck me as I sized up this mind-boggling display out in the road. There must be some things in our home that could easily be dispensed with. Equally there were things in my own wardrobe I would be more than happy to be rid of especially as most things were either too small, too tight, or simply too worn out. So far as I was concerned three quarters of my own second-hand wardrobe of hand—me—downs from committees or latterly from dear cousin Hanni, were eminently disposable and once gone, might persuade Mutti to employ her ever-present ingenuity, to obtaining some better clothes for her youngest daughter.

As it was, she hardly ever looked through my clothes unless I drew attention to something. And so it was that every so often we arrived at these shops with paper bags filled with old socks, knickers—yes, my very own knickers if I ran out of wares! And counting our loot we made our victorious way to the Granada to enter the world of dreams with a cry of "Eureka!"

On the opposite side of Woolworth was a chemist shop which sold the most desirable Coty and Max Factor cosmetics, as well as Elizabeth Arden and Helena Rubinstein. At no time would I be able to treat myself to such luxuries whereas Trudy was far closer to financial independence. Bedford, we were told, was the town where John Bunyan had been incarcerated. I knew little of John Bunyan and had not yet learned about him. But to me Bedford was already special enough with its beautiful river-side, its cinemas and glamorous shops. It was bright and alive, where Hitchin was gloomy like Shefford and Biggleswade, with a horrid butcher shop in the market square with whole carcases of pigs and rabbits, their tragic heads slumped beneath them, as well as chickens and turkeys and beef and lamb halves. I loathed that butchers'.

Mutti treated me to the cinema occasionally when she had sold one of the items she had bought at one of the antique or second hand shops in Hitchin and then taken to London to resell. Sometimes she would save up and buy a finer article at GATWARDS, the antique shop in the Market Square next to the butchers' and when she found a good buyer for that, she would actually make a decent profit. It would never have occurred to me at the time that I had picked up the idea of selling second-hand items from my mother. I simply sold rubbish until my stock was entirely exhausted. Trudy had run out of goods long since, so we both depended upon my skills.

It was on one of those precious outings with Mutti, freshly baked buns in a bag bought at the bakers by the bus-stop, that I saw the incomparable Errol Flynn in Elizabeth and Essex with his co-star Bette Davis at the Granada Cinema, to me the height of luxury. There was little doubt about it—I came out of the cinema in a kind of trance. I was not yet thirteen and yet I experienced an attraction to the star I could not explain. His commanding beauty, the way he slapped the queen audaciously on her behind with that inimitable Flynn grin, I was smitten; and all this to the most beautiful musical accompaniment. I am not sure I even remembered the buns. Erich Korngold's magnificent musical score must have had more to do with the overall magic than I would have been aware of too. I was certainly not familiar with the composer's name then, nor could *I have foreseen* the way his music would stay with me throughout the years. Flynn and Korngold (soon to be eclipsed in 'The Sea Hawk'—I had discovered two gold-mines with one stroke at the age of twelve!

Those war-time bus-rides to and from Bedford via Cardington, whose forbidding barrage balloons looming in a dark, cloudy sky, added to the breathtaking contrast of the Granada Cinema's lustrous ambience, taking hold of one as soon as one stepped through its gilded turnstiles blinking several times in sheer disbelief. The restaurant up a thickly vermillion-carpeted stairway to one side was entirely out of the reach of the likes of us. One day who knew—one day! But it was so glamorous just to walk up those stairs and peek into this unattainable luxury.

It was here too that I first beheld the stunning Hedy Lamarr as she walked down an endless staircase with other beauties she totally overshadowed with her incomparable beauty. "You stepped out of a dream—"went the music from the Busby Berkley musical: "you are too beautiful to be what you seem."

I drank in every word and took it for gospel. She was too beautiful to be real. How I longed to have her long, silken raven tresses instead of my increasingly frizzier mop due to coldwater washes. Her face with its chiselled features and her tall, lithe, slender figure floating along in a gossamer gown—o' yes, that was how I wanted to look.

And then there was Gene Kelly, who unlike Fred Astaire, was so handsome and manly even though he could dance to make your eyes water. The glorious music by Jerome Kern or Richard Rogers or Gershwin, though I was unaware of their names at the time, filled me with startling joy. I cherished these occasions, eagerly listening to the fresh new sounds and marvelling at the skill of the great Gene Kelly as he danced and sang in the rain. The film-world held me completely in thrall and I would escape there whenever the real one became too painful, even if only in my dreams.

I would stumble out of the Granada Cinema into the streaming Bedford sunshine with tears still in my eyes. The tune and words of the song I had just heard Deanna Durbin sing so beautifully, still filling my head. And it was not really the film's story that had brought on the tears, as I found that hard tocomprehend. But the words of the song, the beauty of the singer's voice and appearance would never leave me:

"Spring will be a little late this year "sand the sublime Deanna and what I had not really gleaned from the contents of the movie became fully clear to me in all its sadness, just as Erich Korngold's music had been a vital part of Errol Flynn's attraction for me.

Chapter Fifteen

CHICKENS & APPENDICITIS

The Blitzkrieg raged and people were killed daily in London. Those terrible 'Doodlebugs' had become the latest torment as apparently the overhead plane's engine would suddenly become eerily silent seconds before it dropped directly upon what was beneath—with devastating consequences.

It was hard for anyone living in the peace of the countryside to imagine, especially if you were a schoolgirl immersed in your own puerile world as I was. The daily carnage was reported on the wireless, yet Pappi continued to travel to London regularly. The East End was torn apart, ravaged by Goering's Messerschmidts. We saw pictures of the Queen and His Majesty King George graciously stepping over ruins to press the hand of those lucky enough to have survived as they stood dishevelled and disbelieving before the rubble that had been their home hours earlier, often still in their night clothes. The Queen in the mid-high heels of her immaculate, fashionable shoes would then smile graciously before carefully taking tiny steps over the rubble as she followed her husband to the next fortunate recipients of the royal hand-shake.

Papi had not taken me to London since the daily onslaught of the air raids although as he returned before night-fall which was when the raids were at their most severe I considered such caution unnecessary. But both parents were adamant. There was no need for me to be at risk as after all, that was the whole idea of evacuation. The trouble was I loved going with my father to meet his friends in the Lyons tea-shop in White Chapel, where they would drink watery tea and eat little cup-cakes or slices of fruit or Madeira cake between their poetry readings and serious political discussions. My father, as was his way, always gave me his portion.

The heated political discussions were way above my head but invariably, the discourse would soon turn to what was really on everyone's mind—the increasingly desperate situation of every Jew trapped by the Nazi web spread-eagled all over Europe and shockingly assisted in their butchery by local internecine collaborators. In Paris people who had considered themselves safe on French soil, were hounded by the French gendarmes without the need of assistance by Germans. It was the same in every captured country. Italy, Bulgaria and Denmark seemed least inclined to play the gruesome Jew-baiting game. But Hungarian and Czech Jews were now in equal peril and the free world once disbelieving or simply unwilling, were now powerless to assist. There was of course one resource left and that was to bomb the increasingly well-documented Death Camps. It was what my father hoped for. It was what some of the Jewish organisations asked for from Churchill. But it was not thought advisable, it appeared—too many inmates might be killed?

My father looked as though he was in constant pain and soon reality took over. His agonising stomach cramps were supposed to be alleviated by Milk of Magnesia, a floury powder he took without complaint. With what right could he or anyone complain here in the safety of good old England? The reminder was a salient one and stopped us in our tracks. Something had begun to dig deep into my subconscious. Why would I have been spared the horror I knew many of my Munich classmates were now enduring. I had never been anywhere near as sweet-natured let alone as beautiful as Steffi Weil. Yet I knew her to be trapped if alive at all. Why would God allow such injustice? How could he—what was he—who was he—was he at all?

I too suffered from cramps but unlike my father who simply drank his medicine and got on with his work, I lay on that couch in comfort even if writhing with intermittent cramps, as I read my way through the world of literature in a kind of haze and wonderment. The doctor, when finally he was called, suggested it might be a bout of appendicitis! Perhaps it might be advisable to have an appendectomy. Papi, as usual when talk of surgery came up, shook his head once it was explained to him. It could surely wait and appendicitis did not necessitate appendectomy, did it? As no-one knew how to translate half of Papi's objections the matter was left hanging in the air much to my relief. My cramps were the perfect foil for my hours on the couch, until Trudy upon her return at week-ends complained that it was time someone else had a turn. Then I would shut my book, move over and insist we had a sing-song with her accordion as the star participant I loved those sing-songs with Trudy and invariably we ended up laughing until my cramps grew seriously worse. But how easy it was to escape back into the world of Thomas Mann's Magic Mountain and suffer far greater anguish with the afflicted heroine or with Emma Bovary on her death bed.

Henny and cousin Hilde had found work in London: Henny in an office as she began to cope with the language and her shorthand-typing had always been exemplary and Hilde as a dental assistant. They were sharing a bed-sitting room in Golders green not far from Auntie Rosel's apartment and how I envied them. But they returned every Friday evening to spend the week-end with us. Here they each had their own room as did I unless Abi was home when I shared with Hilde. She had really begun to look very smart, with her thick, shiny black hair in a perfect page boy. Unlike Henny and me she was blessed with a sleek head of hair instead of our frizzy crop. She also somehow managed to dress in the latest fashion although I thought she often overdid it (which might have annoyed her since I was not one to hold back on my views.) But neither Henny nor Hilde used make-up, so far as I knew though I sometimes suspected that they used powder on their noses, especially Hilde whose nose was quite prominent, whereas Henny's was small and straight but freckled.

Trudy had to attend training with other WAAF cadets at a special camp somewhere in another part of the country. But she would not tell us where. When she was a fully-fledged WAAF she would receive her uniform. We were very excited and proud, especially I as I loved those uniforms. Abi too had put aside exams soon to receive training in the Intelligence Corps. His excellent educational record stood him in good stead now.

Hilde and I had a love-hate relationship. She teased me incessantly and not unlike Mrs Jacobson though unawares, thought I was too vain if I so much as looked in the mirror for longer than a second. But when my little adopted cat fell ill and looked as if she would not make it through the night, it was Hilde who stayed up with me all night and helped give her sips of warm milk until she showed signs of improvement. I could not help crying every time I looked at her. Papi too stayed with us for a while. But the cat survived and I was forever indebted to dear Hilde and began to see her in a more favourable light. As it happened, the cat we had thought a Tom, turned out to leave us a present in the outside toilet of four beautiful kittens. My excitement was intense but to my horror, first one squeaky little furry ball then the next, went missing. As they could not have walked more than a few steps those first few days, I was as mystified as I was miserable. By the end of the week, all four were gone.

It was Mr Swingler who chose to enlighten me. The cat had eaten her kittens! My feelings for that particular feline would never again be the same though in my heart of hearts I never quite believed it. My opinion of my erstwhile far from appreciated cousin, however, had changed dramatically in one night.

One early morning I awoke to wild clucking and crowing, emanating from right below my window facing our back yard. Leaning out the window I could scarcely believe what I beheld. There were at least six chickens and one cockerel in a fenced enclosure that must have been put up furtively whilst I was asleep.

I did not know how to interpret this sudden husbandry as of us all, Mutti had always shown the least interest in animals. Well, I thought, Mutti has decided to rear chickens. But we were never short of eggs here. In fact my parents sometimes brought a few to London for my maternal grandparents who were staying temporarily with Auntie Rosel. Presumably Mutti planned to sell more eggs; it was the kind of thing she would do to make a little more money.

Chickens—of course I would offer to help whenever possible. If there was one thing beyond doubt it was that I had time for any and every animal. I didn't even mind spiders and I was never hysterical like Henny when I saw a mouse. Abi was too eager with the mouse-traps and I was unhappy about it but there was little I could do. My big brother was master of 'mousing' and any other pest-control necessary. I think he rather enjoyed it. But as he was not home much and would soon be in the army permanently, I gritted my teeth especially as he always helped me with my Maths. As it was, he could not taunt me with a dead mouse as he could Henny. I was not so delicate. My naughty big brother took full advantage of poor Henny's squeamishness, however, which seemed to cause him no end of amusement. Even Mutti sometimes joined in his laughter. He had also picked up some very strange remedies for chill-blains from which both Henny and I suffered. But we firmly rejected having our feet soaked in our own urine! Sometimes Papi had to step in when his shenanigans grew too wild and even I required rescue.

Henny had passed the age of twenty-one and there was much talk of her finding a husband. All mention of the handsome, blond young artist son of my father's friend Sochachevsky was instantly quelled by Mutti. But I knew that my sister nursed a secret longing to make friends with the attractive and apparently brilliant painter. The Sochachevskys were not merely poor, but agnostic and such an alliance was simply out of the question so far as my devout mother was concerned. As it happened the young man soon went to war and Henny's romantic dreams of him never materialised. Papi did his best not to become involved as was his diplomatic way though it was through him that she had met the charming Maurice and it was quite obvious that so far as he was concerned, an alliance with his childhood friend's family would be more than welcome. As it was the young man had a girl-friend so Henny had to make do with her romantic fantasies of Maurice.

Hilde had nursed her own secret fantasies since the age of twelve but she had no idea where her idol was or even if he was alive. At an exceptionally young age Yitzchak FRIEDLANDER (later known as ESCHEL) had already attained a post in the Munich REICHENBACH Synagogue as Cantor. His voice was remarkably fine and he had managed also to steal my twelve—years old cousin's heart as well as quite a few other nubile maidens' I believe. He was a diminutive Hungarian youth but according to HIlde, his impish charm and panache were irresistible.

Hilde had matured early and she had a lovely deep singing voice too. Right then my dear brother was not averse to her womanly charms, more developed and buxom than any girl around. Martha had long returned to London and if he suffered love-sickness he certainly did not show it. But Mutti kept a wary eye on this unwholesome new romance.

As Henny was the easiest to rile and upset she seemed destined to suffer the brunt of family taunts. Abi was the chief offender and at this stage in her life, working in London and rushing back home Fridays, then being expected to help Mutti with Sabbath meals and general housework, she sometimes exploded uncharacteristically. I was upset for her and tried to interfere between Mutti and her on one occasion, afraid that Mutti would clout her as she had used some very rude language and Mutti did at times resort to a slap or two. I stepped between them feeling immensely brave and self-righteous and not entirely unafraid of ending up as the recipient of the punishment. There was little doubt that of us all, Henny was the most obedient and least difficult and of course, she rarely upset the parents. But sadly, she was too easily offended by the most trivial things and would burst into torrents of tears. Fortunately the little three-some scuffle ended with my stressed mother telling me not to be so silly and warning Henny not to be so rude, as indeed she had been.

Of course every-one of us would flee to Papi for comfort if Mutti had been a little too harsh in judgement even though we knew full well that all Papi would do was beg all parties concerned to remain calm. It was hard on Mutti but I'm not sure if any of us understood at the time except Hilde who was a bystander. Someone had to keep her burgeoning brood at bay and it was never Papi. Maybe Abi sensed Mutti's difficulties—or was it that he knew he could get away with murder. I loved all my siblings dearly but at the time my heart went out to Henny above all, as it seemed she was in a state almost every week-end and only Hilde seemed never to upset her, whereas I was far from squeaky clean either.

It was special and awe-inspiring to watch Mutti prepare for the Friday night Sabbath. She would place her meticulously polished, gleaming embossed silver candle-sticks salvaged from our precious Munich home, fed with tall white candles, at the top of the table. The old familiar velvet green embroidered cloth covering the CHALLA (plaited egg—loaf) forever redolent of poppy seed from the Challah, candles lit and hands placed over her face. Her head loosely covered by a white lace shawl, while she said her prayers with the electric lights extinguished, gave the room a mysterious, enchanted glow. For a moment one could almost believe that something good, magical might take place and set the world to rights once more. Prayers over, she would wish all present "Gut Shabbes!" and we would approach for our kiss. I loved these traditions and scarcely associated them with the religion that was drummed into me by Dr Grunfeld.

It had been obvious to me for quite some time that Papi's idea of our religion was not in the same league as my mother's. They might belong to the same team, but they had very different ideas of reaching their goals. As for me, for the past year and more, I experienced serious problems with any form of trust and belief in God, the more was revealed of the horrors befalling my people. I knew that these Polish Jews were some of the most devout and clean-living human beings anywhere on earth. They sought neither comfort nor wealth; all they sought was God, to reach him, to study his laws and ideas. They were of a similar calibre as my grandfather Israel Dov the Scribe my father revered. They came from similar backgrounds and had never wondered further than Krakow, Warsaw, Lodz, Wilna or the muddy 'Schtetls' outside these cities.

These guileless devout souls were not greedy for worldly advancements. They were unsophisticated to a fault and without any secular ambition. Why would God punish them? These Polish Jews were the most devout of humans; their trust in God was implicit, childish. But where was their God? They had never assimilated as the more mundane Jews of so-called more civilised, advanced countries had, nor sought high positions vying with their non-Jewish compatriots. And what good was their absolute devotion now? Why were they being punished? Why were Jews being punished so hideously? And if it was something God disapproved of—then how did he come to the decision of who would be spared? I argued with myself over and over but the reply was always the same: the whole religion thing made less and less sense. All those prayers fell on deaf ears and that was because there were no ears to hear.

Deep down I could not believe there was a God—and that sudden realisation shocked and frightened me. What if there was? Would I be punished as I had always been taught if I did not adhere to my people's faith? I began to experiment secretly little by little with further transgressions; almost as if I was climbing a mountain and missed out small steps one by one. If nothing happened I could venture further. But it was more than I dared say to anyone excepting Trudy. Mutti would have had a fit or worse, put her hand to her heart as though about to have a heart-attack—and Papi? I trod with care. As it was, the kind Mr and Mrs Swingler would act as our Sabbath 'Goyim' and light our hearth in the winter as well as switch on lights even if at times I stood in for them with Papi's definite covert knowledge. If my canny mother was aware too she never let on.

Our over-zealous religious instruction, hammered into our heads as with nails of fire and brimstone, did little to endear these laws and customs to me. Dr. Judith Grunfeld (known as the Queen) who took it upon herself to ascertain that her students would honour every minor petty law for the rest of their lives merely brought out in me every rebellious streak I possessed.

Unlike Trudel I was shrewd enough not to argue during discussions after the lesson. In all fairness, religious zealot that she was, knowing that so many of her students would never see their parents again, Dr Grunfeld must have considered it her absolute duty to instil in them every iota of faith she could sum up. And in that she certainly succeeded with the younger ones like my friend Helga who had come from a totally free-thinking household. This smouldering worship of God and his commandments were the comfort and compensation obviously fulfilling her needs. Her teaching of the 'OLAM HABA' (the next world) was ambiguous. Jews did not believe in an after-life per se but they believed that the Messiah would come and then the living and the dead would be reunited. So did we believe in an after-life? I never elicited a definite reply and I was careful enough not to press further. I for one even at that age could not imagine all the dead of all the centuries coming back even in spirit. Or did she mean only the righteous? After these lectures I returned home more confused than ever. As for the 'OLAM HASEH' (the present world) that seemed the most despicable of all in those dark, grisly news days.

Often in pain I was determined to keep it secret as I did not want to see any doctor instinctively convinced there was nothing seriously wrong. My school-work apart from all English subjects including English Literature was far from satisfactory. Mr Schuller, the new young Maths trainee teacher was perfectly adequate for anyone with mathematical ability. That, however, did not include me. Mr Schuller, a fresh-faced, shy young man with a club foot, was as ill at ease with me as I was with him. It was certainly not his fault that I made little progress as even Abi's patient efforts proved to be useless. Algebra made sense. Arithmetic was doable until it came to Fractions. But Geometry and even worse Trigonometry were unattainable heights whose first rungs I would never even reach, no matter how hard my stalwart brother might push. The real trouble was that my mind at that time was simply unwilling to accept any more. I had learnt a great deal in a very short time and I was fortunate that my German, unlike my classmates' was absolutely perfect thanks to my non-stop reading. So I was left with two terrible gaps. But a great respect and love for my brother was cemented as he would sit up half the night on his leave, press warm milk upon me and try so pitifully hard to hammer the unfathomable into my impenetrable brain. All I could think of was how much he must love me and how much I would always love him even if he insisted that urine was good for chilblains.

As I was obviously gifted for languages I decided a Correspondence Course to bring my French up to scratch might be the answer after all, if my parents were able to pay for it. This was made all the more desirable as the school had just announced that Matriculation could be taken in two separate parts at different dates. Thus it would be advantageous at least to pass the first half consisting for me of English Literature, German and French, as those were my chosen languages and take Maths and English at a later date. Dr. Levine approved the decision heartily as he considered me his top English student and thought I showed real talent in my essays, frequently reading them out to the class. I also excelled in Literature and was asked to act pieces from Macbeth (one of my chosen Shakespeare plays with Twelfth Night and As You Like It), as well as demonstrate how to put into my own words and set to précis pieces that most of the class could not comprehend. But where was my brain when it came to Geometry?

When I told Solly of my decision his face lit up. He congratulated me and told me that I was obviously getting some sense in y 'thick head'—compliment enough. But that did not stop him from stuffing snow-balls deep down my neck as soon as he could find enough snow to form into a ball big enough to soak me through; nor to tell me to" keep my wool on!" when I complained vehemently. It was certainly a phrase of the day but I took it personally and secretly found it offensive because my hair was so thick, long and—woolly.

As he was an excellent ping-pong player and I enjoyed the game enormously I would sometimes come to the White House after school to play. I was the only student who lived in Clifton now. I was also the only student whose parents had escaped from Germany and resided here in the country, though several like Solly's father lived in London. As no mother was ever mentioned only his sister Esther, I took it his father was a widower.

This set me apart socially as I missed a great many social, mostly religious functions I purposely evaded. But it also gradually deprived me of my small social circle unless I made a great effort to walk to Shefford twice or three times a day. Unfortunately even Helga and I grew apart though whenever I did make an appearance she would loyally be at my side. I suspected that we were both a little in love with Solly but that was more than we were able to confess to each other. A kind of innate inhibition about sex and personal feelings seemed to gag us both. But our friendship was still solid if a little bruised and awkward when Solly's name came up. Did he know? Did he like her better than me? She was very pretty with her long, very straight black hair, pale complexion and fine dark eyes. And she was much more disciplined and popular with the other girls. What was more she took part in all activities including girls' football. And perhaps most surprising of all, although emanating from a totally agnostic and untraditional background, she now eagerly embraced the most rigorous religious laws.

CHICKENS

It all came to a head with the chickens, though my fairly obvious rejection of religious traditions I had formerly embraced without a word, certainly added to it. It seemed to get worse by the day. Everything I did was wrong. Mutti was angry with me at the slightest provocation it seemed to me. My poor mother, at such difficult times even her youngest seemed to slip from her grasp. At the thought of it now I feel very guilty particularly as she was also undergoing early menopause. Naturally such matters were not discussed nor would I have understood them with my ignorance of biology. Nothing personal or sexual was ever discussed! But at the time I was convinced that the fault was never mine and all I had to do was seek my father's understanding—which was invariably given.

And still no-one seemed to take much notice of my cramps. As if they were another of my not infrequent exaggerations. Admittedly in every other way I had grown into a pretty fit, strapping teenager in the shortest time, with ruddy cheeks and a healthy glow. No-one, not even Papi seemed too anxious.

Yes, the serious rows with my mother certainly came to a head with the chickens. There they were that morning much to my delight. Did Mutti bring them here to please me? She knew how much I loved animals. These noisy, clucky little birds would be delightful to get to know. And the fresh eggs would not come amiss either, especially as the grandparents would be coming on a visit soon.

Mutti's reaction was somewhat subdued at my irrepressible enthusiasm, almost as though she was embarrassed. Papi made no comment at all before he left for London. The news of the allies' advances was wonderful. The Russians had taken back Stalingrad. So far as I was concerned Stalin was wonderful and so handsome and avuncular. Not for nothing was he called 'Uncle Joe'. The Russian Army Choir, frequently heard on the wireless, was simply inspiring and dragged you with it through snows and ice—to victory. With Russia, America and Great Britain advancing on all fronts the war was as good as won. And yet there was little joy for Jews. There were few who did not know of the unspeakable atrocities by what were once considered civilised, well-educated people. Moreover people who such a short while ago were next-door neighbours of their victims. I was filled with loathing for them all when I dared think about it.

Little wonder that in our household, no-one was particularly jovial. But when Trudy was home she and I could sneak off and be as silly as we needed to be. We had our sing-songs. I preferred Deanna Durbin and her songs to Judy Garland's. I loved her sweet, gentle, lilting voice as I loved Martha Haftel's. I would whistle the songs and Trudy would play her accordion. For a short time we escaped into our much-missed careless juvenile world.

We hitchhiked to Bedford and I would produce yet more knickers and socks for sale. Strolling along heady with success after these sales we simply could not stop laughing and my cramps of earlier changed to cramps from laughter. We much preferred the rides in jeeps with the handsome Yanks, to lorries or even private cars in which we felt less safe. Of course we told no-one we had hitch-hiked and we never had an unpleasant experience. If the Americans made overtures to Trudy she was well able to handle them. As for me, it never occurred to me that they might be flirting with me too, these big, handsome Yanks. They called us Blondie and Blackie, as Trudy's recently bleached hair looked so glamorous.

No-one enlightened me as to the true purpose of the chickens until one afternoon I returned from school and found the chicken enclosure empty save for small rivers of blood. I do not remember what terrible language I used to abuse my poor mother who was still in her hat and coat having just returned from Letchworth where she had delivered the chickens to the kosher butcher shop. Presumably Abi had helped her transport the chickens as he was home. So now the chicken quandary was solved. The kosher butcher-shop had agreed to buy a certain number of chickens from my mother and had put her in touch with the 'SHOCHET' the man entitled to slaughter the animals according to Jewish law (Schechita). A new batch was due to-morrow, after the yard had been cleaned. Somehow my mother had managed to time the procedure during our absence.

"I hate you—I hate you!" Was all I could yell over and over glaring daggers at my mother, before running to my room and throwing myself on the bed, my face awash with tears. After about an hour I walked into the living—room to announce that I would be leaving for London in the morning. I still had enough money saved and would stay with Henny and Hilde. I could not live with such a heartless mother.

My mother was very pale and let me continue ranting. She looked exhausted. Abi was outside sweeping the yard.

"Have your supper." She said eventually.

"We'll talk when your father gets back."

"Nothing to talk about" I shook my head.

I could hardly understand my own misery. But it was very genuine. It had welled up inside me and it would not be quelled. I felt at that moment that I could no longer live with my mother. She had transgressed every boundary in my book of morals. She had betrayed me.

"Does Papi know?" I asked hoarsely. Mutti nodded. I could scarcely believe it. Surely my good, kind father would not be an accomplice in something so dastardly?

I made my intention very clear to both my parents. I was leaving. What about school? I would try to get into RADA, the Royal Academy of Dramatic Art, zenith of stage and film training. I was determined to become an actress and for that, who needed further education? My education was superior to the average already. I was sure Vivien Leigh had not bothered to pass her matriculation exams.

I knew my father was suffering from stomach ulcers and he looked unwell and tired most days. I hated to hurt him but I felt betrayed by both my parents even though they had tried to explain that the money from the chickens would help everyone in the family obtain at least a few things out of reach at present. I did not understand nor did I want to understand. School—we were pretty much left to our own devices these days, to study and attend classes as required. Only the religious instruction lectures including Jewish History were compulsory. As it happened that was the one area in which Dr Grunfeld really did excel. But these lectures were frequently straight after the Sabbath so that I could not possibly make it there in time. At least that was my excuse.

Papi begged me to be sensible; to try to remember what times we were living in. He understood my disgust and he did not really approve either, he confided. Stubbornly, self-righteously I shook my heavy head of frizzy hair washed in cold water and soap. Papi had helped me with it a couple of days previously as usual. It was time I left. If only my poor father didn't look so miserable. But I was mystified by the anger that would not be stilled within me at the slightest provocation. I knew too deep down, that I was being unfair to mother whose life had been turned upside down and who was so bravely facing up to any and all challenges with her inimitable strength and courage. But why of all things, did she choose to go into the kosher chicken trade, for goodness sake? Could anything be more disgusting?

APPENDICITIS

Early Sunday morning just after day-break, I packed my cardboard suitcase, far larger than necessary, with my handful of dresses, jumpers, skirt and underwear. Shoes—just the flimsy pair I would be wearing, no stockings. I left on tip-toe and closed the back-door without a sound. My heart beat very fast. I dreaded causing my father pain, not once considering mother's feelings. It was she I wanted to punish. And I dragged the heavy suitcase through the fields with cattle still peacefully dozing, the wind sharp as knives; along the seemingly endless Pedley Lane, a very uncouth dirt-road through to Clifton Road into Shefford, towards the Ashby Hall and well past the dozing pigs and ducks of the Coopers' farm. Further on I dragged the heavy case into Shefford until I reached the small station. I was wearing my best summer dress and open sandals. The wind beat mercilessly against my bare legs and arms. I bought my ticket to Hatfield from where I would have to change to the Birch Bus. A soldier assisted me onto the train with my case. My cramps had started again.

At Kings Cross I boarded a bus to Tottenham Court Road, sinking into the seat with a sigh of relief. The conductor had assisted me with the case making some crude joke I scarcely understood. I felt strange: the pain had ceased but I could feel moisture between my legs. I ignored it as I alighted with suitcase, helped once more by the conductor at Tottenham Court Road Underground Station. As I walked into the station I could feel the warm trickles down my bare legs. Aghast I stared down my legs—they were streaked with blood.

"O' no—I really must be ill!" I mumbled to no-one in particular. This looked serious. I had absolutely nothing with which I could quell what I now felt was a flow of blood as I rushed into the Ladies in the station. There I grabbed what was fortunately an abundant supply of toilet paper and stuffed it into my blood-soaked knickers. The paper was hard and rough. Was I dying? Tears poured down my cheeks as I dragged my suitcase down the escalator towards the Northern Line. There was a terrible ache in my stomach and in the small of my back. I had to get to my sister and cousin's digs as soon as possible. And although it was not yet five o'clock and they would not be back from work, it was the only place I could think of. I could not possibly descend on my Auntie Rosel in the state I was in with my pathetic suitcase.

Yet Henny and Hilde had no idea I was coming of course, as my parents had no way of communicating with them. They did, however, have the use of the house phone. Yet I had no idea of the number and they would at any rate have still been at work. I could have shortened my journey had I known there was a connection at Kings Cross Underground Station without going across London by bus to get the Northern Line. But I was totally unfamiliar with

London and far more attracted to buses where one could at least see where one was heading. I might, had I but been aware of it, also found a number thirteen bus all the way to Golders Green from Oxford Street or Regent Street.

Somehow I arrived in Alba Gardens, Golders Green, having walked from the terminal along the long Golders Green Road, blood soaking the toilet paper and trickling down my legs again, which smarted with the relentless wind and the wet blood—to save the bus fare from the station. My hands were raw from dragging the overloaded suitcase. Now Mutti will see. Serves herb right if I die!

Finally I reached the house, gratefully set down the suitcase on the porch and rang the door-bell. A tiny old man with a few tufts of white hair and a wizened but friendly face, came to the door and stared first at me and then at the large suitcase in undisguised surprise. I explained who I was and that I would like to rest in my sister's room until she arrived. An equally miniscule, white-haired old lady joined him at the door and immediately bade me enter. Their accent was endearingly Dutch as was their name. I left my suitcase in the hall and ran up the stairs where they both pointed to the room my sister and cousin shared.

"Would I like a cup of tea?" I shook my head, miserably aware I smelled of the blood, hoping their sense of smell was less acute than mine. All I wanted was to cleanse myself but I could not simply invade this lovely old couple's house and use their bathroom knowing that Henny and Hilde were allowed only one bath a week. Fortunately there was a large sink in their bed-sitting room with towels and all necessary where-withal for a good wash-down, which is what we were accustomed to. But it was all so pristine and how could I soil their spotless little room in this way? If there was one thing we had in common, it was our relentless quest for cleanliness and our abhorrence of dirt and squalor irrespective of difficulty or inconvenience. I had returned to my natural instincts after my short lapse during the Kindertransport.

I stood there on the threshold of Henny and Hilde's room, about as miserable and helpless as I had ever been. What should I do first? I could not use their towels and mess everything up. I would have to go to the toilet again. There would be paper there surely. As it was the cramps were quite crippling now.

As in answer to an unspoken prayer I could hear the familiar foot-steps racing up the stairs as she called out:

"Mellale—"and found me on the bed in tears.

"Hilde," I said, "I'm really sorry—I'm ill and I'm—there's blood—" She went up to me, stroked me and told me to come to the sink as she handed me flannel and soap and took out a huge wad of cotton wool.

"Our Mellale is a big girl now—you've got your period at last, MASEL TOV!" She patted my cheeks. At that moment I truly loved my frequently too judgemental cousin.

Henny arrived soon after, but by then, with Hilde's help, I was reasonably cleaned up and had calmed down. No-one had even hinted in all this time, what might be causing my cramps. No-one had ever thought to put me wise. Even then, with all the adult literature I had devoured, I had no idea of sex or how a child was conceived let alone born. It is inconceivable to-day and maybe it was even unusual then in a household not short of females.

Henny phoned from the one house-phone downstairs and left a message with the Swinglers for the parents, that I was safe and would stay here that night. She was determined I should return in the morning and was quite cross with me for causing the parents such anxiety. She mentioned in passing that it had made Papi ill. Hilde managed to calm us both and suggested we enjoy my visit and then we would talk sensibly. I could sleep in her bed with her to-night. But Henny insisted I share hers. It was good to know they both loved me.

Meanwhile we enjoyed a supper of sardines on toast and I was given a tall glass of hot milk and generally mollycoddled, before Henny and Hilde began their serious discussion with me. They were hardly overstocked with food and even milk was limited as they had to count every penny. I was touched by their generosity and sympathetic attitude but deep down I already knew that I would return. I wanted and needed my parents as much as they needed me, especially Papi. I was, after all, a young woman now, whatever that meant. Though I loathed the idea of having to go through years of this kind of torture, I was nonetheless relieved that the cause of all this foul blood was nothing more serious. Appendicitis—so much for the doctor's knowledge. It also became clear to me why some girls in class were impossible to sit next to. We had always put it down to body-odour and frankly showed little tact. But it was obviously due to menstruation and insufficient hygiene. In a way it was the same thing, wasn't it? Would I end up smelling like that?

But my sister and cousin were now more than ready to shower me with advice. Hilde said that first thing next morning she would go down to the Chemist to buy me my first packet of Sanitary Towels. My dear cousin, with whom I so frequently quarrelled and made up, was as good as her word. Both Henny and Hilde now overpowered me with instructions when Hilde returned with the awkward, uncomfortable contraptions that I would be doomed to wear between my previously free, ample thighs, against which they would rub atrociously. Until many months later, I discovered a softer brand when I could afford to buy them or simply used cotton wool which was far kinder if giving less protection.

My first flight from the coop had come to an aborted landing. It was not to be the last attempted escape, however, nor sadly, the last serious skirmish with Mutti. Did I not love my mother at that time? It seemed not as we so vehemently disagreed about everything and worst of all, if only I had had the sense or sensitivity to see it: Papi increasingly took my side and Mutti, like a beleaguered enemy, stood alone trapped, whereas I egotistically seemed to bask in my increasing victories.

"Let her be—she is only a child after all," would be Papi's final comment no matter what the argument. And from him being 'only a child' was a welcome observation whereas I would have flown at anyone else who had the audacity to call me a child.

But the truth was that the one talent my mother seemed to lack was insight into her growing daughter's psyche. Whereas Papi had always, throughout our growing years, somehow reached the right equilibrium, Mutti was too much engaged in the more mundane tasks of making sure the roof over our heads was not merely existent but comfortable and secure. Was it even fair of my father to lap up all our affection? But it was what he thrived on and Mutti selflessly made do without, because at no time did she doubt his true love and affection for her. Her love and admiration for him was equally never in doubt through all those troubled times. They might have arguments when tempers were at their most fraught but no-one who saw them together could doubt his admiration for her or hers for him.

Hess was in jail after his farcical arrival in Scotland. I would have liked to tell someone from school how close I had stood to him; how well I remembered his coal-black, manic stare, the only pair of eyes I clearly still recalled of that bunch of murderers. None of the others in that march-past, not the strutting, over-stuffed showman Goring, the insignificant, club-footed Gobbels, or the rouged Fuhrer with the clown's moustache—but those black eyes from hell had registered. I would have liked to tell Solly, Helga, Jock or particularly Dr Levine that I had been in touching distance of this devilish bunch. Instead I spoke of it to no-one as it seemed utterly irrelevant to-day, when the war was coming to a victorious end yet Jews were still being murdered by the thousand daily. I simply stored it with so many other occurrences of the last years in my secret compartment, where I might pick at it at leisure later on—or never. I do not recall even speaking of it to Papi or Trudy who had shared the experience with me. It was not something to be proud of after all.

If there was one thing I now finally understood, it was how much the Yiddish language and its entire culture meant to Papi; how much those who had breathed life into the language were part of his own being without which he could not imagine life. The Jewish religion was one thing and I would hazard a guess that it was in his case adhered to more out of loyalty than true conviction. But Yiddish, the language, its literature, its traditions, the people who spoke it, lived it—they were his raison d'etre. In fact they were his true faith.

Josef Hillel Levi had been immersed in his MAMME LOSCHEN all of his adult life. But I, of whom he had once said to my mother after an argument: "she is my life!" only opened my eyes more fully as I grew into my mid-teens. And that was as I watched aghast as he visibly wilted under each new report of atrocities committed. It was also the time when the names of Auschwitz and Bergen Belsen, Buchenwald, Treblinka and their heinous colleagues became common coinage.

It was natural enough for every Jew blessed with freedom, indeed every human being worthy of that name, to be weighed down by the horror of the slowly, too slowly emerging details of what had and was still taking place in Poland and other parts of German occupied Europe. But it seemed that every new bulletin was another stab at my father's already fragile health. These were his friends, his colleagues, the cream of Europe's Yiddish artists, poets, writers being bit by bit erased. German Jews had always looked down upon the Jews from Poland and Russia—the OSTJUDEN. Yiddish was not for them the language of art and culture; in fact for them it was not a civilised language at all. For them it was no more than a ghetto language. They had shut their eyes and ears to the art and honesty, above all warmth and humour of Sholem Alechem or Sholem Ash, yet to which Josef Hillel Lowy, (Levi) though educated, enormously well-read and immersed in every aspect of musical and literate culture had given his life and soul. Now they were crushed and he with them.

I now look back on my part with shame. But being raised in the German mould with German culture to the fore, I too secretly could not accept Yiddish as being on a par with other European languages. I did not then find the beauty in it that my father did.

I had hoped that one day father would begin to write in English, so that all the world might recognise his talent. How stupid of me—how blind!

What world was I thinking of? His world was being systematically destroyed and what was foremost in his mind was to keep it alive, not to let the butchers stamp out this precious culture entirely.

It was not the best of times to be self-obsessed, egotistical, vain and proud as I think I must have been. In other words: to be a young girl on the cusp of womanhood in love yet owing to back-ground and upbringing, unable to betray the slightest emotion as though it were something to be ashamed of. It was a strange, confusing time for me as it was for most Jewish youngsters of my generation. A part of me was mesmerised by this new world and life into which I had miraculously been dropped: the glamour of the films and their magical music. My days and nights were filled with the stunning Errol Flynn riding into the sunset accompanied by the equally enthralling music of ERICH WOLFGANG KOPRNGOLD without whose contribution I could hardly imagine the perfect features of Flynn in 'Robin Hood', 'Elizabeth and Essex', 'The Sea Hawk,' or 'Captain Blood'. It was indeed a very confusing time and there were moments when I was secretly ashamed of myself. But these did not last long.

I would have liked to walk with Solly along 'Lover's Walk' by the river in Shefford as some of the older, less inhibited students had done; as Abi may have done with the lovely Martha or Trudel with Imre Sarkany, though she never let on. It was de rigueur to hold back, to curb one's desires and natural instincts. I use the word desire loosely as I had no longing or desires of any sexual nature whatever. I still had only the vaguest anatomical knowledge as we received no biology lessons. My dreams were simply of romance—a gentle kiss and holding hands as Judy Garland and Mickey Rooney did. Decent, respectable

One just had to wait to grow older and more uninhibited as my sister Trudy was. For me it was simply impossible to wed the world of film and music which I soaked up so greedily, to the real world right outside. How could life be so beautiful and romantic and at the same time so hideous? That world of death and suffering was one I wanted to shut out. Yet the phantom that refused to go away was one that had begun to stalk me a few years back but had now become more troublesome: why was I here and not in Poland with the others? Why had our train turned back? I was so unworthy! I didn't even believe in God.

Oddly enough I did not discuss such matters even with Papi. But at least there was no need to hold back on my love for my father any more than he did. My mother would have to wait a long time for similar emotions—but time was on her side and they assuredly would come.

There was great excitement at the prospect of the arrival of my maternal grandparents Opa Aaron and Oma Chatsche. I had only seen them very briefly at my cousin Hanni's wedding and now they were to stay with us a whole week. They would have my parents' bedroom furnished with the enormous twin beds brought over from Germany. During the week when Henny and Hilde were in London, there was plenty of room. At the week-end, with Trudy and Abi away, I would simply sleep with one or other of the girls. I looked forward enormously to our reunion as I loved my grandparents dearly. Fortunately there were no chickens in the yard. Mutti had obviously suspended operations, but only for the time being as what to me was a hideous practice, turned out to be a financial fillip.

But sadly I had found another bone of contention between Mutti and myself and one, I believe Papi and Trudy also if not so vociferously championed. And that was the matter of my sister Henny's new suitor. It was strange really, why I the youngest, had set myself up as Henny's champion. Maybe to my credit, I understood that Henny though she grumbled a lot, was definitely the meekest and in many ways the nicest and easiest of us to get along with. One could always get around Henny. But that was certainly not the case with Abi, Trudy or me. Whatever gave me the idea that Henny needed my protection let alone championship, I shall never know. I always sensed that she was vulnerable in a way that the rest of us were not and in danger of being taken advantage of as the rest of us could not.

Of late she had acquired a very eager suitor by the name of Willy Trenner. Not that it was any of her doing. She was far too modest and shy to flirt openly. Willy was a diamond merchant from Antwerp who had been widowed in his early youth and was eighteen years older than my sister. He had been introduced to her and dated her in London and come here to Clifton twice. He always behaved impeccably; always brought me chocolate and smelled heavenly as he used some expensive French Toilet Water I loved. "The perfect gentleman" as Hilde put it with a longing sigh.

Willy was exceedingly dapper, debonair and very self-assured. He was also immaculately and expensively dressed. In other words the kind of suitor a mother could not possibly object to as he was also wealthy. How wealthy who knew, as to my parents at the time the smallest bank account must have seemed gigantic. Henny would be set up for life. Above all he seemed genuinely attracted to this modest, sweet, innocent young woman not yet twenty-five.

But I knew that Henny hankered after that handsome young artist son of Papi's childhood friend the poet Sochachevsky, blond, tall and slender. I had never met him but according to Henny's description he put many a film-star to shame. So how could she possibly marry Willy even if she had only had the briefest rendezvous with the charming Maurice? Trudy and I had long, secret discussions all of which ended with the conclusion that Henny could not possibly marry the fragrant, mundane Belgian with the impressive diamond signet ring, but so far removed from all our dreams of love and romance. Nice as he was he was too old. Papi said little but Hilde, whose own romance with Abi had been clinically aborted by Mutti in her inimitable way, seemed to be wholly on Mutti's side. Yes, she at least was enormously impressed by Willy. So much so that she said if Henny refused him, she wouldn't be averse to setting her cap at him herself. She saw something good and decent and dependable in him, we silly girls were too blind to see. To do her justice she was certainly the most sensible of us all and she also had great influence over Henny.

"Could it be money?" Trudy suggested cynically with me nodding wildly in agreement.

"No," insisted Hilde "you silly geese, but a good, decent, loving husband—they're not that easy to find and at such times when all our lives have been thrown upside down. And anyway, what's wrong with money?"

Henny like Papi said surprisingly little. In fact it seemed she had less to say than any of her siblings or cousin. But she looked suddenly prettier, with her clean, unmade-up complexion, her straight little freckled nose and slim figure. Her blue eyes had a new sparkle. She let others fight her battle but she herself simply stood by and enjoyed fray. Now she was centre of attraction. I wondered if secretly she was actually falling for Willy and simply wouldn't let on. He certainly never seemed to lack the right words or compliments not only for Henny but for every female member.

Mutti baked and when she did each Friday for the Sabbath breakfast and tea, there was no-one to rival her except her own mother. There was an apple cake and a plum cake as well as her standard chocolate 'Gesundheitskuchen' (marble cake) my personal favourite. But it was pretty obvious that this week-end the cakes were more manifold and more carefully selected. I guessed before being told, that Willy Trenner would be visiting. She looked more relaxed. I noticed that her ample hair was showing signs of grey but her flawless complexion, like her daughter's without a scrap of make-up, was still unlined. Somehow she too seemed more relaxed. Maybe the mere thought of her eldest daughter finding a suitable husband who could care For her adequately, took a huge load off her mind. Even Papi could hardly disagree with that. But of course I could and had the audacity to say so more than once even though I loved the compliments Willy paid me and found him agreeable in every other way—but not as my sister's suitor.

Chapter Sixteen

VISITORS EXAMS

Henny was engaged to Willy and wore her gleaming diamond solitaire with undisguised panache. She seemed changed, more poised, self-confident, less impatient with me. I suddenly dreaded losing her. She was after all my eldest, my 'good' sister where Trudy was my 'dangerous' sister, the one who might lead me astray as Dr Gruenfeld had cautioned my mother. I had no idea of course, what she had meant but I was secretly most intrigued by the thought. To be with Trudy was never dull but could be dangerous. To be with Henny may not have been exciting, but it was always safe and dependable.

My three months' French Course was at an end and Matriculation loomed. I did not think I could pass French although all my marks were very encouraging and I had picked up more in those well-spent three months than in the entire past year with Mrs Jacobson. I knew too that I had a natural gift for languages as I did for music. What was more, I liked French as I thought it elegant. I had picked up English faster than most of my class-mates. I enjoyed pronunciation and loved the sound of French and Italian. It would be quite nice if I passed—though of course, ultimately I would become an actress, no doubt about that, hopefully a famous one. At the back of my mind there was, however, a niggling caution that acting was a little superficial for someone who had after all, just been snatched from certain death.

Abi had been enlisted in the Intelligence Corps and now found himself somewhere in the country (I believe it was Bridge North) and was granted little leave to begin with. We hardly saw him but he was proud to have been accepted. He too had mastered the English language with remarkable skill although his accent remained unmistakably German. But he had had a head start as he had benefited from several years of English tuition at Gymnasium.

Trudy had arrived one day in her attractive powder blue WAAF outfit with the hugely becoming, jaunty cap that suited her lovely, flawless face to perfection. She had grown taller and slimmer. I had helped her some months back one week-end, when she had doused her straight, very fine shoulder-length chestnut hair in peroxide and left it for what seemed an interminable time to do its bleaching best. Once it was washed out—and we had heated umpteen kettles—we rolled it into a pageboy and waited for it to dry with beating hearts. Would her hair fall out? One heard the most horrendous stories of ladies who had bleached their hair and ended up bald. Trudy bald—o' dear Lord! Mutti was out on some errand, or this operation would have been unthinkable. But lo and behold, my sister was transformed into a film-star when excitedly I combed out her hair for her roller by metal roller: an ash blond film-star, a veritable Betty Grable. When we walked down Clifton Church Street and the Yanks drove past, there was an almighty choir of whistling and yelling. I was so proud of her I nearly burst.

"Blondie, "they shouted and even added: "Blackie—meet us at The Golden Lion!"

But no, my sister did not lead me astray though I would not have been averse to that drink in the Golden Lion, Clifton's most buzzing pub at the end of Church Street. Tree-lined Church Street on the left side of which lay the commanding, medieval old church and church yard I had had to pass umpteen dark nights with all manner of ghostly images in mind suddenly seemed to have come alive too. The Golden Lion was a kind of resurrection after one reached the end of interminable Church Street, the eerie grisly-grey gravestones behind the gloomy dark walls never far from one's mind. Suddenly there were bright lights blazing ahead and voices crooning or shouting in booze-enhanced abandon. Maybe Trudy went to the pub later in the evening; I would have given anything to have been there with her.

Trudy would receive love-notes from various admirers in the RAF. One went "you'll be so nice to come home to

You'll be so nice by the fire." quoting the popular song of the day.

"He's asking you to marry him, isn't he?" I exclaimed excitedly. Trudy merely shook her head smiling broadly. Or another went:

"You'll never know just how much I love you—"but my sister had set her sights on someone else as she now had the opportunity to meet so many new people. You could tell she was in her element. Imre Sarkany had long left and had made no effort to contact her.

Because I had always been told I was pretty and often even beautiful, I did not at that stage give my appearance too much thought. It actually did not occur to me that I might not be. Or that it required special attention. I had grown quite tall and certainly rounder but I was slim still, with a tiny waist. My hips had, however, spread out thanks to Mutti's generous cuisine but my breasts were changing at a snail's pace. When I complained that I ought to have a brassiere, Hilde chuckled and said:

"With those pimples you don't need one!"

She meant no harm; it was her way and normally I would have struck back with some equally ironic remark about her breasts as they were exceptionally voluptuous for one so diminutive, but this time her remark niggled and I just swallowed hard. I recalled that Hedy Lamarr or Vivien Leigh did not appear to be very full-bosomed even in maturity and comforted myself that that was the ideal way to be. My sister Henny too had small breasts whereas Trudy's had definitely blossomed.

Most of the girls at school including Helga and especially Jock who looked practically matronly at fourteen, already had perfectly female shapes. In fact some looked twice their age as there was a melancholy about them owing to the fact that they had no idea of their parents' fate. They looked like girls who had become women too soon. But I did secretly wonder why the upper part of my body was so reluctant to make a significant appearance. Yet in all, I was happy enough with the way I looked apart from my hair whose bulk and frizz, especially if I was caught in the rain, seemed a life-long affliction. It did not occur to anyone at the time, that such a voluminous, healthy head of hair could with a little know-how and money, be converted into my crowning glory. As it was most people said they envied me my thick, long, curly top. In a year or two I still hoped I would magically grow into a second Hedy Lamarr or Vivien Leigh. They would remain my two indisputable icons. I certainly had an optimist's view of my future. Mutti said I was lucky (MASELDIG) and I fully believed her. Didn't she always turn out to be right in the end? Unfortunately my darling father found it hard to see the brighter side of anything these days. Even his fathomless stock of lieder and beautiful classics seemed to have shrunk. He had exhausted his joi de vivre so early and it did not return. Yet he never objected to my dream of stardom as did Mutti.

It was strange, shameful really how little interest or comprehension on my part there was for all those glorious final victories like D. Day when so many brave young men went to their early death. Almost as though I was saturated with all war-time gore of every sort and walked securely off into my own favourite world: that of films, their music and their beautiful stars. And there was always that other, fascinating world of my father's varied literature which I was devouring with unseemly greed. I was interested in everything except the ugly present. Maybe too it was because Papi talked of little else. And of course there was always that impish monster playing hide and seek with the Jewish refugee's conscience: there but for the grace of God—God?

Victory in Europe Day (VE DAY) had come and gone. There were parties in many homes and in some of the streets in Clifton, Shefford, Stotfold, Arlesey, Biggleswade, Letchworth and surrounding villages. There was bunting, balloons and Union Jacks were displayed proudly but there was little celebration in our home. Not one balloon and though we would have happily displayed the Union Jack we did not own one, though the Swinglers had one flapping happily in the wind from one of their windows.

None of us liked flags, I think. The mere recollection of Munich swamped by the cursed red Swastika flags could still make our hair stand on end.

We knew that even at this final hour there was no end to the murder and the scale of the horror was almost daily becoming more evident, with the Russians having liberated Auschwitz and the Americans Bergen Belsen. People spoke on the wireless and pictures emerged on cinema screens and television. I was glad we had no access to those little television screens I had seen at the Hales. The pictures in newspapers and the cinema were enough. And they haunted no matter how hard I tried to push them from me.

I had heard that towards the end Hitler had encouraged young boys to fight. I thought of my admirer who would now be just a year or so older than me. Had he fought and killed? Was he himself dead? Munich had been bombed relentlessly. And if not, did he know what had been done to his Jewish compatriots? Had he finally learnt to hate Jews too? I somehow could not connect him with the Nazis. I just hoped he had not openly opposed them. I hoped too that there really was hell so that all the Nazis would burn there for ever. As for Mussolini, in my ignorance I somehow felt that he had not deserved quite such a ghastly end. And why had they killed his mistress? I had seen no marching automatons in Merano on our visit there and the Italians had seemed so harmless and charming. Surely Mussolini could not have been as evil as Hitler—no one could. Of course I knew nothing Of Abyssinia or the Fascists' ruthless onslaught on anyone remotely connected with Communism. Dr Gruenfeld had taught us a great deal of ancient Jewish History but next to nothing of present day European or American History.

It was a pity I could not be part of the celebrations in London. But the pictures on the cinema screens of the countless thousands milling around Piccadilly Circus would have deterred me even had I had the opportunity. I hated crowds. There were unwashed, miserable crowds at the jail and on the train to Poland. Since then I found it impossible to connect jostling strangers with anything remotely enjoyable.

Oma and Opa were coming. We were excited; Mutti and I more than Papi. Papi was never one for visitors. He liked his peace and quiet and that would not be too forthcoming with my vivacious chain-smoking Opa. But I simply could not wait. It had been so long since I had been together with them and I loved them dearly, especially Opas's impish sense of humour—true Jewish Chutzpah, never hurtful, just naughty and hilarious.

The grandparents were living with Auntie Rosel but there was talk that they would come to live with us once we found a suitable house in London. It was no longer a pipe-dream as my industrious mother, like the proverbial squirrel, had gathered the pennies and pounds after purchasing precious little trinkets and a few more important pieces and managed to sell them at profit. She was now planning to become a diamond broker, as Willy had introduced her to colleagues at the Diamond Bourse in Hatton Garden and Mutti had taken to the whole process like a duck to water. Everyone spoke Yiddish there so there was no language barrier. Our very own house in London! Mutti told us with mixed pleasure that as her future son-in-law persisted in calling her Mutti, many members in the Bourse had also begun to follow suit. Did I still not realise what a remarkable woman my mother was? Or was it that my poor father resembled a fox trapped by a pack of hounds when business was mentioned let alone discussed, even though he appreciated his wife's acumen. The subject was and would never be anything but anathema to him. Not only did he not covet riches, he gave me the impression he despised those who did.

Mutti had a predilection for upmarket North West London and Papi loved only Whitechapel and the rest of the East End, still buzzing with Yiddish chatter. His friends Avrom Stenzel and Ben A Sochachevsky, Lysky and most Yiddish actors and artists all lived nearby. Esther Kreitman, sister of Fuchs and Bashevis Singer and herself a fine poet, lived in Hampstead and Papi had taken me along to her home. Whilst they read each other's poetry, I ate her delicious almond biscuits and twiddled my fingers, staring out at the leafy garden. I suspected that I might be acting as chaperone as Esther was charming and she obviously thought the world of Papi. He gave frequent poetry-readings in the East End at Adler House and other similar modest Jewish venues. This of course was unpaid work but it meant a great deal to him and his appreciative audience. These were elderly, shabby and strained as they had just survived years of bombing and running to and fro Underground Shelters. Generally Stenzel and Lisky made an appearance and afterwards there would be tea and honey 'Lekech' or other delicacies from Grodzinsky's the Jewish bakers. My father alone was immaculately dressed. I believe he was also the only one happily married. Avrom Stenzel had mysterious romances that were not discussed at home and Sochachevsky's marriage was certainly strained as a rubber band pulled to the limit. Even I was embarrassed by a most unpleasant skirmish I had witnessed on a visit there with my father.

As for Lysky with his startling wild shock of dark chestnut hair and even more diminutive stature than Stenzel, he often appeared with the same pleasant, reserved woman who seemed content enough to let him do all the talking. Both Stenzel and Lysky had a predilection for a drop or two of strong liquor. But I looked askance at the impoverished audience so appreciative of my father's talents. I wanted better for him—I was growing into a snob, in spite of my father's obvious humility and love of modest life-style.

For Trudy and me the grandparents were a sneaking look back at a pre-war, pre-nightmarish Munich we could scarcely admit we still hankered for. But for us, the two youngest, Munich was a synonym for blissful, fearless childhood. Trudy yearned for it so much that she volunteered to join the American Army in Germany to be stationed in a Munich smashed to pieces. Abi and Henny, on the other hand, wanted none of it. Their recollections were bitter and far from sweet and even I could not comprehend Trudy's heartfelt sympathy for the city and its inhabitants when our own hearts bled for our b brutally murdered people. Sympathy for the people who even if they did not know all the gruesome details, were still more than sufficiently involved in the escalating cruelty meted out in the early thirties to the Jewish population since the rise of Nazism? Sympathy for the Bavarians who so raucously cheered Hitler every step further in his way—the people who made him Chancellor! I certainly could not share my sister's sympathy.

Oma and Opa were quite unchanged; they had been in their early seventies and their dear faces looked exactly as they had done previously: old. They did not grumble about the lovely home they had lost simply delighted to be here, alive with us. And grandpa Opa was as incorrigible as ever, his harmless if very dated jokes making us laugh and never failing to annoy poor Oma as much as possible. The only trouble was that Papi did not feel like laughing at his or anyone's jokes. I believe he was particularly shocked at the fact that Opa, blowing his heady, yellow nicotine clouds, could sing and joke at all, aware as we all were that Uncle David, his wife and young daughters had not been heard of since the start of the war. They had been living in Lodz and then were presumably moved to the Ghetto there. After that there was nothing more—But Opa, the eternal optimist like his daughter, was certain that any day now there would be news—good news. Mutti, like Oma, was disinclined to speak of it at all, though there was definitely an air of melancholy about Oma and her sweet, childlike blue eyes were more clouded. But she did not complain and went on humming in her chair when there was nothing to say. This little grandmother simply hummed from morning to night but never when there was company or a conversation in progress elsewhere. In other words she seemed to hum to amuse and cheer herself and was probably unaware that those very hushed hums were at all audible. What she hummed was never a discernible tune or song.

I loved her as I loved the humming. I had recently begun to wonder if her humming was not a means of shutting out her husband's banter and the trials of the world at large. She was gentle, never aggressive unless provoked beyond endurance by her mischievous husband; she was the perfect grandmother who could bake the most amazing pastries if given half a chance. Of course she must have missed her elegant Munich flat over the GEBSATTEL Bridge but I never heard her speak of it. Uncle David and his young family were undoubtedly constantly on both their minds. Yet in their seventies they had been miraculously spared the horrors. Was it conceivable that David and his family had not? I like to think that Opa was putting on this act of insouciance as much for himself as for us all. Being so utterly different, they both had their own weapons to deal with the harsh realities.

It was a lovely day and the grandparents sat in deck-chairs basking in the warm sunshine. Mutti had borrowed the chairs from the ever-helpful Swinglers and I joined on the grass. Papi sat a little apart with pencil and pad on his lap. The talk was of Henny's wedding and the possibility of finding a house in North West London as Henny would be living there. Willy owned two houses in North West London. His brother Emile and his wife Janey occupied one of these. The other was rented out in two flats at present, but Willy and Henny would live in the downstairs flat which would be freshly papered and generally refurbished to Henny's taste. The flat upstairs was rented to a charming young newly-wed couple Mary and Charles Gabrovitch (later changed to Gabb.)

To Papi North West London, particularly Golders Green was the kind of milieu he most wanted to avoid. Jumped up nouveau riche with one major ambition: to make more money.—It was no good; he would never throw off that idealistic, unrealistic dream of a more equal society and above all one to whom art and culture were more important than fine dwellings, clothes and jewellery. He managed to feign delight at Henny's impressive diamond engagement ring. It was for Henny's sake, of course. Papi always did things for our sake, as did Mutti in her way. The lovely ring was double the size and many times the value of the one Mutti wore on her finger when he had saved every penny to buy the alluring Miriam the ring that would prove his undying love. There was no getting away from it: I realised more and more that my father was an incorrigible idealist whose faith in humanity was rapidly crumbling. He was also a genuinely moral man in every sense of that word without the constriction of stifling religious rules or superstitions. All those marvellous operatic and classical music pieces he had softly sung with full lyrics throughout my life and I had unwittingly soaked up, seemed to have shrunk away in shame or despair. He hardly emitted a note nowadays though he listened avidly to music on the wireless still, especially if the tenor Richard Tauber whom he had known in Munich was on or as a little later, Tauber had his own programme.

I believe it must have been my mother who from the start chose where we lived, because our home in the Schweigerstrasse was undoubtedly more posh than Papi would have chosen. And I must admit that for once I was on Mutti's side. I dreaded the thought of living in a battered East End as opposed to leafy, elegant Golders Green with fine shops and the lovely Hampstead Heath close by. I prayed secretly that Mutti would pull off this miracle as she had pulled off so many others. I was not all that unlike her. But I still fought with her.

Henny's wedding dinner would be at the kosher Kedassia Restaurant in the East End close to the synagogue. Willy's sister-in-law Janey was supervising procedures. She herself was a born and bred East Ender and seemed to have contacts all over the city. She had actually been involved in the couple's initial introduction and had simply fallen in love with my unassuming, modest sister whom from that first meeting she had taken under a wing she would never relinquish. Fortunately Henny appreciated the far older woman's affectionate guidance enormously. It was exactly what she needed in this entirely new life she was embarking on. Besides, Janey Trenner was hard to resist. She was the warmest, most charismatic East Ender one could ever hope to meet. Willy's brother Emile was as reticent a character as his brother and incidentally his wife, was loquacious and urbane. They were both members of the Diamond Bourse and were otherwise about as alike as Laurel and Hardy. In fact you were lucky if Emile so much as addressed you at all. But he was known for his kindness, generosity and piety. He was also a well-respected diamond expert. It soon became obvious to us that the vivacious, generously endowed yet hugely charming Janey was the exact opposite of her husband and was famous and much sought after for her wonderful culinary and hostess skills. Her parties, especially for young, unmarried Jewish couples were much sought after. Though it would have been difficult to squeeze her bulky figure into anything fashionable, with her beaming, welcoming smile and florid complexion there were few who did not fall under her spell.

The time of my Matriculation was drawing ever closer too. My classes at Ashby Hall had come to an end. The only way I would now see my friends would be at The White House where Dr Gruenfeld continued her Jewish History lessons for a short while longer and where we could play ping pong and generally get together. The school would be returning to London in the near future.

It never occurred to me to invite even Helga to tea. Our home was cramped and there seemed never enough space or chairs and although we were enormously fortunate to have found it, none of us considered it a real home. As for Solly, maybe he looked for me as I did for him. I hoped so with all my heart. The only admission I would make of my feelings was in a bedraggled little diary. "I love him—"I wrote much to my own surprise, "I really love him!"

I dragged myself into worn, gloomy old Shefford several early evenings to join in the ping pong games. But as they were generally in full swing by the time I arrived and Solly being one of the best players, was fully engaged, I felt foolish sitting around and waiting until his game was over so that he could play with me as he suggested several times. My pride took over and I left. On the long walk home I felt mortified and before long I gave up. Deep down I knew that if I did not make another effort, I might lose the people, especially the one person who had found a space in my heart. But it was not in me, in my nature, my upbringing to swallow pride.

I travelled to London University to sit for my Matriculation. In the vast hall I fleetingly met Solly, Helga and most of the other classmates. I had arrived at the last moment and Solly mumbled something about seeing me later. They had all travelled down together. But as I lived in Clifton and had hardly seen anyone from school for weeks, I had not been included in any of the school's arrangements. I felt shy and estranged when we met: an outsider.

We took different subjects of our choice. My English Literature papers were an absolute gift and I sank into them with real pleasure. I had loved Macbeth and Twelfth Night and had frequently been asked to read from each play by the wonderful Dr Levine. With his puckish humour he had frequently assured me that I read like the greatest Shakespearian actress and as for my written work he was sure that I would one day equal Shakespeare. I knew of course that he was inclined to tease me and yet deep down I hoped and actually believed that he thought highly of my potential and it did me the world of good.

I was not the greatest aficionado of Jane Austen. Her world was a million miles from any I had ever been close to. But she was one of the compulsory authors and Pride and Prejudice, which by the time of the exams I knew almost by heart, spilled from me with the ease of someone who was truly glad to be rid of it. I loved Charlotte Bronte and thought Jane Eire a far worthier project but I had to comply. I had chosen Pride and Prejudice as a last resort in preference to George Elliot's Mill on The Floss which I found even less riveting.

In short, I sailed through the Literature papers with ease. During the briefest recess I caught a glimpse of some of my school-friends. But it was a huge hall and we were widely scattered. I thought I saw Helga but I could not see Solly before it was time for the second round of papers. I would have liked to rush out for a cup of tea as I saw many students did but I did not have enough money. I just had enough money for the journey home.

I would need to return for French and German the following day and I was to stay with Henny and Hilde that night. Fortunately the German paper was the first and I nearly arrived late but I need not have worried. My two-hour paper was fully completed, revised twice and looked over yet again in less than forty-five minutes. There was nothing more to do until my French paper. Elated, I walked past sweating students as I handed the paper in. If nothing else, I had certainly bought a little extra time to go over some French Grammar again. The French paper did not strike fear in my heart and I managed to complete it in the set time, carefully going over it before handing it in. I was able to make use of all the vocabulary I had hammered into my head over and over again and now actually felt quite euphoric as I managed to use almost every of these words and expressions I somehow squeezed into the tightest fit.

It was over. I walked into the milling crowd in the vast hall. We had been told that this was not the usual procedure or place but since the blitz everything had had to be rearranged. I looked about me and with sinking heart realised there was not a sign of any other fellow pupil of the JSS around. I was sad and lonely. I knew deep down that this was truly the end of a momentous period in my life—another end?

I would not know the results for weeks and then only through Dr Gruenfeld who would be contacting me. The results did not much matter so far as I could see. No-one had actually ever explained the importance of passing Matriculation. Abi was the only one who understood the exam's significance but he was not around. For me it looked like yet another phase ending and a new one beginning. The present was not yet the past to regret and the future for a girl confused and egotistical, was a total blur. Somehow the next phase would be dealt with as the last had been. My emotions were as confused as my entire life. But I had my life and for someone of my age I certainly appreciated the significance of that.

Dr Levine and his family had already returned to London. The White House was in the process of being dismantled and the next time I walked into the tumble-down old relic of a building that was anything but white, invariably overflowing with hideous cooking smells and rumbustious mobs of unstoppable youngsters, it was deadly silent though the smells seemed to linger in crumbling walls and crevices. Maybe they were simply immured in my imagination.

I hesitated on the threshold as though held back by an invisible hand. The door was wide open. Not a soul, not a sound. I walked gingerly through hall, dining room and comically small kitchen where so much activity had taken place. I could hear the hilarious gibber of kitchen ladies in their mind-blowing accents yelling, screeching and laughing uproariously.

"Bring the bugger up the stairs!" Mrs Strom had yelled. Because some mischievous boy she had asked the word for bucket had told her bugger. Everyone had been in stitches, even the teachers.

I walked back into the main dining room where Dr Jacobson had held his music classes. Back into the narrow corridor where the small room that had been Dr Gruenfeld's sanctuary, her office was situated; not a soul. We had enjoyed her 'Schiurim' (lessons) there, or at least most of us had enjoyed them. I had rarely been one of them. For a moment I almost wished she was seated there still, upright and regal, her turban bound immaculately over her finely-shaped head, her pale, handsome face just a jot away from a warm smile. And Solly would be sitting close by, sometimes stealing a furtive look over at me.

It was true. We were the only refugees left in the hospitable Bedfordshire villages of Shefford and Clifton and any day we too would be gone. We were to stay here until Mutti had finalised the purchase of a link-detached house in 3 Hodford Road, Golders Green, a grand address by any standard, only a main road away from Holders Hill Park and the Heath. Only a stone's throw away from every refugee's oasis: Hampstead and Swiss Cottage already reverberating with German, Yiddish, Polish and French in its continental—style restaurants and Patisseries.

Mutti had taken me to see the house the day after my exams while I was staying with Henny and Hilde. I entered the beautiful, wood-panelled hall with parquet flooring and stood there speechless. The staircase was elegant, wide and of similar panelling along its walls that seemed to reach up to heaven they were so broad and high compared to anything I was accustomed to. Mutti eyed me, not used to such silence from her 'chutzpadig' daughter.

"Nu—"My response was to embrace and kiss her.

"It's—it's simply fabulous!" Was all I could say before I went on to explore the lovely hall, the sitting room, dining room, kitchen and pantry. I opened the kitchen door and there beside it was the outside toilet and beyond it a wonderful stretch of lawn surrounded by tall trees.

"Such a large garden—it's simply wonderful!" I exclaimed as she came up behind me.

"Look, look" I cried breathlessly "there are even rose—trees just like at the Lichtigs!"

Mutti's generally pale face was flushed with pleasure. We returned through the French doors of the dining room and I ran up the wide staircase with its fine balustrades two by two, to discover a generous bathroom, separate toilet next door, three spacious double bedrooms, one to the front and two to the back of the house and one good size single bedroom front-facing.

After the years of primitive accommodation to put it mildly, with no hot water even in Clifton Manor, our present haven, this house seemed to be just another phantasmagorical invention of my overactive imagination. I loved the area, so leafy, quiet and elegant. There was a cinema just minutes away on the main Finchley road and buses, buses, everywhere to take us into town, out of town, into our new world. A fine Synagogue was at the end of the road on the other side. Papi had to love this, surely.

Mutti had done it. She had somehow scraped together the pennies after years of chicken farming she must have hated just as much as we and above all, inspired purchasing of small, seemingly insignificant antique objects a few of which apparently turned out to be veritable treasures upon resale.

Henny and Willy's house as well as Janey and Emile's were only a short bus—ride down the long Golders Green and Finchley Roads respectively. They were also easily within walking distance. And yes, one of the double bedrooms would be set aside for the grandparents. The second one in the back would be mine and Trudy's when she returned from Germany and the front double bedroom would be the parents'. The smaller front bedroom would be let out.

Yes, now London beckoned with more allure than I had ever dared hope. I would be torn from a countryside that meant far more to me than I realised at the time. But I was alive, the hideous Germans had not managed to murder us and a new life beckoned. I was all of sixteen years old.

Chapter Seventeen

HENNY'S WEDDING. LONDON OUR NEW HOME

SOLLY

Only days before we were due to leave Clifton for good the unsettling reality hit me with a powerful punch. For nearly six years I had been part of this rural unsophisticated, honest farming community, in spite of its dependence upon pig farming and general animal husbandry I had grown to love it. To me the entire practice of using living creatures as though they were inanimate objects was cruel, inhuman and unnecessary when there was such a plentiful crop of every kind of vegetation and fruit. But humans were greedy gluttons even if they called pigs greedy. And gradually the place had come to mean almost as much as once my birthplace had done. The lovely scent of hay, the berries on the bushes in the little lanes; the high, sun—bleached corn in the meadows leading to the silvery brook that was almost a river, where under Hilde's supervision I had swum against parental permission; the stench that had gradually become a familiar, even welcome odour of the ill-used trusting cattle—now I would be leaving it all behind.

No-one else in the family felt about Clifton as I did. Trudy disliked it. The others were not much more enthusiastic. But they had not arrived here at the age of ten after having been thrown about hither and thither as on a choppy ocean to finally land here dizzy but unharmed. The war had washed over me but now I had reached my mid-teens and a more serious awareness took hold of me. I was excited but also a little apprehensive at what life held in store for me. London—the mere thought of living there permanently made my heart race. But I hardly knew anyone there of my age. I longed to meet new people—Londoners. But in my undiminished optimism, it never occurred to me that I might have to seek these new adventures at least as much as they might seek me.

I received a letter of congratulation from Dr. Gruenfeld, informing me that I had passed all three of my Matriculation subjects, English Literature and German with Distinction and French with an A. Both parents were still shell-shocked at ever-increasing news of the horrors of the camps and hardly gave it the kind of attention they would once have given such an achievement. I myself was particularly pleased that I had mastered French so quickly and hoped to keep up and improve my knowledge of that language as I enjoyed its elegance and lovely tonality. I vowed to hitch-hike to Paris as soon as I found a girl-friend willing to come with me. Many young students hitch-hiked but of course I would not tell the parents of my plans; at any rate they were in the nebulous future, as were all my evolving dreams.

It seems that the entire war years were wrapped in the songs of that period. With sponge-like efficiency I soaked up every tune within hearing as well as their words, nonsensical and trite as many of them were. To me they had more relevance than any of the actual occurrences as they were far easier to grasp. And most of them, especially the American songs by Irvin Berlin, Richard Rogers and Jerome Kern, were able to reach a young girl's romantic fantasies. I had left my early self behind in Munich, my friends, my teacher, my beautiful, comfortable home, a far larger chunk than I was aware. The next phases were spasmodic and I accepted everything—but superficially. Songs and music of every genre, just as, it would seem once was true for my father, could reach my very being whilst an icy outside world was pushed aside.

HENNY MARRIES WILLY

I was given the princely sum of seven pounds with which to choose a dress and shoes for my sister's wedding in London. It really seemed a most generous sum of money to me and I was sure I could purchase my dream dress and elegant high-heeled shoes as well and have a little over for a Coty lipstick I was determined to wear on this special occasion. After all I was a young woman now and it was time to make the most of that newly acquired status just as Trudy had done

I had seen a most enchanting lavender-blue dress in the window of Rose's in Bedford. The gorgeous mannequin looked like a princess in the kitten-soft woollen frock, fitted to the doll-like waist and billowing gently out over tiny hips. I could envision myself in that dress as I stood for ages outside staring at the mannequin, too shy to enter the posh store with its snooty sales personnel. It was the sort of frock any film star would be proud to wear. I felt certain that five pounds or thereabouts would be ample. The dress was not priced in the window.

It did not occur to me that I was not even dressed in my best Sabbath clothes which consisted of a nice angora jumper I had recently inherited from Henny, who in turn had inherited it originally from our cousin Hanni. There was also a new (for me) Gorray skirt I had been given from who knew where. But I was not in my Sabbath best.

Instead, I wore an old dress that was too tight and short and betrayed umpteen bad wash-days as well as perspiration marks under the arms as I had begun perspiring. My legs were bare, a sign of poverty if ever there was one if I had given it the slightest thought. The pair of crepe-soled shoes Mutti had bought me a year earlier that had been such a bargain from the down-market shop further down the street, were probably the one acceptable sartorial item. I had worn them incessantly since, however, and they looked it. My hair was as ever a mass of frizz. I doubt if my entrance made the impression I would have liked.

But a coward I was not as I walked in, head held as high as I knew how. No-one rushed to greet me as was custom. In fact it seemed as though I was being deliberately ignored with plenty of sales personnel all looking the other way. So instead of being approached I had to approach the first person who caught my eye. It was demoralising as was the manner in which my request to see the dress was treated. I was immediately in formed of the price: ten guineas, though I had not asked for such information. I swallowed hard but now I was rattled and took the obvious insult with what I hoped was perfect equanimity.

"I would like to see the dress." I repeated. The tall, thin woman all in black took her time. Then with the utmost reluctance she brought the dress down from the first floor instead of inviting me upstairs where the fitting room was situated. My face was flushed from the insult but I was an obvious refugee and it was not the first time I had had to swallow an insult almost always from a girl not much older than myself.

The woman held the lovely dress aloft as though I might pollute it. I studied it with so much longing and felt the material. It was unbelievably soft to the touch. The thought of having something that gently caressing against my flesh was of course too good to be true. Every single garment I had ever worn, even angora, scratched against my sensitive flesh with the intensity of a saucepan—scraper.

"Did you say ten guineas?" My voice sounded alien, hoarse. I was known for my deep voice, but now I sounded as if someone were choking me. The cynical smile was broad as she nodded without as much as a yes madam.

"I'll think about it." I said without looking at her as I walked out of the shop into the fresh air. I let out a deep sigh as my eyes watered.

I could not recall ever wanting a garment that much. Never mind about the humiliation. Pride was something refugees could not afford. That time in FRANZENSBAD when my dear Mutti had come to the rescue. Yes, I had craved that lovely coat. But I knew that this time I would have to relinquish such an elaborate fancy. It was a salient experience.

A few doors away around the corner towards WOOLWORTH, was a small, modest clothes shop with shoes, jumpers and dresses in the window, displayed higgledy-piggledy. I had previously ignored it as I knew full well it was not where I had hoped to buy my first brand new grown-up dress in England. I was my own boss, with money in my pocket and I had to return with a dress. The beautiful, seductively soft woollen dress at Rose was a far-off dream I must forget. But this shop; it was so ugly and bald. There was nothing to tempt you inside its unadorned little show-room with a linoleum covered floor, a steep staircase leading to a poky fitting room—except the realisation that here were the clothes a poor refugee with a five pound note and a little over for shoes, stockings and maybe even a lipstick could afford!

I found myself in that fitting room trying on a dress of the harsh wool I had been battling most of the past few years and of a screaming purple colour. It only just fitted and as I was asked to walk downstairs to show myself to the canny shop-keeper, he clapped his hands in delight.

"Beautiful—"he cried, "You are a beautiful young lady—just the dress for you! You look like a film-star! That colour—it was made for you!" And after he had twirled me around the sole, stained mirror several times more I almost believed him.

It was all I needed to hear plus the fact that the dress cost less than five pounds. According to the shop-keeper he was giving me a special price because I was made for the frock. And wasn't I lucky, they had just the right pair of shoes too: a black suede pair with teetering high heels in which I could hardly walk and that pinched and stubbed my toes. But I was told they looked perfect and I could have both shoes and dress for the much reduced price of my seven pounds with even a pair of stockings thrown in—not silk, naturally. It was done. I parted with the largest sum of money I had ever owned, if only for a few hours.

My dear sister Henny wore what was for 1945, just months after cessation of all hostilities, a most lavish white wedding dress which somehow dwarfed her and made her look vulnerable and shell-shocked as though she simply did not know what was going on around her. I had little chance to speak to her when we were seated in the dingy Kedassia Restaurant, naturally strictly kosher. I believe it was a make-shift venue as the original building had been bombed. I wanted very much to hug her but I was seated at a little table with a few other young people I did not know. Now Willy was in charge and whether I realised it or not, that day he was not my favourite person although he was always most charming and complimentary and made a fuss of me.

Trudy arrived late in her WAAF Uniform and was a great success but to my dismay she left early to return to base. Abi was not in Uniform and looked handsome but distant. I think all three of us were overawed by this sudden change in our cosy family set-up. We all knew that it would never be the same again. But we also knew, yes even I, just how fortunate we were. And whether we admitted it or not, we knew too that this marriage of our good, sensible sister would bring her contentment and a standing in the community she so wholly deserved.

My outfit, my entire appearance: an over-painted mouth with the cheapest lipstick from Woolworth, I think it was Ponds (Max Factor had been way above my means), did not exactly have the effect I had expected. I thought I looked very adult and glamorous. What I must really have looked like was sad and cheap; a teenager desperate to look grown-up. I teetered on the most uncomfortable pair of shoes I had ever worn and swore never to wear again. The purple dress most likely did little for my slightly olive complexion and naturally ruddy cheeks plastered with floury powder I had found in Trudy's old drawer. My long, thick, raven page-boy may have been eye-catching, but even I realised that in my sad, tight cheap dress a Hedy Lamarr I was not!

I traipsed up and down those perilous, narrow stairs of the dilapidated old building unsure where I was heading. I felt lost as Papi was entertaining his writer friends. Whenever he caught sight of me he would call me over and I would be patronised by these well-meaning, to me ancient relics of another age. Only Papi looked debonair and very attractive and the two or three ladies of the group would monopolise him whenever possible. Mutti was with the newly-weds looking content but stressed. I do not know if what she wore was new but I doubt it. She had put on a little weight thanks to her own culinary skills as had I, and clothes were certainly not on her list of priorities. She always wore hats outdoors and I liked her so much better without. I believe she was dressed in a navy suit, hat and white silk blouse—smart but hardly eye-catching. But that was the last thing my mother would have wanted at any rate. There was so much to see to, to achieve still and if anyone would manage it she would.

Janey Trenner seemed much more at ease. She too wore a hat but it was jaunty, almost audacious, with its bits of fauna and flora and framing her flushed, chubby, face but above all, it was obviously new and fashionable. Remarkably one tended to ignore all else Janey wore not merely because of her size but because her face could hold you with its vivacity and irresistible joy de vivre. Somehow she ruled over any small crowd she graced. She had captured Henny from the start but I am not convinced if she and Hilde were quite so well-matched any more than she and Mutti. These two indomitable ladies were made of sterner stuff.

Hilde, what did she wear? As with Janey I took little notice of my cousin's attire but she looked charming enough from what I recall, with her trim figure clad most likely in her best grey woollen suit and white silk blouse as was almost de rigueur at the time for an afternoon do of this kind. Her page boy, reaching just below the nape of the neck, was always immaculately styled as she had a smooth, full head of black hair. And she took good care of it so that it always looked clean and trim. Henny and I were the ones with frizzy hair, but Henny's had been suitably tamed and coiffed for this occasion.

We were staying over in London that night. I would sleep at Hildes' who had retained the room she had shared with Henny for the present. She had enjoyed the wedding a great deal more than I had and looked a good deal more elated than any of us siblings. Fortunately she had left her trilby at home though I would not have put it past her to wear it to 'shul' (synagogue). The parents, I believe, were staying in a modest boarding house in Golders Green Janey had found for them. There was the house in Hodford Road, off the Finchley Road, to inspect once more next morning. And there was Papi to persuade as he was not yet won over. The excitement of that day seemed never to come to an end. Not for a moment did I think of how Henny was feeling. She was on her way to her honey-moon destination. Neither Hilde nor I spoke of it. I was far too innocent and Hilde far too discreet.

'THE LONDON I LOVE'

The day we moved into 3 Hodford Road, our beautiful new house in Golders Green, the second phase of my childhood was truly over. In fact so far as I was concerned my teenage could also be safely packed off. I had worn my first pair of high-heeled shoes, worn lipstick in public and born myself like an adult. Until Trudy's return I would have my own spacious room overlooking the verdant garden. My own cupboard and the bathroom with running hot and cold water was next door, the lavatory next to that. The generous gas fire in the room was absolute luxury though we would use it only when it became seriously cold. The house did not have central heating as we had had in Germany but after years of freezing cold rooms and houses with ice-cold water where and when it was available, I think none of us could quite believe our sudden good fortune. Papi smiled a lot those first weeks and called Mutti 'Marieleben', his pet name for her. Yes, I believe he finally saw the advantage of a truly spacious, comfortable and lovely home once more, although at heart he must have felt that no Jew could and should rejoice in anything. For him, as for many, true genuine happiness was a thing of the past.

But rejoice in the house and its surroundings we did. The houses backed on to Holders Hill Park and I would take long walks with Papi, his favourite form of recreation. As the Regal cinema was only minutes away up the road in the ubiquitous Finchley Road, the parents could treat themselves to the occasional night out, something they had not been able to do since those scarcely creditable days of their former life.

Papi really fell for Rita Hayworth in 'GILDA'. It certainly took me by surprise though I should have understood that there would always be a part of him that loved theatre and film not to mention m music. As was his way he came home singing its main song with the words mangled as only he could, so that "put the blame on Mame boys—"would only become recognisable once I had seen the film myself. Though it was wonderful to see him even the slightest bit more like his old self, it was obvious that the Papi of yore would never again return. He was also suffering from stomach ulcers that continued to persist no matter how much Milk Of Magnesia he swallowed or whatever other medicine he was prescribed. He was in pain a good deal of the time but did not complain. He just ate even less than before.

I had lost contact with almost everyone from Shefford excepting Jochwed Heidenstein (Jock) who to my genuine delight, had managed to contact me on our new phone line almost as soon as it was installed and listed in the London Phone Book. I received news of other fellow students and invited Jock to come and visit. Solly's name did not come up as Jock was not interested in boys and had no idea of my interest in Solly Bornstein. Did I bring up his name casually in passing? Maybe, but as there was little or no information of interest, I certainly did not press further though I would have given a great deal to know what he was doing. Did I dream of him or fantasise of a future where we would be together? Hardly, Solly was not dream material. He was not glamorous and I had not reached the stage where I imagined myself married with children in a happy ever after scenario. And yet he was and remained somewhere deep down and was far from forgotten.

As I have said, my childhood and early teenage was at an end and with it these Memoirs must of necessity come to an end too. Yet as I found it so hard to discover the real me for several years, experimenting with the person I thought I was, to the person I might eventually become, dreaming of a glamorous thespian career and then again falling under the influence of all the serious, unforgettable literature I had swallowed so greedily; the terrible fate of so many of my class-mates in Munich, my teens were a prison I needed to escape as soon as possible. And the London I now explored by bus and foot from one unfamiliar square, monument or theatre to its sprawling parks, filled me with love, awe, admiration and fear. Where did I belong?

Long ago I had admitted to my diary that I loved Solly. After seeing a great many romantic films and reading even more romantic novels, especially Jane Eire by Charlotte Bronte, I knew that what I had felt for Solly was very different. It had nothing to do with sex about which I was still pitifully ignorant. And yet the feeling, the flutter when his name was mentioned or I thought of him, remained.

I was the baby of the family and my parents would always treat me just that bit more leniently and maybe favourably. I knew it and expected it but it did not help me mature. Abi was the only one who took me more seriously even confiding his romantic problems in me. But I still did not get on with Mutti who was not at all encouraging in my quest to win a scholarship to RADA (The Royal Academy of Dramatic Art in Gower Street) and certainly the most prestigious School of Drama in the country. I did not doubt my ability. However, I was not sure deep down if that was really what I wanted to do with my life. I had always written the odd short story and poem and loved writing. Papi was a writer and he was the person I most admired. No one in our household yearned or even aspired to riches. Papi had laid the foundation long ago of disdain for greed and voracity. Shakespeare had created the monster Shylock and Dickens Fagin. Jews were never like that and must show the world as much. He had grown up in poverty in Krakow surrounded by study and piety. That was the way to be.

And now Papi, who might himself once have hankered after a theatrical career, was encouraging me in my thespian aspiration. He had met a lady who taught elocution and he took me to see her. She agreed to give me a short course free of charge. I have no idea where or how Papi had met her but she seemed more than happy to oblige. She was English obviously and did not even understand Yiddish. But somehow she had become a part of Papi's circle and they had formed a friendship. She lived in The Frognal in Hampstead only a short bus ride away and at a pinch I was prepared to walk there. After all, when you have traversed miles and miles of Bedfordshire countryside, walking is not an obstacle. And this wonderful lady was prepared to help me get on the ladder of my dream after a brief introduction.

I enjoyed these visits enormously. I drank in the entire area around Hampstead and Swiss Cottage. Not only were the streets abundantly tree-lined. But the Finchley Road that took in part of Swiss Cottage, abounded with continental patisseries, restaurants, cafes and clubs literally spilling over with refugees. The Cosmo, The Dorice—magic names I longed to be taken to by some suave gentleman, preferably resembling Anton Walbrook or Charles Boyer. It would come soon enough, if not in the guise of such heart-throbs. But for me at that time it simply could not come soon enough.

My elocution teacher lived in a spacious, high-ceilinged flat on the ground floor of a large, dilapidated Victorian house. So far as I could tell she lived alone. But of course I was not in the least interested in other people's affairs. I was probably one of the least inquisitive youngsters one could wish to meet.

Miss M's flat was furnished exactly as expected: frayed crimson velvet chaiselongue and armchairs with matching equally shabby and faded cushions. The walnut furniture was huge and cumbersome and displayed endless, dust-encrusted antique ornaments. There was a constantly crackling, spitting, fetid coal fire in the old, black grate. Altogether that huge room never quite warm enough, always sooty, held and still holds my affection. It belonged to a distant, unexplored world I had never and would never inhabit. I would try desperately not to choke on the smoke and succeeded most of the time, improving my diction from visit to visit until I myself could tell that "how now brown cow" sounded very Sybil Thorndike, even Vivienne Leigh!(Never, however, quite without that slight foreign intonation.)

I would go there on my own after Papi's initial introduction. She was a Miss so even I could deduce that she was a spinster. Her clumsily dyed black hair wa starkly fake and unflattering in an aging face. Her cheeks were rouged in an otherwise white face and altogether she looked the part of the faded actress which I believe is what she was. But her dark eyes were bright and alight as she spoke and taught with affection and interest. I liked the way she looked. It was how I envisaged the face of an aging thespian right down to the heavy black fringe obscuring part of her pale forehead. I thought her very old when she was probably no more than in her late forties. And she was a brilliant teacher filling me with mounting confidence. As will be obvious she is one of the only people whose name I do not recall, perhaps even never knew as I called her Miss with the reverence shown a prized teacher. The obvious explanation had to be that Papi, who had not yet mastered more than a handful of English words, had never been able to pronounce her name and thus entrust it to me.

The exam consisted of a choice of any female speech or oration from a Shakespeare play. I chose Lady Macbeth, the only of the Bard's plays that had ever appealed to me though I had taken 'Twelfth Night' and 'As You Like It' at Matriculation, which had been Dr Levine's choice of tuition. I could also choose a speech from any play and I chose one of Strindberg's, just about the darkest, surely least quoted the examiners had ever been confronted with. I was very dramatic in my rendering to be sure and I must have had a fairly strong foreign accent still which did not come amiss for a foreign play.

I had entered for a full scholarship. But at the back of my mind was yet another notion: I loved writing stories and had written several only to tear them up. Dr. Levine had always encouraged me; could I become a journalist? That would surely be a good, honourable profession? Yes, life was full of possibilities now that I was no longer a school girl and the war was over. The 'lights had gone on again all over the world' so far as we knew. (Quoting from the war-time song: 'When the Lights Go On Again All Over the World.) I had a great deal of confidence in myself and felt that whatever fate had in store for me now, it was certain to be for the best.

1945 was coming to an end and I was on the threshold of seventeen. The scholarship would decide my entire future life. I cared—but not enough as teaching and writing also attracted me. The letter came just before Christmas. I was offered a partial scholarship with ten pounds to pay per term. I read and reread the letter. Unaware how hard it was even to pass the ordinary entrance exam failed by some of the finest future stars, I shook my head stubbornly and arrogantly.

"No Mutti, "I said proudly as she stood there uncertain as to what to say, let alone to do. "It's alright—I can't expect you to pay that. It doesn't matter!" And as Papi looked so crestfallen I actually added:

"Pappele, you did your best—IT DOESN'T MATTER!"

And that was that. My disappointment was tinged with relief. Fate had once again stepped in to decide my future. Or was that the start of my running, running away from the slightest obstacle instead of facing it head on?

Had my mother been less traumatised by what had transpired in her own life and my father physically stronger and less broken as a man by then, I believe they would both have made sure that I would take up this once in a life-time offer from the Royal Academy Of dramatic Art. As it was I stood in our kitchen in Hodford Road holding the letter with a form included that required filling in. I spoke with conviction even if there were tears in my eyes.

"No, you can't pay" I repeated magnanimously feeling very self-effacing. "It doesn't matter!" Did I mean it or was it just another act?

Both parents looked at me and said nothing more. None of my siblings were at home. Maybe if Abi had been present he might have had a hand in changing my fate.

"Anyway, there are always repertory companies." I remembered to add more for my own benefit as I don't think either of my parents had the faintest idea what I was talking about.

I accepted a post soon after in Horley, Surrey, as a student teacher in a Jewish Boarding Prep School. My hair was very long and a striking raven black finally tamed into a fashionable page boy and the girls told me that their parents said I was beautiful and looked like Hedy Lamarr. I did have large green eyes and unusually thick, curling lashes. At the age of seventeen I thought all my dreams had come true. Who needed RADA! I was attracted to one of the nephews of the headmistress and it seemed he reciprocated the feeling. Above all I enjoyed teaching the little boarders who hung on every word I uttered and I made friends with the senior girls only a few months older than I.

But there it was again or still: inhibition, pride or simply innocent lack of any experience. The young man I felt attracted to, scarcely older than I was equally gauche and tongue-tied. We would stare at each other. I would blush and once in a while we might exchange a few words. I liked his thick black moustache. But Solly was never far away, a kind of remote precious part of that childhood I was sure I had now left behind. It had never occurred to me to make an effort to take a bus or tube and travel to Stamford Hill, where I knew all the old class-mates would occasionally meet up as they worshipped in the Synagogue which was part of the old Jewish Secondary School. That old Jewish Secondary School was once again a proud resident of Stamford Hill. As it was it seemed I was the only one of our old class resident in Golders Green!

I was lonely again or still. Days off were spent wondering around the neighbouring countryside on my own, with the occasional treat in one of those lovely old county Inns slowly, o' so slowly supping on the smallest portion of Plaice and chips. But to sit with other people and at last able to pay for my meal from my meagre earnings, made me feel very adult and more—It gave me a feeling of accomplishment. If I was stared at by the occasional equally lonely gentleman or even spoken to, I would simply ignore it and put it down as part and parcel of a young woman's reward for not being unattractive. At the same time I was extremely wary of strangers. The girls had told me that Mulek, the heads' nephew, had let it be known that he found me very attractive. I was thrilled and was perfectly happy to leave it at that. Maybe I hoped as he obviously did, that one of us would finally make a move. Meanwhile I dreamed of romance. It would all come, of that I had little doubt.

I had not seen anyone from my class for a year. Helga and I had not kept in touch. I simply lived too far away in every sense. Whereas most of my class-mates did not stray from their religious belief and its upkeep, I had made little secret of my growing scepticism. Of course Palestine was on everyone's mind. Suddenly the country that was our saviour became a demon. Why would they, how could the British stop Jews returning to the land they had longed, prayed for ever since the destruction of the temple? "Next year in Jerusalem!" we sang at the Seder every Passover. Millions of those chanting voices had been stilled for ever. What fiendishness to refuse the EXODUS entry to the port of Haifa, crammed to the stifling brim with sick women and children! I was torn apart.

I loved England with an overpowering sense of admiration and gratitude. But I loved my people too with an equally strong sense of loyalty and never being able to rid mysels of that open unhealed wound of degradation inflicted by the Germans. I had made up my mind long since that this feeling had nothing to do with religious belief. I thought it was a historical right but Papi had always maintained that there would be terrible bloodshed as the Arabs had resided there for centuries.

Papi felt as he had always done. Palestine was not ours indisputably. I would argue with him as was my way. But his words were never lost on me either. Undoubtedly after what had happened since the war, a country of our own was the only comfort (if there is such a thing after the deliberate genocide of six million Jews) that might eventually inspire the remainder with hope and a renewed belief in humanity. And the vast majority of Jews in this country and the States prayed for the eventual legitimate establishment of our own country. They were going to call it Israel. I felt like crying. It sounded too good to be true. It felt and sounded right.

Maybe for Papi, though even he had become more enthusiastic, a country of our own no matter where, was too late. Of course it was. His world had been destroyed. Since the Warsaw Ghetto Uprising in 1943, my handsome, debonair father steeped in world art and culture whether music or literature; an idealist with unshakable morals, had gradually changed into a world-weary man in physical and mental agony. Having heard of the unimaginable cruelty of the murderous German soldiers well before it had become common knowledge, what his journals had related was inconceivable brutality against helpless, defenceless men women and children. These satanic creatures were bent on exterminating every Jew in Europe. Where were Churchill and Roosevelt—why was outrage so hushed throughout the world?

Not only that but with it the precious, unique Yiddish culture was in danger of dying too as it was OSTJUDEN who had clung to and enriched that language. Now it was mooted that the new State of Israel would adopt Hebrew as their national language. This was the final blow. His entire life's dreams and ideals lay in tatters. Yiddish was the foundation-stone of the entire cultural voice of these razed Eastern European Jews.

I would go on adoring the nobility of my father, his pure idealism, as he had done his father's; though in my case it threatened at times to stand in the way of my own relationships. What I did not realise at the time was that to love a father this much meant inevitably tat you sought him in every man, in every close relationship for the rest of your life. And that you would never find him again.

As for Mutti—I needed to grow up a great deal more to value her full worth—but we were both fortunate to be granted that time.

The following demands relating as it spelt the final termination of my adolescence. A new Mella slowly reluctantly emerged.

Jochewed Heidenstein (Jock) was one of only a couple of class-mates who phoned me occasionally. It was easier to phone me as we were on the phone whereas most of the girls or boys lived in rented accommodation with shared phones. But I found it puzzling and touching that Jock, who was my absolute antithesis in every sense, should make such an effort to keep in touch. From the start she had always found the comfort in religion I so resolutely discarded from the age of twelve. But then it was not difficult to see why she needed an anchor as her parents had sent her and her siblings away to safety on the KINDERTRANSPORT, themselves remaining behind and never a word from them since.

It was during one of those much appreciated calls that Jock mentioned in passing that of course I must know that all of the boys of our form had gone to Palestine to join in the fight for liberation.

"No, "I cried excitedly, "I had no idea—how marvellous!"

There was a weighty pause. "You mean you really didn't know? In that case you won't have heard about Solly? "

"Solly—I suppose he went too." I interrupted even more excited at the sound of his name.

"O' yes—but—he was killed!"

"What are you saying—MY Solly? But, but—"

"Yes, they had only been out there six weeks when he stepped on a land-mine!"

"O' God—"then after another long pause: "I loved him—"I heard myself say out loud. "I really loved that wonderful boy! Why on earth—just him" I don't recall what Jock replied. She must have been quite taken aback by my outburst. Pupils of the Jewish Secondar School were not accustomed to such passionate outpouring.

I had spoken from the depth of my being, surprising even myself And I had called him 'my Solly' when I had never had the courage to reveal my feelings while he was alive. Would it have altered anything? Could I have stopped him? Of course not . . .

Tears, I don't think so. But a life-long sore and longing for a love that never was and probably never could have been.

EPILOGUE

Josef, Hillel Levy died April 2nd.1955 at the age of sixty-four. He had been seriously ill two years earlier with a burst stomach ulcer. I returned from Berne Switzerland, where I had been teaching English to the children of the Ambassador of Siam, (Thailand) having left my first husband in 1951. My mother and I stayed at the small Cottage Hospital for several nights as it looked increasingly more serious. Papi was delirious much of the time and there were times when he called out my name in bloodcurdling volume, heard throughout the hospital. His sonorous voice took on eerie, other-worldly tones. His words have echoed in my head throughout the years:

"Mella, ich will weren varbrennt!" (I want to be burnt (cremated))! And he would repeat his plaintive plea over and over.

I understood full well why he addressed himself to me and not to his wife. It was against the orthodox doctrine of Judaism and no orthodox cemetery would inter ashes of the deceased. My mother was a traditionally orthodox woman. He knew she would not—could not acquiesce. Did he really believe I could induce her to change her unshakable, life-long belief? That haunting voice—my poor, delirious Papi!

I held his fine hands in mine, almost unable to look at his ashen face and nodded agreement with a beating heart and tears streaming down my cheeks. My mother was mercifully out of hearing or so it seemed. It took me no time to comprehend what he was really saying. It was not that he was rejecting the traditions of his beloved father. It was clearly that he wanted to share the final fate of the millions that would continue to haunt him until his last breath.

But Papi was to survive this illness and live another two years. He had lost weight and was a shadow of his former self. He continued to write and he and mother enjoyed an Indian summer all their own, with mother devoting every spare moment to him. Yet she continued as a successful and respected broker at Hatton Garden. That was how she had been able to pay for her husband's private care at the hospital without assistance from anyone else.

The lovely house was quiet and the garden green and fragrant. All four of their children were gone though Henny and her family lived close by and I too lived nearby in Swiss Cottage having recently left my first husband.

The family were due to meet at the Golders Green Hippodrome where Henny had booked seats for an Italian opera, I do not recall which. (Perhaps I never knew.) Abi, who had married Joy Felkoff was the father of little eighteen months old Anne and few weeks' old Ruth and lived in Stoke Newington, would not be joining us.

I arrived early at Hodford Road to find Papi ready to leave.

"But it's far too early, Papi," I reproached him laughing, as he greeted me dressed in his fedora hat and coat—"the bus only takes five minutes. Why are you all dressed to go already?"

He smiled his wistful, sweet smile. "I like to take my time." He said simply. "I'll meet you there in the lobby."

I shook my head as we kissed.

"O' Papele—"was all I could say as I watched the frail figure in his grey, immaculate Burton overcoat and matching fedora hat retreat down the short garden path and out of the gate into the tree-lined street that joined Finchley Road at the corner.

When over an hour later mother and I arrived at the Hippodrome we were met by Henny, Willy and Janey Trenner but no father. We scattered and each looked in different parts of theatre and lobby. As it was growing late and the performance was due to start I volunteered to wait outside whilst the others could go inside. Maybe Papi had decided to walk all the way as he liked walking.

I stood for a few moments undecided on the stone steps leading up to the theatre before setting off searching the length and breadth of the bus terminal, at the foot of which the theatre was situated.

Almost opposite the theatre I suddenly spotted an ambulance. As though driven by some unseen hand I approached and noticed the open door. I stood undecided.

"Yes Miss," The Driver appeared.

"I'm looking for—I'm looking for my father."

"Your father—o' no—he's not here."

"But—"

"No, the man inside is an old man—he couldn't—"

But by now I hardly heard what he was saying.

"I'd like to see for myself—"I insisted and without further ado I stepped inside the ambulance.

I had never been inside such a vehicle before. Momentarily the entrance part, a kind of lobby, confused me as it was like a small First Aid Centre. The room leading off it was visible only through a half-open curtain. And all I could make out was the corridor and the base of a stretcher. I hesitated before pushing the curtain aside.

"Miss-"

My father lay on that stretcher in his best coat and gleaming polished brown shoes; his eyes were closed and he was obviously not conscious.

"Papi—"I cried as the man walked up to me in surprise. I kissed the face of the sleeping figure several times.

"Will he be alright?" I asked. "He—it's my father!"

"We're taking him to the Royal Free Hospital." Was all the information he would supply. Papi had been taken off the bus in the terminal having apparently fought for breath on the bus with no help available until an ambulance could be called. What I did not know was that my beloved father was already dead when I found him.

Marie, Miriam Lowy published father's collections of poetry and essays posthumously with the help of the Yiddish poet Lisky. She survived her beloved 'Jossele' by thirty-six years and passed away April 23rd. 1990 at the age of 94 having continued work at the Bourse in Hatton Garden into her early nineties. She was the rock of our family.

Chana Henne Lowy, nee Bienenfeld, died in Clifton, Bedfordshire on August 4th 1941 of a sudden cold that turned to pneumonia. She was senenty-nine years old. The most pious person I would ever know.

Aaron Tennenbaum resided in New York with grandma Chatsche at Ida and Paul Theilheimer's home after having lived with us for several years at Hodford Road. Aaron passed away at the age of eighty-six and Chatsche (Helen) lived with Ida and Paul in Miami Beach and passed away at the age of ninety-six in New York. She remained the sweetest lady to the end.

Abi Lowy and his wife Joy (nee Felkoff) had two daughters Anne and Ruth. Abi and Joy, a devoted couple, died within months of each other, Abi in April 2001 aged eighty-one and Joy in January 2002 aged seventy-five. She was one of my dearest friends.

Abi had begun working life after demob as a Maths teacher but later followed Willy Trenner and his mother into the diamond bourse where he became a successful and highly respected diamond broker.

Henny Trenner survived Willy over twenty years but her health took a violent downturn from the day Willy collapsed suddenly of a heart-attach at the age of senty-two. Willy was well-known and a sought after diamond merchant, frequently assisting young people to get started in the trade. He was a devoted and well-liked family member.

Willy and Henny had two daughters Annette and Elizabeth. Henny passed away in December 1998 aged seventy-eight within days of delighting in the birth of her first great grand-child.

Trudy (Trudel) Natapoff married her GI Marshall Natapoff but the marriage was later dissolved. They had two daughters Karen and Laura. She passed away in the United States September 1999, aged seventy-five.

David Tennenbaum and his entire family, wife and three young daughters were murdered by the Germans and it is believed they all met their deaths in Auschwitz. No trace has been discovered.

Rosel Bernstein (auntie Rosel) lost Uncle Bernhard early in the war years. He died of stomach cancer in London. The entire family had escaped to England not long before. Her children Hanni and Abi predeceased her. Abi died at the age of forty-nine and Hanni in her early fifties. Hanni had settled in Haifa with her handsome solicitor husband Max whose bridesmaid I had been at the age of eleven. Auntie Rosel died at the age of eighty-six.

Auntie Ida married twic and had two children: Bernie Erteschick from her first husband and Rochelle from Paul Theilheimer. Aunt Ida passed away in the States at the age of ninety-eight.)

Hilde Stiel married her childhood love Yitzhak Friedlander (later changed to Eshel) and they remained a loving, inseparable couple until passing away within months of each other in Israel at eighty-eight and ninety-two respectively. They had a son and a daughter.

Trudel Roth (Stiel) and Kuno her charismatic dentist husband, whose tiny bridesmaid I had been in Munich before their emigration from Berlin to Tel Aviv, had three children, two girls and a boy. They both died in Tel Aviv.

Louis and Jani Stiel survived the war in Nice and later immigrated to Israel where they were respected teachers. Louis married but Jani remained a bachelor.

Topsy (Ilse Herzberg) rediscovered me in 'Weiss's' in Golders Green in 1949 when she mistook me for Trudy as this was the first time we had met since she left Stotfold. I was trousseau shopping for my wedding to Richard Adler (later dissolved). Our friendship blossomed for many years until Topsy died of lung cancer in Israel in1990 aged sixty-two. She never married. We had become the closest of friends.

Lehrer Berlinger committed suicide early in the war thus mercifully escaping the horrors of the death camps. I do not know the details but I have never forgotten him.

Solly (Solomon) Bornstein met his early death in Israel where with his entire class he had volunteered to fight in THE WAR OF ATTRITION in 1947. He had been there barely six weeks when he stepped on a land—mine. He was not yet eighteen years old.

Chaim Joachim Stiel, my cousine Hilde's father who had not wanted to leave with his sons, was murdered in Buchenwald in 1941.

Martha Haftel married Hans Schlamme and became a well-known singer and entertainer in the United States. Sadly she died of a stroke on stage in New York aged sixty-two. Her Yiddish records are greatly treasured.

Having shaken off the shackles of religion, I still treasure beyond words the priceless memories of these religious Jewish traditions thanks to my father's modest, loving, open-minded manner. And I treasure the country Solly and thousands of others gave their life to regain. So soon after the slaughter of the millions, with no place for the few survivors, our pride in shatters, it seemed so right, so fair. Is there anything in history, any event that still bears the same connotation fifty, a hundred years later than it did originally?

As stated at the front of this Memoir, it is dedicated to my dearest niece Ruth Lawy, (nee LOWY) Abi and Joy's youngest daughter, who has been far more than a niece to me and has always been at the ready with printer and computer if help was needed. Her brilliance with anything technical far exceeded not merely mine but most people's I can think of. Ruth had been plagued by her illness since her early twenties. But she bore even the final, escalating trials with a stoicism that left everyone around her filled with admiration and humility.

Sadly we lost her on November 5th 2010 at the age of 55. Her illness stretched over thirty years but her beauty, her courage and her love for life and her husband, relatives and friends, seemed to leave far fitter people way behind. She and I had forged an exceptionally close bond and I thought of her more as a daughter than a niece.

_____ABOUT THE AUTHOR_____

Melanie Lowy is the author of the novel MARTHA'S BOOK OF SONG. Her novel NEMESIS is due to be published later this year. She has published poetry, reviews and articles in several papers and lectured for seven years annually at Oxford on her father JOSEF HILLEL LEVY'S Yiddish poetry. She has ghosted several novels for a well-known surgeon. She now lives in the English village to which she was first evacuated at the age of ten, months before World War Two. Melanie has been a vegetarian for over fifty years.

Printed in Great Britain
by Amazon

84489634R00171